THE
Schuylkill

Potdstown

Perkiomen creek

Wissahickon Creek

nixville

Norristown

alley Forge

Conshohocken

Philadelphia

THE *Schuylkill*

PREFACE
TO THE 2004 REPRINTING

First published in 1951, J. Bennett Nolan's The Schuylkill provides a snapshot of the region's history and serves as a valuable educational tool. It has been reprinted in the original format by the Schuylkill River National and State Heritage Area as part of their educational outreach program.

The Schuylkill River National and State Heritage Area is one of twenty-four Congressionally designated Heritage Areas in the United States and one of eleven Pennsylvania State Heritage Parks.

Established as a State Heritage Park in 1995, the Heritage Area expanded its reach in 2000 when Congress enacted legislation that recognized the Schuylkill River Region's contribution to the American, Industrial and Environmental Revolutions. Heritage Areas combine preservation of historical, cultural, and natural resources, recreation, and education with tourism and small business development in strategic initiatives to enhance the economy and quality of life of local communities.

In 2003, a management plan was approved by the U. S. Department of the Interior in support of this basic purpose and established these goals of the Schuylkill River National and State Heritage Area, resource conservation and enhancement, education and interpretation, recreation, community revitalization, and heritage tourism.

The Schuylkill River Heritage Area is managed by the non-profit Schuylkill River Greenway Association located in Pottstown, Pennsylvania. Established in the 1970's to foster development of green space along the river, the organization has adopted the Heritage Area's mission, "To conserve, interpret and develop the historical, cultural, natural and recreational resources related to the industrial and cultural heritage of the Schuylkill River Valley."

Kurt D. Zwikl
Executive Director
Schuylkill River National and State Heritage Area
Pottstown, Pennsylvania

www.schuylkillriver.org

October 2004

Reprinted from the original 1951 publication with permission from Rutgers University Press.

THE

Schuylkill

BY

J. BENNETT NOLAN

RUTGERS UNIVERSITY PRESS

NEW BRUNSWICK, NEW JERSEY

TO MY FATHER

James Nolan,

THE BRIDGE BUILDER

OF THE SCHUYLKILL VALLEY

A PROLOGUE OF APPRECIATION

The writing of this book has entailed an embarrassing and mounting debt of obligation. In all the river towns I found sympathetic collaborators eager to impart the valley lore of their own particular neighborhood. Editors, librarians and curators, former navigators of the canal, local historians and journalists, all vied in interested cooperation. Empty phrases of gratitude, we are told, are the exchequer of the poor, and yet my own sense of debit arises not so much from lack of appreciation as from the fact that an attempt to name all of my devoted helpers would swell the book to undue proportions. They and I must accept the accomplishment of the task as the only reward.

FOREWORD

LONG AGO, in the year 1795, my maternal great-great-grandfather, a young lawyer fresh from graduation at Franklin's college in Philadelphia, rode up the Schuylkill to make his home in the frontier village of Reading. His meager store of law books was at his saddle-bow; his clothes were following by stage. Pausing on the hill at the eastern approach to Reading, he looked curiously down upon the place where he was to live and die. Below him were the valley, the rim of western hills, and the loops of the river in the rays of the setting sun. That night in the tavern, writing to his father in Philadelphia, he said: "The river here is like the descriptions which I have read of the Links of Forth below Stirling."

Half a century passed and then, after the bitter famine years, my Irish ancestors on the paternal side arrived in the valley. Stonemasons and stonecutters, these Nolan brothers threw three bridges across the Schuylkill and one across the mouth of the Wissahickon. Honestly and sturdily constructed, they may endure for centuries, monuments to the ardent young Celts who built them. I take a modest pride in these bridges and in the careers of my bridge-building forefathers.

I was born by the Schuylkill, swam in its waters, and fished from its banks. Later in my many trips up and down the river I grew to know it and to love it. I mourned the defilment which I saw creeping along its valley; I rejoice in its present regeneration.

Strange that of the many travelers—Swedish, Dutch, French, German, and American—who have followed the winding trail along the Schuylkill's banks or pushed their canoes upon its surface, not one has left a description of the stream as a whole. Although there are narratives dealing with certain sections of the valley, no complete account exists.

When I set myself to the work it was with a pleasurable anticipation now amply fulfilled. If what I have written here serves to give a fuller appreciation of a romantic stream, I shall be well content of my task.

J. BENNETT NOLAN

CONTENTS

1. Hidden River

2. Anthracite Valley

3. The Pleasant Land of Berkshire

4. Below Neversink

5. Nation's Shrine

6. Gorge of Schuylkill

7. Fairmount

8. Urban River

9. Crossings and Navigation

10. River Regeneration

I

HIDDEN RIVER

CHAPTER 1

Hidden River

WHEN Henry Hudson first tacked by the sand spits of Henlopen and while buffaloes still wallowed in the dales of eastern Pennsylvania, the inhabitants of the Schuylkill Valley were Lenape Indians, mostly of the Unami tribe. Their tribal insignia was the turtle. They were not warriors like the fierce Mohawks or crafty Onondagas, but a race of fishermen and trappers, indolent and comparatively peaceful. Paddling their canoes up the Schuylkill River each spring, when the shoals of shad leaped northward to spawn, they pitched their summer wigwams, fished in the river, and hoped that the truculent Susquehannocks to the westward would not raid their valley.

Vaguely they knew that they had drifted eastward from the Mississippi. "We came hither many moons ago from the valley of the Father of the Waters," said one of their chieftains to the Moravian missionary, John Heckwelder.

They were scarcely a numerous tribe, these Schuylkill Lenapes, perhaps not more than two thousand; and they were clustered for the greater part in the lower valley, although they had villages in Berks and Mont-

gomery and in the stretch of river above present Phoenixville.

A nebulous uncertainty shrouds the identity of the
first white man to gaze on the waters of the Schuylkill
foaming down through the laurel copses from the
Tuscarora hills. Some maintain that the enterprising
Etienne Brulé, Champlain's guide and interpreter and
the first pioneer from beyond the seas to enter Pennsylvania, came over from the Susquehanna for a short
sojourn there. Others assert that when Henry Hudson
sailed up through the Capes of Delaware in August 1609
he penetrated as far as the mouth of the Schuylkill, and
that the Dutchman Cornelis Mey (for whom Cape May
was named), who came four years later, was told by the
Indians that there was such a stream.

However, the probability is that the first European
navigator upon the waters of the Schuylkill was Arendt
Corssen from Leyden, who drifted up the stream under
the silver flag of the Dutch East Indies Company. He it
was who gave the river its name, Schuylkill (*Skokihl*, or
the Hidden Creek). For tradition has it that the mouth
of the stream on that summer day, three centuries ago
when the Dutch explorer first saw it, was partially hidden
by tall bulrushes.

Corssen's original view of the river was at its junction
with the Delaware, just where the gigantic derricks of
League Island now dominate the great Navy Yard. Here
the stream has a width totally incommensurate with its
actual size. It is not likely that he attempted to sail far
up a stream so full of shallows that even the shad which
came up each spring had to leap over reefs and barriers.

The earliest map to indicate the Schuylkill definitely
is Peter Lindestrom's map of New Sweden made in
1644, the chart which hung in the Royal Council Cham-
ber at Stockholm and was burned in 1697. Fortunately, a
reduced copy had been made. Even Lindestrom, pains-
taking cartographer that he was, was only able to follow
the Schuylkill's course for about ten miles from its mouth.
The name which he gave it was *Skiar eller linde Kill*, or
the Linden Creek. The Lenapes called the stream
Ganshowahanna, or "Falling Waters," a descriptive as
well as euphonius name. Still another Indian name was
Manayunk, meaning "where we drink."

Schuylkill is among the very few American rivers
of which it can be claimed that the flags of four nations
have successively flown over it. Its waters have mirrored
the gold and buff of Sweden, the rampant lion of the
Netherlands, the crouching leopards of the royal standard
of Great Britain, and the stars and stripes of the United
States.

The Dutch and Swedes, first settlers in Pennsylvania,
were not too ethical in their dealings with the Lenapes,
and appropriated sites for forts and trading stations with
little regard for the rights of the red men. Practically no
trace remains of the sporadic occupation of the Dutch on
the lower river. Little besides the names remains of the
Swedish settlements.

When the valley came under English rule and was
granted by Charles II to William Penn in payment of
the money owed by the Crown to his father the Admiral,
the tribes were greatly concerned about the treatment
that would be accorded them. However, when they were
convinced that "Onas" (their patronymic title for Wil-

liam Penn) was prepared to treat with them for the purchase of their lands, they were reassured. Consequently, in all the settlement of the Schuylkill Valley there were only a few sporadic Indian outbreaks—brawls rather than skirmishes.

Actually, Penn had rested nearly three decades in his grave at Jordans before final settlement was made. His agents met the assembled Delaware Sachems at the Manor of Stenton near Philadelphia on August 22, 1749, and legally acquired the lands which are watered by the upper courses of the Schuylkill River. All details of the transaction were scrupulously correct, for it was the boast of the Penns that they always paid for their lands. The blanketed chiefs professed to be satisfied and were only impatient for their dole of calico, flintlocks and rum.

The Schuylkill, almost alone among American rivers, lays claim to the rank of a proprietorial stream. The patroons of New York were overlords of parts of the banks of the Mohawk and the Hudson, the Calverts of certain sections of the Potomac, but the Schuylkill was a Penn river from source to mouth.

William Penn was quick to appreciate the advantages of his watercourse. In a letter to the Free Society of Traders as early as 1683 he wrote: "Schuylkill being 100 miles boatable above the Falls and its Course Northeast to the Fountain of Susquehanna is like to be a great Part of the Settlement of Age." He brought with him an influx of English, Welsh and Irish Quakers, gazing with eager eyes at the fatness of the river lands and appropriating everything in sight.

In those early days the Penns were popular in the

valley. There was no great pressure for ground dues and no break with the mother country to give patriotic tenants an excuse not to pay rents to an English landlord. When John Penn, dubbed by popular acclaim *The American* because he was the only one of the Founder's sons to be born in Philadelphia, came back from his education in England, he was met at Gray's Ferry below Philadelphia and carried into town in triumph upon the shoulders of a rejoicing multitude "which included many Indian Chiefs."

William Penn frequently commented upon the similarity of the Schuylkill to his own beloved Thames, and perhaps this induced him to take a canoe voyage up the river during his second visit to Pennsylvania. Little is known of the details of this trip, but he seems to have penetrated deep into the wild back-country.

Scarcely a hundred and twenty-five miles in length, the Schuylkill of Penn's day seemed destined for nothing more than a placid bucolic course, flowing past orchards and wheatfields and bearing upon its bosom crude shallops carrying up-country flour to the seaboard. Certainly, in that early period no rash prophet would have dared to predict that the twenty-one-hundred square miles embraced in Schuylkill's watershed would one day be inhabited by three million people. It was the discovery of anthracite coal beneath its headwaters that altered the river's destiny.

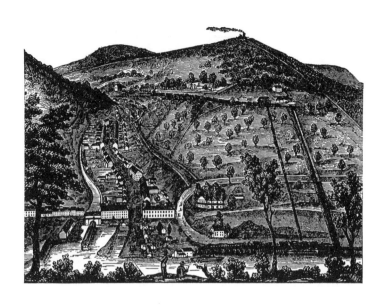

2

ANTHRACITE
VALLEY

CHAPTER 2

Source and River Head

THE sources of the river Schuylkill lie in eastern Pennsylvania in Schuylkill County, a district rich in deposits of anthracite coal. In all America there are only two considerable accumulations of hard coal, and they are both in Pennsylvania. One lies for the most part in this same Schuylkill County and the other about seventy miles to the northward in the valley of the North Branch of the Susquehanna.

Many years have passed since Governor Hoyt of Pennsylvania, bending over a geological map of the Schuylkill anthracite field, exclaimed "Why, it's just like a fish!" The mouth of the gigantic "vertebrate" faces eastward at the boundary line of Schuylkill and Carbon Counties. The two extremities of the tail straddle the Wiconisco Creek fifty miles to the westward on the borders of Dauphin County.

In the keystone state of Pennsylvania, mountain ranges run like mighty walls from the southwest to the northeast. Only in the southeastern corner of the state is the land comparatively flat and agricultural. In this region, in the counties of Schuylkill, Berks, Chester, and Montgomery, is the Schuylkill Valley. The Moravian cartographers, two centuries ago, contemptuously dubbed

8

the wild country north of the Appalachian Wall as the *Wilderness of St. Anthony*. The smiling dales to the east were often referred to as "the German Counties" because of the Teutonic cast of their settlement.

When Schuylkill County was carved out of northern Berks County in 1811 and became a separate district, it seemed likely to rank always as another forest county with hilly surface affording a minimum of tillable land. But an astounding discovery made some twenty years earlier was eventually to change the face of the countryside. The vagrant Yankee trapper Necho Allen had kindled his campfire on a ledge of black shale; in the morning the entire slope was aglow. Everywhere men began to speak of deposits of carbon buried beneath the forests which engirdled the sources of the river. However, many years were to elapse before the discovery would be commercially exploited.

The mineral wealth, whose development has so largely destroyed the original beauty of the Schuylkill scene, runs in seams, or veins, sometimes elevated two thousand feet on the summit of the mountains and at other times the same distance below the floors of the valleys. The geological formations of Schuylkill County are in the Upper Silurian, Devonian, and Carboniferous Ages of the Paleozoic System. Anthracite, or "stone coal" (a name said to have been invented by the Moravian missionary Heckwelder and now little used), is the carbonized product of a primeval vegetation so profuse that a coal seam of six inches represents the deposit of twelve hundred years of the most luxuriant tropical growth.

A contour map shows that of all the Schuylkill Valley

counties, only Schuylkill County is traversed by mountain ridges. The rampart of the Blue Mountains forms the southern boundary of the county. This Blue Range is the highest of the ridges and presents an almost impervious wall penetrated by the Schuylkill River through the single opening of the Port Clinton Gap. Northward, beyond a countryside still agricultural and still rural, rises a second ridge, the double-crested chain known as Second Mountain; here the coal fields begin. A narrow red-shale valley intervenes, and then comes the line of Sharp Mountain with its continuations, Locust Mountain and Broad Mountain. Broad Mountain, the despair of the pioneers, was for a long time an almost impassable barrier, negotiated for the uses of commerce only after the invention of the inclined plane. The lower ranges are less formidable. The tributaries of the Schuylkill are able to pass through Second Mountain in five narrow gaps and to pierce Sharp Mountain in eight places.

Through most of its fifty-mile course in Schuylkill County, the river is divided into the East Branch and the West Branch, which join to form the main stream just north of Schuylkill Haven. The sources of the East Branch, the more important of the two, are the many springs which lie hidden in the hills of Tuscarora near the present coal metropolis of Tamaqua. More than a century ago a tourist made his way up through the underbrush to record: "It is remarkable, that before reaching Tuscarora, we see the river Schuylkill disembogueing its whole volume of water through a wooden box, not more than two feet square, and so feed a single saw mill; such is the humble beginning of this majestic stream."

About that same period, in the autumn of the year
1833, the eccentric naturalist Raffinesque, born in the
Levant, whose career had taken him over most of Europe
and North America, climbed up the Tuscarora slope. He
has left the following description of his observations: "I
found two rills that are the source of Schuylkill. The
maps erroneously show a lake as the source. This lake has
no existence, merely a small mill pond often dry."

The East Branch flows in a southwestwardly direction
down the long valley which is flanked on the north by
Locust Mountain and on the south by Sharp Mountain.
As the tourist drives along this blackened stream where
breaker succeeds colliery and culm banks succeed washery,
it is hard for him to visualize the lovely agrarian setting
of other days when the up-country watercourses were
used to turn the mill wheels that ground the farmer's
wheat. No one had as yet driven unsightly tunnels
through the grain fields; the rich mineral deposits lay
undisturbed.

The first settlers who paddled up the river in the
middle decades of the eighteenth century—men like
Peter Orwig, who founded Orwigsburg, and Martin
Dreibelbis, who located at present Schuylkill Haven—
must have envisaged a continuation of Berks County beyond the mountains, agricultural and Teutonic, with red
barns and sturdy stone farmhouses. As these pioneers
turned their plows at the end of the long furrow and
looked up at the savage hills to the northward, they
could appraise only the wealth of lumber which the
untrodden slopes represented. As they gazed at the
Schuylkill, swollen after the spring rains, they could

deem it merely an easy medium for the rafting of pine and hemlock, chestnut and oak, down to the Philadelphia market.

These early farmers, many of them just disembarked from the immigrant ship which had brought them from the Rhineland, certainly never suspected that the discovery of the new fuel was to bring in its wake a horde of immigrants from Wales, Ireland and eastern Europe, whose labor would transform and blacken the pastoral setting. The silhouette of the graceful tower of the old red Lutheran Church still loomed against the horizon; the oriental dome with the double cross of the Eastern Rite had not yet appeared.

In that halcyon period each isolated farmhouse on the East Branch was a separate, self-supporting unit. When the farmer had assembled sufficient wheat and whiskey, dried peaches, flaxseed, hides and furs to warrant the journey, he joined a convoy to the market town of Reading. There must be at least six wagons in the caravan, for no one ventured to essay the trail alone for fear of the wild beasts and wilder Algonquins. In descending the steep hills, trees were cut and attached to the wagons as brakes. The bottoms of these descents were usually strewn with heaps of faded saplings, the discarded brakes. Once arrived at Reading, the farmer would trade his harvest for Spanish-milled dollars or would exchange it for indigo, tea, cambric, muslin, weaving-fixtures and nutmeg.

There are still valleys in lower Schuylkill County where coal has not been found and where the wheat-fields roll back to the mountain wall with no breaker to disturb the serenity of the landscape. In such a neighborhood is McKeansburg, oldest settlement in the district. Near McKeansburg is the location of the desolate glen known as Teufel's Loch, or Devil's Hole. Here dwelt the hermit magician Paul Heim, who had studied the occult arts at Paderborn before coming to America. Heim had brought with him two powerful books of magic, the sixth and seventh of Moses, from which he evoked spells. The spells were used not only for the discomfiture of the Iroquois, but also for the confounding of the many witches who abounded in the valley. Instances of the machinations of witches are contained in the curious book, the *Hex Kammer*, copies of which are still to be found in the garrets of remote farmhouses on the banks of the Little Schuylkill.

A miller of the East Branch of the Schuylkill was much annoyed by a black cat which frequently attacked his apprentices. At length one apprentice, bolder than the rest, armed himself with a sharp axe and slashed off one of the cat's forefeet. The next morning the miller's wife was found to have lost one of her hands.

At Orwigsburg lived a witch who had a familiar spirit. When mischievous boys came to rob her fruit trees, she whistled and a large black snake sprang out and drove the boys away.

A Locust Mountain settler whose cows were afflicted by a witch filled a pan with milk from the affected animals. Then the family, armed with sticks, gave the milk a thrashing, scattering it over the floor. When the pan was empty, the witch expired.

Are these tales still believed? It is difficult to say. The advent of the radio and modern scepticism has played sad havoc with old-time credulity in folklore.

But not so very long ago, by the fireside in the lonely cabins as the sharp winter blast blew down from the Broad Mountain, these legends were gravely related.

Surrounding Teufel's Loch are the wild mountains: Wolf's Head, Wild Cat, Sheep-nose, and Prowling Bear. Nearby is the site of Heinrich Boyer's castle, a fortified farmhouse in which the neighboring settlers took refuge during the French wars, when there was a threat of an Indian foray. Near McKeansburg was the location of one of the last of the Pennsylvania encampments of the once powerful Delaware confederacy. These Lenapes remained here until well into the nineteenth century, and the Indian children played peaceably with the whites. The warriors, formidable no longer and smelling of onions and cheap whiskey, haunted the taverns, while their squaws made baskets and chairs, which they peddled down the Schuylkill Valley as far as Potts Grove. Old settlers told of how these aborigines caught the language of the settlers and talked to each other in broken Pennsylvania German.

As the East Branch flows down through its valley, the banks become more utilitarian and its waters are no longer clear. Middleport is a coal town, founded by the pioneer Caleb Parker, who constructed a crude dam on Silver Creek and propelled his machinery by water power. Parker never thought seriously of steam and yet he must have had some premonitions of mineral riches, for in 1849 he began to scratch the vein which is now part of the great Primrose Mine. These deposits could scarcely be ignored, for in the very bed of the East Branch the black fuel formed ledges plainly visible in the stream.

Necho Allen had made his discovery half a century before Caleb Parker's time, but there was little immediate result. It was said that the tavernkeepers of Reading had used stone coal and that it burned with a red glow in their Franklin stoves. The enterprising German engineer Lewis Wernwag, whose career was to be so intertwined with the story of the river, was said to have used anthracite successfully in the operation of his mill at Valley Forge. The blacksmith Jacob Whetstone burned it in 1795. Others who used it in that early period were the miller David Berlin of Valley Furnace, Philip Ginther of Mauch Chunk Mountain, and Obadiah Gore the Connecticut pioneer. Judge Jesse Fell of Wilkes-Barre first experimented with hard coal in his house grate in 1808.

Nevertheless, scepticism toward its use prevailed. Had not Colonel Shoemaker driven some wagon loads of coal down the stony road to Philadelphia and peddled it vainly from door to door, finally dumping most of it into the Delaware? And had not the senator from this very district, Frederick Fraley, declaimed to his fellow legislators at Harrisburg: "There is no coal in Schuylkill County, only a lot of worthless black stones that will not burn."

An important early advocate of anthracite was Abraham Potts, son of one of the founders of Pottsville, who erected his Black Furnace in 1826 on the East Branch to the north of the present town of New Philadelphia. Potts experimented for a long time with the use of anthracite in smelting iron ore. He had only dubious success until one day he was visited by a traveler from the southland, who introduced himself as the Reverend Frederick W. Geisenheimer, a Lutheran clergyman re-

cently arrived from Mulheim in Germany. Potts was
at first not convinced that his clerical visitor could be of
any assistance in the solution of his problem of puddling
iron with anthracite. However, he soon perceived that
the pastor was a very able metallurgist. In 1833, when
Dr. Geisenheimer took out the first patent for smelting
iron with anthracite and hot blast, he was acclaimed as
the leader in his field in the entire world. The partners,
Potts and Geisenheimer, continued in their experiments;
and such was their success that on a summer morning in
1836 they were honored by a visit from the Governor of
the Commonwealth, Joseph Ritner, who rode up on
horseback all the way from Harrisburg to witness this
new process for making iron.

At the junction of the rushing East Branch with Mill
Creek stands the flourishing coal town of Port Carbon,
once so prominent as the northern terminus of the Schuylkill Canal. Port Carbon's pioneer was the same Abraham
Potts. He came here in the lumbering days when the
confluence of the two streams made a pool so clear and
limpid that each spring the shad and rock fish made
the long journey from the Delaware to spawn in its
waters. Indeed, Potts first attained prominence not as an
industrialist, but as a fisherman. His monumental catch
of five hundred lamprey eels at the mouth of Mill Creek
was long a piscatory tradition in the neighborhood.

Two years before the canal came to Port Carbon in
1828, Potts had begun to dig coal and had constructed a
railway, one of the first in America, fitted out with
wooden rails. The cars were drawn by horses, and old
Jake Heffelfinger came down from Middleport to witness and record the marvel:

Abe Potts had a horse hitched to thirteen cars ready to take them down to the river. I said, "That horse can only draw 1½ tons. You have at least 20 tons." He said, "The nag'll do it." And it did. Then Abe said "Some day we'll send coal by railroad all the way to Reading." I said, "Come into Pottsville and we'll find a place for you in the crazy ward."

Port Carbon boasted that from Tom Ridgway's wharf more coal was shipped than from Pottsville itself, but this period of prosperity did not last very long. The inevitable seeping of coal dirt began to clog the channel to the southward despite the frantic dredging of the Navigation Company. Canal shipment from Port Carbon ceased as early as 1853.

Port Carbon and the Mill Creek Railroad are interestingly connected with the career of the Franco-American philanthropist and financier, Stephen Girard of Philadelphia. In 1830 Girard, with many qualms, was induced to buy a tract of timberland in the Mahanoy Valley from the old United States Bank. The sellers suggested vaguely that there might be coal on the tract, but Girard's purchase was induced primarily by the lumber rights. And since this lumber could best be marketed by bringing it down to the head of canal navigation at Port Carbon, the crude railroad which he built, scarcely more than a tramway, was frequently called "the Girard Road."

In 1831 Girard deemed it advisable to get a report on the tract; and accordingly, up this same Mill Creek on a stifling summer day panted the luxurious William J. Duane, his trusted agent and lawyer. Girard had promised his agent that he would accompany him into the wilderness. However, as the financier traveled very little in the last twenty years of his life and was very comfortable in his house on Water Street in Philadelphia, he decided that Duane should go without him, as the agent was a younger man and could better endure privations. Duane went alone, facing other problems besides the heat and mosquitoes.

"In these wild mountains of Schuylkill County," he wrote, "I could do nothing without Jake Alter of Pottsville who speaks the only language that is known or spoken here, the German." Writing from the foot of Broad Mountain, he enlarged upon the difficulty of cutting a path "through undergrowth which averages eighteen feet in height."

Neither the wealthy principal nor the querulous agent dreamed of the actual value of the coal lands so acquired. Girard at his death ranked as the richest man in America, leaving an estate of five million dollars. In the inventory these "timberlands in the Mahanoy Valley" were a negligible item; indeed, they lay almost forgotten until the period of the Civil War, at which time some inkling of their real worth seems to have permeated the Board of Trustees. The subsequent development of the Mahanoy "timberlands" has increased the total of the estate to eighty million dollars. From the revenues derived from these coal lands come most of the funds supporting the school in Philadelphia which immortalizes the Girard name.

A lively picture of the East Branch at Port Carbon is given in the account of a traveler from Bucks County who visited it a century ago. "Here, in the midst of forests and swamps, is quite a flourishing town, sprung up as it were by magic, with regular streets laid out, running over and under numerous railroads. The stumps in the streets showing, that but yesterday a dense forest, and impassable swamp existed, which the enterprise and physical force of man, have compelled almost to vanish, giving place to the cheerful hum of business. The wharves are covered with large bodies of coal, and boats were constantly arriving and departing, to discharge and take in their loading."

CHAPTER 3

Epic of Anthracite

BORDERING the East Branch as it courses swiftly westward below Port Carbon, paralleled by the new Tamaqua Highway, huge culm beds break the skyline. These formidable heaps of waste contain much coal which was hastily discarded in the old days of plenty and prodigality when the mines were first opened. Now the dumps are being combed to meet the needs of a more prudent generation, a process which does not make for beauty any more than do the strippings which disfigure the slopes. About half a century ago the idea was conceived of stripping off the surface and scooping up the coal as from a gigantic cheese. Unfortunately, the authorities have never insisted upon reforestation after the coal has been taken out, and the scars remain.

The stripping of the surface land often leaves tempting masses of unmined coal within easy reach and invites the pirating, begun some decades ago, which even the Pennsylvania legislature and governor seem powerless to check. The unemployed miner, whose family must live, sees near his shack coal belonging to the company. Temptingly enough this coal is on or just below the surface, so the miner piles it up, loads it on a truck, drives it down the valley, and makes his sale. The fact that it is not his coal to sell apparently matters little. The aggrieved coal companies complain that redress is difficult where the community is so sympathetic with the offenders that often the local grand jury will not find a true bill and the petty jury will not convict, no matter how conclusive the evidence.

Lawlessness is not peculiar to any community, certainly not to the upper Schuylkill Valley, and yet the story of hard-coal mining is not a peaceful one. The valley of the East Branch once acquired unsavory notoriety as the stronghold of that ominous criminal association, the Molly Maguires, which, nearly a century ago, spread a trail of murder and intimidation throughout the district. Indeed, it was at one of the sources of the East Branch, Kerrigan's Spring, west of Tamaqua, that the three leading Mollies who had just murdered John P. Jones, Superintendent of Lansford colliery, were reposing in fancied security when the vigilantes from Tamaqua captured them. Their trial and conviction ranks as the beginning of the end of the conspiracy.

The reign of terror under the Molly Maguires may be said to have been inaugurated in 1862, about the time when the first draft wheels were set up for the recruitment of the Northern Army. The desperadoes who made up the leadership in the Mollies openly defied the draft, remained at home when their neighbors went out to fight the Confederates, and reveled in their career of crime. It is claimed, however, that the origins of the Mollies are to be traced to similar criminal bands of conspirators of an earlier period, operating in Ireland, whence most of the Mollies came. Many of the members of these bands, sometimes known as "White Boys," sometimes as "Ribbon Men," carried on their depredations in the coal fields of Pennsylvania after the immigration to America.

In their infancy the Mollies were termed "Buck-Shots," and not considered very formidable. However, as their numbers grew following the influx of foreign miners, they became a real terror. Arson in the properties of such coal companies as were deemed unfair, and assassination of mine superintendents who endeavored to curb their influence, became more and more common. Alibis were easy to establish as the juries were often composed of men who were either Mollies themselves or sympathetic to that association. Archbishop Ryan of the church to which many of the Irish Mollies belonged thundered excommunication, and an association of the Catholic clergy of the coal regions under the name of the "Sheet Irons" was formed to combat the criminal conspiracy.

Despite these measures, violence in the coal regions increased until Franklin B. Gowen, president of the Reading Railroad and a former member of the Pottsville bar, called in the Pinkerton Detective Agency. Pinkerton dispatched to Schuylkill County the detective James McParlan, alias James McKenna. McParlan, himself an Irish Roman Catholic, gained admission to the order, obtained a knowledge of its secret workings, and finally denounced its leaders.

In all the history of this district so rich in legend and tradition, there is no more striking figure than that of the prosecutor Franklin B. Gowen, in the courtroom at Pottsville, May 4, 1876, as he confronted the accused and declaimed to the tense hostile auditors: "Is there a man in

this audience looking at me now and hearing me de-
nounce this association, who longs to point his pistol at
me? If so, I tell him he will have as good a chance now
as he will ever have again."

The malefactors were duly hanged, but it is one of the
tragedies of Schuylkill Valley history that Frank Gowen,
the able executive who brought law and order to the distracted regions and who flashed like a comet across the
financial and commercial horizon of his period, should
lead the Reading Railroad to the brink of financial ruin
and then die by his own hand in an obscure hotel room
in Washington.

A detailed account of the relations between capital and
labor in the coal regions of the upper Schuylkill would be
monotonous. Strike was succeeded by settlement and settlement by strike. The first general labor disturbance in
the coal regions arose in the summer of 1842 through dis-
satisfaction with the starveling miner's wage of $5.25 a
week and with the twelve-hour working day. In July of
that year the peaceable citizens of Pottsville were startled
by the appearance in the streets of a battalion of grimy
miners armed with clubs and other weapons. A local
Paul Revere rode down the valley to Orwigsburg; and
presently a militia company, the gallant and obese Orwigsburg Blues in full martial panoply, appeared in Pottsville, whereupon the strikers dispersed.

The strike of 1850 after the great flood of that year
had temporarily inundated the mines, and the strike of
1868 when the Workingmen's Benevolent Association
began to agitate for a shorter day (the miner was getting
$13.50 a week by this time) were prefatory to the "Long
Strike" of 1875, which stopped all work from January

until June of that year. Then followed the Knights of Labor strike of 1886, which ended in lugubrious defeat for the poorly organized miners, despite the bravado of the local bards who defiantly chanted:

> *But stick and hang brave union men*
> *We'll make them rue the day*
> *They thought to break the K. of L.*
> *In free Americ-a*

The setback in the Knights of Labor strike nevertheless led to effective organization of mine labor. This organization began in 1899 with the arrival in the coal regions of young John Mitchell with his soft voice, burning eyes, and clerical attire. The test came in 1902, and both sides settled down defiantly for a long struggle. The operators erected stockades and brought up from subterraneous depths their mules, who, blinded in the unaccustomed sunlight, rolled happily in the pastures. The miners paraded with banners: "We are slaves now, but Mitchell will make us free." Mitchell and the priests implored for order.

Just at this inauspicious moment an ambitious Reading lawyer, George F. Baer, who had gotten himself elevated to the presidency of the Philadelphia and Reading Railway, took occasion to blandly assure the complaining miners that they might well leave the questions of their wage and living condition to the benevolent magnates whom God had entrusted with the operation of the coal fields. A flood of satire and caricature in the press of the period greeted this naïve proposal, at which criticism "Divine Rights" Baer affected to be greatly aggrieved. It was his conception that the miners should go on heaping up coal, to be presently translated into dividends, and that in hard times they should draw the belt a notch tighter and hope for the best as their ancestors had done for centuries in the bogs of Connemara. However, to the underfed miner living in the hovel, which was termed a "company house," erected upon the barren wind-swept patches of Schuylkill County, the suggestion of a recurrent trust in an all-providing Deity offered small consolation.

In October the peremptory Theodore Roosevelt summoned all parties to the White House and demanded a settlement. Out of this conference, which led to a victory for the strikers, emerged the present Board of Conciliation.

John Mitchell with his long black coat and white tie is remembered not so much by his statue in Scranton, dedicated by John L. Lewis in 1924, as by the annual Mitchell Day, October 29, upon which anniversary the jubilant miners sometimes unite in the old-time chorus:

> *It was Baer and Morgan done it,*
> *And for it they'll repent*
> *For I don't intend to work a tap*
> *Till I get my ten percent.*

> *Here's health into the Union*
> *Which is very strong and sane,*
> *Likewise to the conductors*
> *On Johnny Mitchell's train.*

Throughout the account of strife and unrest Celtic names predominate, but this has altered with the passing years. When the mines were first operated, the miners were English and Welsh. Then after the famine years in Ireland, 1846 and 1847, came the flood of Irish labor. Immediately the effigy of the rollicking, devil-may-care Celt in knee breeches and caubeen began to appear in American caricature. The appearance, habits, and even the language of these newcomers was strange to the old inhabitants. A German farmer, straying into a tiny chapel above Minersville, was surprised to hear the priest reciting the Litany of the Saints with the responses all made in native Irish. But the Irish, once so distinctive a stock, have since been largely assimilated. A new flood of immigration, this time from the Baltic lands, has followed. Over the tavern doors and store fronts where Kelly and O'Brien once predominated appear the names of Lithuanian proprietors.

CHAPTER 4

Mountain Capital

CURVING now to the southward, the East Branch approaches the Pottsville area and skirts the town of Palo Alto, hanging on the slope and commemorating the Mexican War victory. Somewhere under Palo Alto runs the illusive Mammoth Vein, the despair of prospectors, the exact course of which appears never to have been determined. One of the causes of Franklin B. Gowen's financial downfall was his costly failure to reach the Mammoth Vein by the expensive shafts which he sank at East Mines near St. Clair. Gowen had financed his venture in England and the contemporary satirists were quick to pounce upon him.

Frank thought himself clever and very discreet,
And choosed for his foreman a regular beat,
Who said he could sink him a shaft all complete,
And bottom the vein at fourteen hundred feet,
But the Great Mammoth vein not yet has been found,
In Franklin B. Gowen's big hole in the ground.

Now John Bull for his money will roar I'll be bound,
And his army and navy will soon be around,
But his forces we'll sink with his ten million pound,
In Franklin B. Gowen's big hole in the ground.

On a hill south of Palo Alto the statue of Henry Clay, the Mill Boy of the Slashes, looks affably down upon the thriving town of Pottsville. This dominating statue gives Pottsville a certain individuality. Without it, the place would be just an upland county seat, another coal town. Curious visitors are continually asking what Henry Clay is doing here in the Schuylkill hills. They are reminded that Pottsville was an iron city before it was a coal city. Clay battled vigorously for a protective tariff, and so in the year 1852 the grateful citizens erected this statue.

Pottsville is not an old town as Pennsylvania settlements go; Reading and Lancaster had full graveyards while Pottsville's site was marked only by the mill of the unfortunate Neiman family, who were murdered by the Indians. The location at the junction of East Branch and Norwegian Creek was much used for the assemblage of the long rafts by which timber was dispatched down the river in times of high water, but the neighborhood remained in comparative obscurity until 1804. Then Lewis Reese and Isaac Thomas built a small charcoal furnace on an island in the stream near the site of the old Neiman mill. Both Reese and Thomas had lived in Reading.

Presently another citizen of Berks County, John Potts, came from Oley and erected the Greenwood furnace and forge. Potts apparently had more vision than his predecessors, for in 1816 he drew up a plan of building lots and gave the town his name. The name has endured even though Jacob Zoll, a grumbling old tavernkeeper who had come up from Reading at an early period and built a log house on Norwegian Creek, was still protesting in his

ninety-eighth year that the place should have been called
Zoll Town.

At the time of its founding, the advantages of the site
of Pottsville were considered only from the standpoint of
its proximity to the stream and its availability for rafting
lumber and conveying iron ore to the Philadelphia market. Curiously enough the presence of anthracite deposits
at this location seems to have been better comprehended
overseas. In the Scull map published in London just before the American Revolution, the site of the future
county seat is marked with the magic name *Coal*. And
later a French map, issued by the cartographer Jacques
Nolin, contains the legend *Charbon de Terre* at the confluence of Norwegian Creek and the Schuylkill, while
American geographers still considered Pottsville a lumbering town.

In its first years, John Potts' modest settlement crept
up the slope, rather doubtful about its future. Then came
the canal, bringing with it visions of astounding prosperity. The Pottsville *Miners Journal* of October 3, 1829,
suddenly awake to the impending advantages, gleefully
called attention to the culinary delicacies brought in by
the new canal boats returning from tidewater:

> Last week our city (in miniature) was enlivened by
> the cry of "Sea Bass, Fine Fresh Sea Bass," which had
> such an effect upon the visages of our mountaineers that it
> would have been a fit subject for the pencil of a Hogarth
> to imitate. Had any person been so presumptious as to
> have asserted 7 years ago that so delicious a food as Fresh
> Sea Bass would adorn the tables among the hills of
> Schuylkill County, he would have been set down as a
> madman and sent to a lunatic asylum. . . .

As the town grew, the jubilant citizens began to dream of an inland metropolis, a second St. Louis. One enthusiastic orator declaimed that: "From this port clears a fleet of more than four hundred vessels, a fleet more formidable than that which bore the Trojan War. For anyone, from Cape Cod to New Orleans, to say that he had not heard of the renowned town of Pottsville would sound as marvelous as if an Arabian declared he had never heard of Mohamet, or Mecca, or Kauba, or the Holy Well. Scarcely a valley, however remote from the rest of the world, that has not heard of Pottsville."

The elation which followed the completion of the canal was nothing compared to the excitement which ensued when the use of anthracite as a commercial fuel began to be fully comprehended. In the Spring of 1830 a migration came from the south that was comparable to the Gold Rush to California:

> Fortune kept her court in the mountain of Schuylkill County and all paid respect to her. The Ridge Road was well traveled. Reading stared to see the long column of immigrants and her astounded inhabitants looked with wonder upon the groaning stage coaches, the hundreds of horsemen, the thousands of footmen who streamed through the ancient and respected borough and on for the Ultima Thule, Orwigsburg. Nine miles beyond Orwigsburg lay the town of Potts, the land of milk and honey.

Pottsville has declined somewhat after attaining the zenith of its prosperity during the boom years of anthracite development, and yet it is likely to rank always as an important and interesting town. From the river-bed this mountain capital straggles up the hill much as the old town of Edinburgh mounts from the Nor Loch.

There is also a suggestion of San Francisco, and in ascending Monument Square one listens instinctively for the clang of cable cars. Pottsville is more fortunate than Nob Hill in that its old houses are more numerous and better preserved. Some of the stately doorways on Mahontonga Street are suggestive of the mining aristocracy, the Pattersons and Potts, Ridgeways, Towers and Shippens, who once dwelt here. These were the patricians who worshipped at fashionable St. Luke's Church, drilled with the Pottsville Blues, drove their families out to Tumbling Run on Sunday afternoons, and took the stage to Philadelphia when they needed a new suit of clothes.

Their ancestors, who came up the Schuylkill when Norwegian Creek was still turning the wheels of primitive sawmills and when Orwigsburg was the county seat, lie buried behind the Egyptian pylons which guard the entrance of Charles Baber Cemetery. Norwegian Creek, once so beautiful, is now merely a sewer, flowing down through a tunnel; but some of the façades of the stately pioneer houses survive to proclaim the glories of the period when Coal was King.

Downstream, on the southern fringe of Pottsville, appears the suburb of Mount Carbon, formerly known as Rum Hollow. This was once a separate settlement, important enough to be a trade rival of the larger city. Now the foundations of its hotel, the Mansion House, classed in its time as one of the leading hostelries of Pennsylvania, are scarcely to be traced. The gardens which attracted visitors from Philadelphia in the summer months have disappeared, leaving only vague legends of departed state and of celebrities like President Ulysses S. Grant and Dom Pedro of Brazil, who once alighted there.

On the box-lined walks and about the old-fashioned cast-iron fountains of these same Mansion House gardens, in the late eighteen fifties, played a swarthy undersized boy who was vacationing at the hotel with his mother, the widow of the exiled Emperor Iturbide of Mexico. A few years later, when the French under Napoleon III sponsored Maximilian's brief reign in Mexico, this same lad was held up before applauding thousands in the palace at Cuernavaca and solemnly proclaimed as Maximilian's successor, the future Emperor of Mexico.

Another guest, who lived at the hotel during the last years of his life, was Necho Allen, discoverer of anthracite. From all accounts he was rather a pitiable figure and grateful when anyone bought him a drink. He would probably have been much astonished to learn that his name was to be perpetuated in the pretentious Necho Allen Hotel at Pottsville.

Mount Carbon for many years was the northern terminus of the main turnpike to Reading. At first, passengers were conveyed across the Schuylkill in a ferry; later there was a covered wooden bridge, which was carried away by the flood of 1850. Mount Carbon Dam, built in 1817 by the engineer Wernwag, was breached by the freshet of 1818. When the Reading Railroad came up the valley in 1842, Mount Carbon was its first terminus, although eleven years before that time it had had a railroad of a sort which ran up upon wooden rails to the mines on Norwegian Creek.

The East Branch, once past Mount Carbon, rushes through the narrow gorge which for a long time was Pottsville's only connection with the south. In the early period the river was crossed and recrossed by a bewildering succession of covered bridges, each looking just like its predecessor. When the "Little Giant," Stephen A. Douglas, came up to make a speech at Pottsville just before the outbreak of the Civil War, he protested that he had crossed the stream eleven times in four miles. Into this ravine, at a later date, were crowded the highway, the canal, and two railroads, the Reading and the Pennsylvania. When the canal was abandoned, a trolley line was built upon the former towpath. Up to a very recent time muskrats could be observed each winter building their houses in the stagnant waters of the deserted canal bed.

Flowing in from the eastward, its sources lying very near the old Catawissa Road—"Catiwessy" it was called—comes the well-named and sparkling Tumbling Run. A century ago the Bavarian artist Gustav Behne came up from Reading to paint the Run. He pronounced it the loveliest rivulet in either Europe or America. It was long the center of a highly prized and much frequented pleasure park, but the picturesque boathouses which once lined its banks exist no more.

When the Schulykill Canal was first projected, the engineer, George Duncan, inspected the stream and laid out the Tumbling Run reservoir with a capacity of two hundred and twenty-five million gallons, a most important adjunct to Schuylkill navigation. This dam, begun by Duncan and completed by his competent successor Edward H. Gill, was deemed able to withstand any flood. Nevertheless the freshet of 1850, a catastrophe comparable to the Johnstown Flood of a later date in Western Pennsylvania, proved its undoing. The dam broke and from the high ground above the Norwegian Creek the awe-struck spectators saw the yellow wave swirling down the narrow gorge to Schuylkill Haven, leaving a long swathe of destruction. This gorge goes by the singular name of Cape Horn, a title given it, it is said, by a Schuylkill boatman who had served on a whaling ship in the Arctic seas.

Sometime in the year 1769 a young lawyer from Reading came paddling up the Schuylkill in a canoe to inspect a trace of timberland in this locality which had been offered for sale. He was lithe, red-haired, and spoke with a strong Scotch accent, as well he might, for he had recently graduated from St. Andrew's before coming overseas to practice law in Pennsylvania. The Dutch farmers who conferred with him in broken English were amused by his appearance and strange guttural speech.

This raw stripling was to become a delegate to the Provincial Congress, was to set his bold signature to the Declaration of American Independence, and to rank as one of the greatest legal minds of his period. The name of the young lawyer later appointed as an Assistant Justice of the Supreme Court of the United States was James Wilson. In the end he bought the tract of timberland and his visit was to have historical consequences.

When the fleet of our French allies lay at Newport in 1779, it was found that some of their masts needed replacement. A request for material was brought to the attention of the Continental Congress. James Wilson, then a member of Congress, bethought himself of his Schuylkill Valley trees and sent a certain Dennis Leary, Captain of Marines, to appraise the timber.

The captain got as far as Reading, where he remained

well satisfied in a comfortable tavern until prodded by
Wilson to further action. Then he took his detachment in
boats up to the present site of Pottsville and found the
bodies of the Neiman family, lately murdered by the Indians. These corpses he buried. At this point Leary, rather
jittery it would appear, was joined by a Tory scout whom
he suspected to be in the British interest. He wrote to
Wilson at Philadelphia: "I was warned that I should take
care of myself or he (the Tory) was determined to scalp
me. On this I had him bro't to Reading where the man
is now in gaol."

Despite Leary's nervousness, he appears to have made
some progress, for Wilson wrote shortly thereafter: "The
express who came with Captain Leary's letter tells me
that a number of very fine masts are cut and ready to be
hauled to the river. Many more may be procured if protection is afforded to the workmen, but it is easy for the
savages to render the masts useless by cutting or notching
them. I have not the least doubt but that the Minister
Plenipotentiary of France will apply on this occassion to
Congress for larger guards."

A concrete highway runs down the gorge just below the
slope where a scarlet Indian head, painted high on the
rocks, marks the spot where Leary cut his masts so long
ago.

Farther down the gorge, facing the almost abandoned
Reading Post Road which it once dominated, stands the
Seven Stars hotel, presenting its rather forlorn outbuild-
ings to the new highway. When Captain Conrad Minnich
conducted the hotel, it was an important stagecoach stop
for travelers proceeding from Reading to Fort Augusta
on the Susquehanna, while Pottsville was as yet unheard

of. In later years, when the road was made a turnpike, the directors held their annual banquet at the Seven Stars. This Lucullan feast was of such culinary extravagance and washed down by wines of such rarity that the aggrieved stockholders, who rarely got a dividend, complained that all the profits of the turnpike were consumed in the banquet.

CHAPTER 5

Junction of the Branches

OVER the rolling hills to the east of the gorge lies the hamlet of Orwigsburg, not a river town and yet with traditions closely linked to the Schuylkill. For a long time it boasted a port of its own called Orwigsburg Landing, later Landingville, the spot where the Lenape chief Bohundy ruled over an extensive Indian community. Despite its inland location Orwigsburg once ranked as a boat-building center. Craft of fifteen tons burden were constructed here and jubilantly rolled down to the Schuylkill at Landingville in haywagons decked with flags. In this Orwigsburg boatyard are said to have originated the canal boats called "chunkers," which were built in two sections for the launching. These "chunkers," rarely seen on the Schuylkill, are associated with Mauch Chunk, from which they derive their name, and with the Lehigh Canal.

In 1811 when it was decided to cut a new county out of Berks in the wild district north of the mountains, an eager rivalry over the location of the county seat developed. Water power counted for much in those days, so the astute citizens of Orwigsburg dammed up all the streams in the vicinity, pending the arrival of the commissioners who were to make the choice. When the com-

37

missioners arrived, the village was bisected by roaring torrents, which so impressed the visiting dignitaries that they chose Orwigsburg as the county capital. A tavern served as the first courthouse. For want of a jail the culprits, on trial days, were chained to trees where, irrespective of weather conditions, they remained until their case was called.

When the first court was set up in this new county of Schuylkill, all the young Reading lawyers rode up to assist in the ceremony—and get some business. They were a notable group: Charles Evans, the distinguished philanthropist; Frederick Smith, later Attorney General and Justice of the Supreme Court; and Samuel Baird, whose son was to be the first curator of the Smithsonian in Washington. It was a bleak winter day, and the cavalcade was much beaten upon by gusts of rain as they rode through the gap. Once arrived at Orwigsburg, they were glad to accept the hospitality of the Widow Bartlett, who had two daughters, Louisa and Lavina, both comely, wellbred, and frugal. It is said that when they made excursions down the valley, they took off their shoes and stockings but modestly put them on again before entering the village.

Lavina Bartlett married a Pottsville advocate, Charlemagne Tower. The lawyer so prospered through astute investments in coal lands that he was able to educate his namesake for a diplomatic career. The younger Tower became Ambassador to Berlin and St. Petersburg, and drifted far away from the humble setting of his Orwigsburg grandmother. When he returned from his Russian post to live in Philadelphia, he brought with him a *kavass*, or body servant. Whenever he went calling, this *kavass* would open the door of his barouche and then stand in the vestibule with folded arms until "Excellence" reappeared.

Orwigsburg is a village of frustration and disappointment. Had coal been discovered in the neighborhood, it might have retained its place as the county seat. Unfortunately it was and is in a district purely agrarian. As early as 1831 Pottsville began to push its claims, and in 1851 the removal of the county offices was effected. The old courthouse long stood in the Orwigsburg square, but that, too, has been pulled down.

On the final stretch of the East Branch before it joins with the West Branch to form the main stream, the site of the once imposing Five Locks, which all travelers admired a century ago, is now scarcely distinguishable. The beautiful Waterloo gardens have disappeared. Anyone who has the curiosity to see the beginning of the main stream can push his way through the underbrush to the peninsula, just under the suburb of Schuylkill Haven known as Irish Flat and east of the extensive Cressona plant of the Aluminum Company of America. Here the waters of the West Branch are absorbed after flowing twenty-five miles from the springs in the hills of Barry Township.

The countryside about Barry Township, source of the West Branch, has still something of the beauty of its primeval setting. It is in the northwest corner of Schuylkill County, not far from the lonely mill which the pioneer Alspach operated when the neighborhood was covered with the original white oak and when buffalo wallows were still to be observed. In the year 1790 the map-maker Reading Howell explored this area and described the upper reaches of the West Branch as a brook "abounding with trout and shaded by dense foliage of white pine and chestnut . . . a body of pure water from hundreds of mountain springs—so refreshing that the traveler, though not thirsty, is tempted to drink the sparkling fluid."

These conditions existed before the discovery of coal and before the gigantic stripping operations disfigured the once beautiful banks of West Branch. For the disfigurement (and perhaps the prosperity) of the district may be said to date from 1828, the year of the establishment of the Mine Hill Railroad, with its crude roadbed, over which horses drew the coal cars down the Branch to the head of navigation at Schuylkill Haven.

West Branch divides into two fairly large brooks, the northern flowing through Minersville, and the southern, called on the old maps the West Branch, through the coal town of Llewellyn. The emporium of the upper West Branch is the town of Minersville near which, on Wolf Creek, the first coal breaker in the valley of the West Branch was set up by George Bast in 1833. Before this the settlement was a relay in the highway from Reading to Sunbury. Travelers coming up the Mahantongo Valley stopped at the tavern, then called the Half Way House, to refresh themselves and feed their horses. In those days the place was called Reedsville, and it is so marked on most maps issued before 1830.

When Ike Zerbe kept the Half Way House, he decided to change the name of the tavern to the General St. Clair—Arthur St. Clair was a much-admired Revolutionary hero in the coal regions. The sign, containing a portrait of St. Clair, was to be painted by Squire Rutter, who lived down the road near Roxborough, and was to be delivered by Harry Dry, who drove the Reading stage. Rutter became confused in the execution of the order. Accordingly, when Dry drove up and proudly exhibited the completed sign, the disappointed tavernkeeper said:

"Why, this is General Wayne."

"So it is," said Harry. "But I'll fix it."

Groping into his saddle bags he produced some paint and lettered the name *General St. Clair* under the portrait.

The bed and course of the upper stream can be followed easily enough along the highway which leads west from Pottsville. To follow the lower stream involves the use of roads and paths not always negotiable by automobile. Above Cressona, the tributaries meet and flow swiftly southward to the junction.

Here at Schuylkill Haven the buildings back upon the water with scant regard for regularity of adornment; nevertheless this clean, thriving town has an air of prosperity, and it is not hard to realize that it was once hailed as a future metropolis of the upper valley. In that period the Haven was the head of canal navigation and no one suspected that the railroad would supersede the canal.

This commanding site attracted the attention of many early settlers. Orwig came here as early as 1747, followed by the pioneer families of Deibert and Dreibelbis. The Quaker John Fincher rode up from Chester County and gave his name to the ford here. An ill-starred expedition this, for in 1763 the Indians murdered Fincher and dragged his daughters across the whole width of Pennsylvania into the "Ohio country." When Colonel Bouquet

defeated the savages at Kittaning, he found the Fincher
girls, who by this time had become Indian in speech and
appearance and only wished to be left with their captors.
This episode suggested the half-mythical legend of
Regina the Indian captive, which has been told in varying
detail in so many localities in southeastern Pennsylvania.

According to the legend Regina had been carried off in
childhood by marauding Algonquins. After the French
had surrendered, her distracted mother sought her
daughter through the Indian encampments. Their pious
German family had been accustomed to unite in hymn
with the refrain *"Allein und doch nicht ganz allein"*
(Alone and yet not quite alone). In the end the daughter who, like the Fincher girls, had become half savage,
heard the notes of the familiar hymn and emerged from
her wigwam for a happy reunion.

Just before the Revolution the site of Schuylkill Haven
was visited by Daniel Hiester of Reading, who was to
serve as the district's first Congressman in 1789. Daniel
Hiester was at heart a lumberman. As he ranged over the
new tract, ever alert for signs of the Iroquois, he noted
with envious eyes the forests of oak and chestnut. Wish-
ing to estimate the depth of the Schuylkill and its availability for floating huge logs downstream, he pushed his
way through the thickets and came upon the banks of the
river about a mile below present Schuylkill Haven. Here
he found a small clearing where the surveyor Benjamin
Lightfoot and three Indian guides were encamped. The
party was engaged in surveying the district, which had
been purchased by the Penns from the aborigines in 1749.

At this period any rumor of the presence of Indians
was enough to throw the entire community into terror

and confusion. However, there was nothing ominous in the appearance of Lightfoot's ill-kept attendants. On the contrary the surveyor, who was absolutely dependent upon their knowledge of the country, had been obliged to protect his charges during the trip up the valley. He purposely took his Indians to Francis Parvin's "to be out of the way of liquor and insults of rude people at Reading. The evening before, James Read, one of his majesties justices, expressed concern lest an accident should befall them."

On the site of Lightfoot's camp by Fincher's Ford a straggling village presently sprang up, and here in lumbering days were assembled the gigantic rafts in which the timber of the neighborhood forests was floated down the river in high water. Then came the canal. The villagers incorporated their town in 1829 under the name of Schuylkill Haven, and complacently sat down to await the commercial growth which had been so confidently predicted. For a time it seemed as if these hopes were to be realized. When the canal was enlarged in 1833, important docks, a weigh lock, repair shops, and mule stables were established at Schuylkill Haven. Lippincott Dock, opened in 1853, had a frontage of three thousand feet; the Dundas Dock, completed in 1846, was almost as large.

As the canal to the northward filled up and became unserviceable as a result of the accumulations poured into it from the mines, and when loading ceased from Port Carbon in 1853 and from Mount Carbon in 1861, Schuylkill Haven grew in importance. The destructive freshets of 1850, 1862, and 1869 caused only temporary breaks in its prosperity. By 1872 the town was the acknowledged head of Schuylkill navigation, but its reign as a canal terminus was to be brief. More and more difficulty was experienced in keeping the channel to the southward open; and finally, in 1888, navigation to Schuylkill Haven practically ceased. Port Clinton, a score of miles to the southward became, in its turn, the northern terminal of navigation. The agitated citizens of Schuylkill Haven joined in a meeting of protest held at Metamorah Hall in Pottsville, but their protests were unavailing. The Navigation Company removed its offices and warehouses. The queen of the river had lost her crown.

A wealth of anecdote survives concerning the Schuylkill Valley boatmen in the days when boats put out each day for Philadelphia. These were best related by old John Bowman of Pottsville, who knew the canal from boyhood.

He told of Billy Bausman of the canal boat *Andrew G. Curtin*, who had made a hundred trips to Philadelphia and was the fattest man on the canal. With a piece of wood back of his head he could read a newspaper while floating in the water. At his funeral no hearse was strong enough to bear his weight, so Yuenglings' beer wagon, drawn by six white mules, was called in to carry him to the cemetery.

Then there was "Nigger" Jim Emery, who always wore his hair in a topknot, with a big ivory needle pushed through it like a cannibal chief. He played "Turkey in the Straw" on his autoharp. When not in jail at Pottsville, he worked for "Ham and Eggs," a notorious virago who kept a house at Schuylkill Haven. "Ham and Eggs" always put a pat of butter in her gin, and when in liquor would brazenly boast that she had had to do with half

the captains who guided their boats through the Five
Locks.

In the period just after the long strike of 1875, the best
storyteller on the canal was Ould Mike Monahan who as
a boy in Ireland had stood in the rain on the hill of
Clontarf and heard the Liberator, Daniel O'Connell,
harangue for Catholic Emancipation. John Bowman remembered Mike very well, and liked to tell of an incident that befell Monahan when he worked on the boat
Governor Bigler under Captain Becker. The boat would
lie in the slip, which is filled up now to make the new
parkway at Schuylkill Haven. Bowman and some of his
friends went down one summer night and Ould Monahan
told them a story about a mermaid who came up the
River Shannon to Limerick and fell in love with a broth
of a boy whom she saw there. She went to a hayrick, shed
her scales, and married the boy.

While Monahan was telling the story, Captain Becker
came up from behind with a bucket of water, which he
had sluiced up with a rope from the canal. He threw it
over Ould Monahan, who fell down the hatchway.

"Why did you do that?" Bowman asked.

"The old liar tells that story different ways," replied
the captain. "Last time the mermaid went to a chapel,
got holy water, and became a saint."

CHAPTER 6

Southward to the Ridge

THE curve of the river below Schuylkill Haven, with the picturesque conical peak of Sculp Hill (called Scallup Hill on the old maps) dominating the landscape to the south, is still passably verdant and beautiful. Fifty years ago, before the hey-day of the coal industry, excursion boats ran down the Eck to the large island which once boasted the finest specimens of rhododendron in Schuylkill County.

The three dams formerly existent between Schuylkill Haven and Landingville are gone, but the stream bed is still full of fairly sizable coal. This coal was washed down in the period when the prodigal operators to the northward rejected all but the larger pieces. Now the Schuylkill in this section is full of dredging boats which suck up the smaller particles to sell as rice or buckwheat coal.

Landingville (Orwigsburg Landing) sleeps lazily by the river which it once controlled. Even before the advent of the canal the town had its importance as the assemblage place for the great rafts. Like Orwigsburg itself the Landing represents disappointment. In the early days of Schuylkill County development, when Orwigsburg confidently expected always to be the county seat, the Land-

ing was intended to play, on a minor scale to be sure, the
part which the port of Wilmington now does for Los
Angeles. But Deibert's boathouses, once so busy, have disappeared and the extensive docks of other days can
scarcely be traced.

Below Landingville and opposite the slopes of Sculp
Hill a succession of rushing brooks, once the delight of
trout fishermen, come foaming down—Red Creek and

Bear Creek and Plum Creek (there are many Plum
Creeks in Schuylkill Valley). The main river, no longer
trammeled by the dams which formerly curbed it, twists
and turns and at times flows back in a northerly direction
towards its source. In this meandering it passes under one
of the most beautiful stone bridges in Pennsylvania, hidden away in the wilderness and conveying the tracks of
the Reading Railroad across the river bed.

Leaving the hemlock-covered slopes behind it, the
Schuylkill glides down to the cut which was once the

450-foot Auburn Tunnel, acclaimed as the first tunnel in the United States. Up from Reading one April day in 1828 came the three Biblically named brothers, Job, Sampson, and Solomon Fudge, the contractors whom the president of the Navigation Company had entrusted with the job. As Job stood fanning himself and looking at the slope through which the tunnel was to pass, he said, "Boys, they say that this is to be the first tunnel this side of England and we've got to do a good job, but I wish you'd tell me one thing. Why do they build a tunnel at all?"

The same question was to be asked many times thereafter, for by laying out the canal one hundred feet to the westward the expensive tunnel might easily have been avoided. No provision was made for a towpath inside the tunnel, so boats had to be laboriously poled through. Finally, in 1857, someone suggested removing the roof, and thereafter the tunnel was transformed into an open cut.

The construction of the Auburn desilting basin and new dam recently has materially changed the scene as the stream flows past the village of Auburn, the western terminus of the Schuylkill and Susquehanna Railroad. Two centuries ago when Pine Creek, coming in from the eastward, was called Bohundy Creek, Auburn was a very perilous outpost on a distracted frontier. It was called Fort Lebanon then, although the fort, which stood east of the river just beyond where Dan Driscoll of Reading afterwards established his nut and bolt works, seems to have offered a very feeble defense. Commissary Young of the British Army, who served at Fontenoy and had a profound contempt for the Pennsylvania militia, came by in 1757 and regarded the earthwork dubiously. He reported it as crowded with refugees and with only three weeks supply of "flour and rum." The commissary also volunteered his unsolicited opinion that "If the French attack this wretched place with rotten apples, it will have to surrender." Luckily the French never came and Fort Lebanon's reputation for impregnability was not tested.

The settlement which developed on the river bank west of the old fort was first called Scotchman's Lock, after a Caledonian emigrant named Hay, who had served in the famous Black Watch and claimed to be a direct descendant of Robert Bruce. When the railroad came along in 1842, another pioneer named Faust suggested the title of Faust Town. The debate over the name became so virulent that Gustavus Nicolls, the youthful superintendent of the Reading Railroad, was hastily summoned from Reading. Nicolls, an Irishman, had been solacing himself on the train ride by reading *The Deserted Village* of his fellow countryman, Oliver Goldsmith. Now as he stood listening to the contestants, his glance wandered to the beautiful stream flowing down between the hills and he murmured:

"Sweet Auburn, loveliest village of the plain."

"What was that you said, Mr. Nicolls?" said one of the town counselors. "Auburn! That's the name we'll have."

At Auburn the towpath shifted across stream and mules were ferried across until, in 1832, a crude bridge was built. Below Auburn three dams, Tom Lord's, Rishell's, and Hummel's, made a long expanse of river surface the delight of amateur boatmen. There is little boating water now, but the plans of the Pennsylvania Department of

Forest and Waters call for a lake of some size to be developed below Auburn, so that after the lapse of almost a century the river may revert to its pristine beauty.

Twisting its way through the bleak hills in a country almost as primitive as when the raftsmen poled their way down, the Schuylkill flows towards the once important canal center of Port Clinton. The village clings to the hillside and embraces the peninsula between the Little Schuylkill and the main river. It takes its name from De-Witt Clinton of Erie Canal fame, but on early maps the location is marked as Old's Forge. The Old brothers came from Womelsdorf in 1804 with capital advanced by their relative, the rich ironmaster George Ege, and established a furnace at this point. Then came the canal. When the northern terminals, Port Carbon and Schuylkill Haven, were successively abandoned, Port Clinton became the upper navigation head, a distinction which it held until the final abandonment of the canal. The last boat to leave Port Clinton's once crowded basin was the *Mary Rose,* which took a load of coal to the state sanatorium at Hamburg just before the outbreak of the Second World War.

Many of the canal boat crews lived at Port Clinton in the months when the canal was frozen over. Canal navigation usually began on St. Patrick's Day and continued until the early part of December. During the winter the boats were laid up and the entire family lived on them. A school was conducted for children, and the boatmen worked at odd jobs or sat about in taverns.

Port Clinton's early history is interwoven with the career of the German economist Frederick List, who later organized the German railway system and was among the first to perceive the possibilities of anthracite coal. List came to America in 1824 as a political exile and accompanied Lafayette, then the nation's guest, upon his triumphal tour. Eventually he settled in Reading as a newspaper editor, made frequent journeys into the coal regions, and acquired a tract of land in the valley of the Little Schuylkill.

With the collaboration of Dr. Isaac Hiester, a Reading physician, List planned the first railroad running up to Tamaqua and prophesied that Port Clinton would one day be a great depot for the exportation of coal. This railroad, like most of the early lines in Schuylkill County, was equipped with wooden rails and the cars were drawn by horses or men. An engine was eventually brought over from England and sent up to Port Clinton in a cart which had been used for carrying marble. The rails had been strengthened for the experiment, but the engine ran off a curve into the stream bed of the Little Schuylkill. This catastrophe occurred near the hamlet of New Ringold, where the Delaware sachem Tammany once dwelt. The news came to Harrisburg just as the State legislature convened, and the amused solons derided the railway and List, "this professor of economy and necromancy." Nevertheless, List's labors had not been in vain. He was back in Germany when the triumphal completion of the road was celebrated on November 18, 1831, by a banquet at Keasby's Hotel in Tamaqua, but he was not forgotten. The toastmaster, Dr. Hiester, proposed the health of "The eminent citizen of two worlds, the present American Consul at Stuttgart, Dr. Frederick List, to whose wisdom and foresight we owe the achievement which we now commemorate."

The waters of the Little Schuylkill flow down from the Tamaquan hills to join the Schuylkill at Port Clinton. The Little Schuylkill, formerly known as the Tamaquan or Beaver Creek, was designated by some of the early map-makers as the main stream. High above the banks of the Little Schuylkill can be found the moldering remains of Fort Franklin, a relic of Benjamin Franklin's brief military career of six weeks in the bitter winter of 1755–56. Franklin maintained his headquarters at Fort Allen, twenty miles to the eastward, a post constructed under his supervision. Twice, at least, he rode over to the lonely outpost of Fort Franklin, named in his honor. As evidence of the Sage's unfailing sense of humor, there survives in his *Autobiography* an anecdote of this same campaign on the Little Schuylkill:

> We had for our chaplain a zealous Presbyterian minister, Mr. Beatty, who complained to me that the men did not generally attend his prayers and exhortations. When they enlisted, they were promised, besides pay and provisions, a gill of rum a day, which was punctually served out to them, half in the morning and half in the evening; and I observed they were punctual in attending to receive it: Upon which I said to Mr. Beatty, "It is, perhaps, below the dignity of your profession to act as steward of the rum; but if you were to distribute it only just after prayers, you would have them all about you." He liked the thought, undertook the task, and with the help of a few hands to measure out the liquor, executed it to satisfaction; and never were prayers more generally and more punctually attended.

The view from Fort Franklin embraces the Hawk Mountain Bird Sanctuary. From the lookout in this sanctuary, fifteen hundred feet above sea level, one gazes down upon the Little Schuylkill, the picturesque Pennsylvania Dutch village of Drehersville, and the great mountain bowl of the "Kettle." Through this gap from time immemorial and as regularly as the autumn leaves begin to fall, hundreds of thousands of hawks, eagles, ospreys and broadwings have passed on their migration south. The winds beat against the side of the gap to engender a mounting stream of air, an unseen roller coaster which the hawks ride at a speed of fifty miles an hour. Great flocks of Canada geese and other water fowl may be seen usually after severe storms to the north. Whistling swans fly by. Loons, sometimes a hundred in one day, pass high over the ridge in flight to Florida.

The phenomenon of this annual migration was familiar to the early settlers, who knew the mountain as *Sparenbarich* (Steep Mountain). The opportunity for easy slaughter attracted unscrupulous sportsmen, and the gap became a veritable death trap, until in 1934 some benevolent bird lovers acquired the mountain and formed the Hawk Mountain Sanctuary Association, the first refuge constructed in the new world for the protection of birds of prey. Indiscriminate shooting in the gap has now ceased, and each autumn the spectacle attracts thousands of visitors from every state in the Union.

Recently, speaking in the very shadow of the peak, a local resident declared: "Soldiers in the far Pacific, marines on tiny atolls far away, have written how their hearts turn yearningly toward Hawk Mountain, that the hours spent on those Observation Rocks, with those quiet valleys spread before them, brought calm and peace to their souls, and healing to their spirits."

Nearby in this valley of the Little Schuylkill are Deer

Lake, the wild and lovely ravine of Moss Glen with its
waterfall, the dale of the Cold Run where the first banks
of spring flowers are to be seen, and the gorge near the
hamlet of Hecla.

The Schuylkill itself now enters the northern end of
the steep Port Clinton Gap. This setting has a distinct
European flavor often noted by travelers. Martin Kaer-
cher, who founded the village of Kercher-town, now
Hamburg, at the lower end of the pass, came from the
valley of the Elbe and compared the gap to the Elbe-Thal
in the steep canyons above Dresden.

Another overseas comparison was made by young
Prince Bernhard of Saxe-Weimar, who had fought at
Waterloo and who visited America in 1826. In the summer of that year the Prince, "curious to see a coal mine,"
traveled up the Schuylkill from Philadelphia in a vehicle
which he called a "rattle wagon." Back in Weimar the
Prince's preceptor, the immortal Goethe, was eagerly following his pupil's American tour.

Writing to the Meister, Prince Bernhard said that
the Schuylkill above the village of Hamburg "reminds
me markedly of our own Rhine above Caub. There is, to
be sure, no Mouse-Tower in the Schuylkill and instead of
the vine-clad hills of our beloved Fatherland (of which I
reflect so often and so fondly) the slopes of Port Clinton
Gap are clothed with groves of beech and oak."

Job Scott, the Quaker missionary who journeyed to
Pottsville just before Prince Bernhard's visit, was no
sentimentalist, and yet he, too, attained a certain height
of poetic description when he wrote: "As I paddled my
canoe up Schuylkill through the great Blue Mountain
Gap, I saw some openings in the forest so carpeted with

laurel that they glowed like a rich Turkey carpet in tints of rose and yellow and heliotrope."

What would be the reaction of the good missionary were he to return to the mountain slope which he described so enthusiastically? Below him engrossing the quiet river level of other days would stretch the expanse of the Kernsville Dam, almost two miles long.

And here, at the lower portal of the gap, Schuylkill shakes itself clear of the mountain bulwark, leaves the domain of anthracite behind, and courses through the fruitful plains to the southward.

3

THE PLEASANT
LAND OF BERKSHIRE

CHAPTER 7

Berkshire

THE Appalachian ridge forms a natural and official boundary between the counties of Schuylkill and Berks. Below the mountain gap the river winds for forty miles through the ancient and historic district of Berkshire, so dear to the hearts of the Proprietary family. The names of the bordering townships, Windsor, Greenwich, and Richmond, suggest the Thames Valley, closely interwoven with Penn tradition. Indeed, Thomas Penn, most enterprising and energetic of the sons of the Quaker founder, always protested that the Schuylkill should have been named the Thames.

Berks County is in the country of that sturdy folk, the Pennsylvania Dutch. The appellation "Dutch," from the German word "Deutsch," is misleading in that it suggests that these immigrants came from Holland. Actually they came mostly from the upper Rhine, from Würtemburg, and from the Palatinate. Successive destructive invasions of the Rhineland by French armies two centuries ago came just at the time when William Penn's land agents arrived in Germany. These agents made promises of liberal land allowances in Pennsylvania, promises not always fulfilled. The expense of the voyage to America could be arranged for by the settler's selling himself into temporary bondage for the first years after his arrival. By his labor during this period the emigrant would "redeem himself," a practice giving rise to the term "redemptioner."

So these Rhineland peasants, despairing of any settled future in their own distracted land, came pouring into the port of Philadelphia, whence they were shipped into the wilderness of the upper Schuylkill. And the counties of southeastern Pennsylvania, whose place names are so suggestive of English settlements, were peopled by Teutonic pioneers, upon whose original language English expressions were grafted to form the dialect, still in common use, called Pennsylvania German. They are a tenacious race, these "Dutch," for although they came into these dales over two centuries ago, they preserve a racial and linguistic isolation which finds no counterpart in this hemisphere except perhaps in some of the outlying parishes of Quebec.

The Schuylkill, in its southward exit from the Appalachian Gap, comes to the site of the former Blue Mountain Dam, now largely occupied by the Kernsville Dam. If one of the veteran canal navigators, Captain Butz of the *Franklin B. Gowen* or Captain Dry of the *Governor Hiester*, should attempt to trace the line of the canal today, he would behold ravaged banks and deserted wharves, a shrunken stream and an abandoned canal bed. The doughty mariner would need only to raise his head, however, to view the glorious amphitheater extending upward from either bank of the stream.

High to the eastward, outlined against the horizon, soars the Pinnacle, sixteen hundred feet above sea level, the loftiest point in this countryside. The visitor who has the hardihood to climb the steep peak will see, on a clear day, the buildings of Allentown, the winding highway to New York, and the hills by the Delaware Water Gap. If it should happen to be springtime, the ridge will be a blaze of colorful glory: rhododendron, wild azalea, and laurel. The glens, both east and west of the Schuylkill, were once a hunting ground for botanists. As early as 1817 the German botanist Bischoff, who boasted that he had fought under Napoleon and against him, noted in this territory plants now very rare or nonexistent—wild senna and meadow-sweet, snow-berry, and goatsbeard.

The game which once made these hills a sportsman's paradise has largely disappeared. A unique race of Appalachian rats, much written about by scientists, inhabit the crannies of the Pinnacle in place of the elk and wapiti which formerly roamed there. The elk had migrated westward even before the white man came, but a century ago bears were so prevalent that they were encountered daily. No political festival nor battalion day was complete without a barbecued bruin. These are no more. Danny Long from the Eck shot the last bear in the woods back of Livingood's mill on the day Lee surrendered at Appomattox. As for panthers, Jake Pflager killed the last one in August, 1874, a monster five feet long. Now only the opossum, the raccoon, the ever-present white-tailed deer, and some marauding foxes remain.

The Pinnacle dominates the curious primitive district to the north still known as the Eck, or "the corner." This was the territory which the early Rhineland settlers dubbed *Alles-Mangel*, or Lack-all, a rugged forbidding country, hard to conquer, easy to defend. Here are still to be found some specimens of the log huts of the early

pioneers, and the folk who live here are the very last to
adopt modern amenities or speech. Only twenty years ago
the luckless hunter who, having become lost, inquired his
way in English, would receive a broad stare and a muttered response in the German dialect. In this same Eck
the interesting and laudable custom of bundling, usually
associated with New England, was practiced within the
memory of the older residents. Barns with thatched roofs,
perhaps the last in Pennsylvania, were to be found here
until recently.

Down the southern slope of the ridge runs that marvel
of geologists, the river of gray glacial stones known as
the Blue Rocks, beneath which flows a mysterious sub-
terranean stream. As boys, we used to ramble over from
the Pinnacle and scramble up upon the rocks. In awed
silence we would listen to the gurgling of this unseen
water and whisper that no mortal man would ever see
its source or outlet.

> *Where Alph the sacred river ran*
> *Through caverns measureless to man*
> *Down to a sun-less sea.*

These highlands form the background of a splendid
prospect to the south. Stretching far down the eastern
bank of the Schuylkill lies the rich agricultural plain of
northern Berks, the townships of Richmond and Greenwich. These are English names, and to complete the
British association there is a Windsor Castle. This, however, has neither turrets, nor battlements, nor royal
standard; it is only a quaint landward country store with
a wide porch where the farmers congregate on summer
evenings to gossip in the kindly Pennsylvania Dutch

vernacular which their great-great-grandfathers spoke, two centuries ago.

Here is a land of green and gold through which winds Maiden Creek, loveliest of the Schuylkill's tributaries, called in its upper reaches by the Indian name of *Ontelaunee*. A cloud of smoke rises over the cement district of Evansville, and spires mark the Teachers' College in the ancient hamlet of Kutztown. Nestling in a curve of the creek is the picturesque village with the curious name of Virginsville (originally *Vergennes ville*), an appellation which evokes much ribald comment from passing automobilists. Few of the inhabitants realize that their village was originally named to commemorate the Comte de Vergennes, foreign minister to Louis XVI and steadfast friend of Franklin's hard-pressed mission at Paris in the dark days of 1778.

Farther upstream is the borough of Lenhartsville, where the townsfolk tell the legend of a grave, silent man of military bearing who taught school there about 1820, and who was really Napoleon's Marshal Ney. Ney, who had deserted the Bourbons to fight under his old leader Napoleon, was captured after Waterloo. History records that the Marshal was executed by a firing squad in the gardens of the Luxembourg at Paris, but the good folk of Lenhartsville stubbornly maintain that he was miraculously saved to come and teach school in the Schuylkill Valley. Old Squire Dreibelbis, who lived to a ripe age and who, as a boy, had seen President Buchanan driving through Kutztown in a barouche drawn by two roan horses, always vouched for the authenticity of the Ney legend. It is true that the squire had never been away from home except to serve on the jury at Reading and

had only a vague idea as to where France was, but he
was a man of excellent judgment. Where is the presuming
sceptic who shall dare to quarrel with the squire's con-
clusions?

West of the Schuylkill the Appalachian rampart is
paralleled by an important east-west automobile highway.
There are traces of an abandoned railway, sponsored by
the house of Vanderbilt sixty years ago.

South of the ridge, in the northwestern corner of present Berks County, was William Penn's Manor of Aldo-
heeno, intended as a baronial estate on the English model,
with Rehrersburg as its capital. William Parsons, the
proprietory surveyor who afterwards ran the original
town lines for Reading and Easton, went up in 1740 to
live in a lonely farmhouse and survey the manor; but
nothing came of the ambitious project. Parsons died,
lonely and neglected, biting his fingers at destiny.

This, like the Pinnacle district to the eastward, is a
pedestrian's paradise, with good paths traversing the
ridge and convenient rest houses. The plateau can be
reached by the steep ascent known as Shower's Steps, a
labor of devotion. The Shower family, living at the base
of the mountain, rolled the huge boulders in place, which
by successive steps make the slope negotiable.

The pass in the hills through which ran the first road
to Shamokin begins at the foot of the steps. The Moravian
missionary Heckwelder rode over this stony trail, on
muleback, in 1745. In a letter to the brethren back in
Bethlehem, he wrote: "My beastial galled me severely at
a point of my anatomy which it would be indiscreet to
particularize."

Two years later another evangelist, the patriarch of

the Lutheran Church in Pennsylvania, Henry Melchior Muhlenberg, mounted the pass. He was young and it was springtime and he was very much in love with Anna Eve, the daughter of the Indian interpreter Conrad Weiser. (Some say that Anna Eve's mother was a Mohawk squaw, although this has been denied.) So on this May day so long ago, Muhlenberg's thoughts took a more inspiring theme than the bodily discomforts which occupied the mind of his Moravian colleague. He writes of his aspirations for the conversion of the wild heathen "and even, if God so wills, of the idolatrous French." But he writes also of Anna Eve, of her grace and beauty, and the home which he will make for her in the new settlement of Trappe, lower down the river.

A half mile to the northward may still be traced the moldering, grass-grown ramparts of Fort Henry, built during the most harassing period of the French and Indian War. At one critical epoch in our colonial history this same ridge seemed destined to be the last line of defense for the preservation of Schuylkill Valley against the inroads of the victorious French and their savage Indian allies. After Braddock's defeat at Fort DuQuesne in July, 1755, when Philadelphia itself was threatened, a line of crude block houses was erected on both sides of the Schuylkill, east and west of Hamburg, and anxious militia sentries watched for the approach of the invader. The visitor of today, from his post at the summit of the Shower steps, looks down upon the sites of three of these forts. Below him is the path where, on a June day in 1757, Royal Governor Denny in scarlet uniform and laced hat, escorted by "fifty substantial free holders well-mounted and armed," rode through the gap to reconnoiter the enemy.

Down this pass was brought the only French prisoner taken in Berks County, Michel de Chauvignerie of Royal Rousillon. At the magistrate's office in Reading the arrogant young officer in his frayed white uniform confronted the village counselors. The Prothonotary, James Read, fumbling for the French phrases which he had learned in his youth at the Academy of Philadelphia, began the interrogation:

"What forces do you muster on the St. Lawrence?"

The Frenchman pointed out to the square where a great sycamore flanked the provincial court house. "We are as numerous as the leaves on the trees."

As the awed counselors listened, they had a vague feeling that the day of wrath was at hand, and their premonition was all too correct. A few weeks later Vaudreuil's raiding parties left a blazing trail of ravished farmhouses along the ridge.

Below the Appalachian ridge the Schuylkill flows southeast past the site of Kern's mill to the bustling river town of Hamburg. *Kercher Stettle* (Kercher's Village), as the Pennsylvania Germans long termed the hamlet, was the capital of the larger tract called Hamburg in the old maps. So eventually the name of Hamburg was given to the thriving village. A modern automobile bridge traverses the stream at the same place where the pioneer Martin Kercher maintained a ferry two centuries ago, and where at a later period Jacob Wolff operated one of the last boat-building yards in Berks County.

Hamburg no longer stresses its river connection. There was a time when its citizens fondly hoped that the advent of the canal would make their town an emporium for the shipment of vast quantities of coal, another Schuylkill Haven or Port Carbon. These hopes were never realized. Indeed, it is hard to guess upon what foundation the aspiration was founded, for no coal has ever been found south of the Schuylkill gap.

Nevertheless, more than one hundred years ago Hamburg was an important enough river station to make it the headquarters for the Boatmen's Association, a labor union whose methods anticipated with curious similarity those employed by the strikers of the present. These Hamburg labor czars imposed minimum wage schedules. When certain boats came down the river manned by crews whose wages did not meet their standards, they stopped the boats and, as a contemporary puts it, "dragged the boatmen with ropes over the ground and also imprisoned some of them." Finally, on July 6, 1835, a riot took place in the village streets and seventeen members of the association were arrested and taken to Reading.

Hamburg was long the social and political capital of northern Berks. Reading, the county seat, was far away; Pottsville was a straggling frontier village. So, on the periodic holidays known as Battalion Days, when the local militia passed in review, Hamburg was a Mecca for mountain chivalry. The taverns were thronged. Bear baiting, panther baiting (while panthers were still to be had), street fighting, and weight throwing were the order of the day. These would-be warriors, fresh from the plough and rather ill at ease in their new uniforms, came early to the muster. There were the Bernville Greys, the Shartlesville Guard, the Orwigsburg Troop, and the Hamburg Artillerists. No one knew exactly against whom these swashbucklers were to fight, but this uncertainty in no sense dimmed the ardor of the home guard. As their serried ranks descended the main street to the fanfare of trumpets and the plaudits of the spectators, the Berks commandos were willing to take on France or Albion, Mexico or John Caldwell Calhoun. It was all in the day's work.

These were the days of glory for the hamlet and for its canal. The latter lies neglected now, with only an occasional rotting hulk to suggest the teeming water traffic of the past. When the Reading Railroad was extended up the valley, it located its Hamburg station across the river from the town. In answer to the agitated protests of the citizens, the officials of the railroad blandly suggested that the town might grow up to their line. This it has refused to do, but nevertheless Hamburg finds compensations for its remote railway station and for the loss of its canal in an excellent network of motor roads.

Just below Hamburg on the east bank of the river there was once a crude chapel, wherein a certain eccentric Doctor Quinadon, from Saxony it is said, preached to the boatmen. The doctor maintained a water cure and primitive summer resort on the mountain nearby, in the glen leading to the abandoned Windsor furnace from whose brook Hamburg now gets its water supply. This was about the time of the gold rush to California, and it was the doctor's custom to force himself into any of the neighboring pulpits which happened to be vacant, expound his doctrines, and give advice to the prospective gold seekers. He was not without martial experience, for in the Seminole War of 1819 he led a detachment of Dutch farmers to fight in Florida. These deluded adventurers somehow reached Pensacola, and then straggled back in small groups to Schuylkill Valley after incredible privations; the miracle is that any of them got back at all.

CHAPTER 8

Country of the Palatines

THE mountain wall fades behind; and over to the westward, in Center Township, rises the graceful front of St. Michael's Church. To the southwest appear the three peaks which form Scull's Hill, the only memorial to the proprietary surveyor Nicholas Scull, who ran the original lines of Berks County. Still farther to the eastward, in Lebanon County, emerges a higher hill often climbed a century ago by a lad named James Lick, a farmer boy of superficial education who loved the stars and studied them from this summit. Now he is remembered as one of the most successful of the Pacific Coast pioneers and fittingly lies buried under the great California observatory which immortalizes his name.

Before the advent of the canal the old boatmen, who knew every reef and eddy of the river, always greeted their arrival at the stretch south of Hamburg with satisfaction, for here the stream, comparatively deep for those days, ran evenly and surely with a minimum of shoals. On the eastern bank there were several resting places where the mariners could moor their rafts or long boats, light their pipes, and partake of refreshment.

As early as 1768 Charles Shoemaker opened a boatmen's tavern in a log house on the south side of Plum

Creek. The place was called Windsor Haven, and a ferry crossed the river at the exact place where the toll bridge was later built. When the name of the hamlet was changed to Shoemakersville, the French cartographers, assuming that shoes were made there in large quantities, listed it as *Cordonier* (shoemaker) on their maps. It was a pleasant place, and in the winter months when the canal was frozen over and navigation stopped, many of the river captains came here to hibernate. In their revels at the old Metropolitan House they developed a robust school of tavern doggerel of which some stanzas survive:

> *When I pulled out of Schuylkill Haven*
> *Danny Deem pulled out ahead*
> *As I went down the Hamburg dam*
> *Old John Wentzel was in bed*
> *On Leesport level Danny fell asleep*
> *Old Wentzel went to hunt him and fell*
> *over his feet*
> *When we tied up to Reading wharf it was*
> *well nigh six o'clock*
> *And the first man I do see is Wentzel*
> *on the lock.*

On this stretch of the river one hundred years ago the ladings at the little wharves which dotted the stream hinted at the iron industry of the district. This enterprise is now only a shadow of its former self, for with the advent of the cheaper Lake Superior ore the lights in the upper Schuylkill Valley furnaces went out one by one. At the beginning of the last century, however, a large proportion of the cargoes of the river boats consisted of iron.

The captains of these river craft could name the forges that lay on either side of the stream. They knew that far into the eastward lay Congressman Daniel Udree's Oley Furnace, and the District Furnace of the Lesher family, and Sally Ann, long operated by burly Valentine Eckert, Lieutenant for the county under the Continental Congress. When the boatmen had further descended the stream, they might observe the steep mountain called Adler's Kopf (the Eagle's Head), below which nestles the homestead of Conrad Weiser. This Weiser homestead has been preserved as a historical shrine by the Commonwealth of Pennsylvania and is now surrounded by a well-ordered park, honoring one of the outstanding figures of our pre-Revolutionary history. For it may be said that in the fateful year of 1756, when it seemed that the French might advance to the Delaware, only Weiser's influence with the few Algonquin chieftains who still sided with the English kept them from throwing in their lot with the victorious enemy.

North of Weiser Park lies Charming Forge. In the year 1763, shortly after the fall of Quebec, this primitive forge was honored by a visit from a pompous gentleman who traveled over the stony roads in a coach and four. The yokels who had never beheld such state whispered that this was the rich ironmaster, Henry William Stiegel, who had come from Elizabeth Furnace in Lancaster County to buy Charming Forge. Back in Cologne on the Rhine, where he had spent his boyhood, Stiegel had not aspired to any title, but now he called himself "Baron" and set up a pretentious establishment. The Baron not only acquired Charming Forge, but bought so much land in the neighborhood that he could walk for a long summer day without stepping off his property. Presently he could be observed pottering about the creek bed and extracting silica and other minerals, with which he experimented in the making of beautiful colored glass.

This was the Baron's period of prosperity. Soon there came insistent hints of financial reverses, and one day the Sheriff came riding over the hill from Reading to sell the domain of Charming Forge at the instance of creditors. Stiegel had an able foreman named George Ege, who had been brought up in his household. At the sale Ege bought Charming Forge, and the Baron went off to teach at a country school. George Ege was a good manager and had the lesson of Stiegel's improvidence before him. As a youth he had once taken a wagonload of rags down the valley to Ben Franklin's printery on Market Street in Philadelphia. At that time the Sage had repeated a maxim which Ege never forgot: "Keep thy shop and thy shop will keep thee."

So Ege attended to business, refused to dabble with colored glass, and prospered. He was even elected to Congress when the capital was still at Philadelphia. It is related of him that he attended a state reception given by President John Adams. A flunky stood at the door and bawled out the names of the guests. This was a new procedure to the ironmaster. When his name was called he was so startled that he forgot his English and reverted to the vernacular: "*Ya. Ya. Ich kumma gleich.*" ("Yes. Yes. I'm coming right away.")

Straddling the stream is the river haven of Leesport, with its reminiscences of the Quaker family of Lee. It was an unpretentious place until the canal was dug and until the Eckerts came up from Reading about the middle of the last century and established a furnace. In the hey-day of the furnace, when the iron business was good, a generation of rough, rollicking iron workers came to live in the comfortless company houses which still survive to testify to the rigors of their lives.

The combat between Bully Rahn of Orwigsburg, representing Schuylkill County, and Bully Zerbe of Reading, the pride of Berks, occurred in this epoch at the Boatmen's Tavern in Leesport. There had been so much contention between the backers of these champions as to their respective prowess, that it was finally agreed that on a certain day the bullies should leave their respective homes and walk towards each other along the canal. This they did until they met at Leesport. The contest was gruelling. There are two versions of the outcome. Each bully was beaten into submission, according to the backers of the other.

The Friends came into this countryside as early as 1737 and established their meetinghouse east of Leesport. Two centuries passed and then the city of Reading appropri-ated the entire district for a lake and reservoir. This proj-ect would have submerged the venerable place of wor-ship. However, there were some public-spirited Quakers still resident in the neighborhood. They re-erected the meetinghouse, stone by stone, on higher ground, where it stands today surrounded by the bones of the early Quaker settlers, the Parvins, Lees, Starrs, and Penroses, re-interred in the new location.

Below Leesport the Schuylkill is swollen by the waters of the lovely Maiden Creek, which flows into it from the east. "Ye vale of Maiden Creek," wrote the Quaker mis-sionary Abel Thomas in 1777, "is fruitful as the demesne

of Jericho or the golden vineyard of Naaman." Fruitful
it has remained. An orchard, one of the most extensive
in Pennsylvania, stretches away as far as the eye can reach
to overlap the Schuylkill and begin again on the western
side.

Maiden Creek, in its turn, collects the waters of Sacony
Creek, where the Indians loved to fish. Here stands the
ancestral home of the Harbaugh family, whose distinguished son, the preacher Henry Harbaugh, ranks as the
poet laureate of the Pennsylvania Dutch dialect. Harbaugh was born in western Pennsylvania but often returned to visit the home of his fathers. In his most important work, a collection of poems published under the
name of *Harbaugh's Harfe*, you will find the kindly
couplet

> *Ich wees net was die ursach is*
> *Wees net warum ich's dhu*
> *N'jedes jahr mach ich der weg*
> *Die alte Heemet zu.*

which might be translated

> *I know not what the reason is*
> *Or why I thither roam*
> *But every year I take the path*
> *That leads to our old home.*

Beyond the high ridge which flanks Reading, on the
east one descries the Irish Hills, Deer Path Hill, the
loftier summits of Mount Penn surmounted by its curious
Chinese pagoda, and Mount Neversink. Here below Leesport the river flows opposite the site of the tavern formerly
known as King Solomon's Temple. Hard by was the

furnace of the Temple Iron Company, which had an early charter so liberal that the corporation could make iron, mine coal, or run a railroad, "so long as grass grows and water runs." George F. Baer, the Reading lawyer, discovered the charter and excitedly took it over to J. Pierpont Morgan, who promptly acquired the stock of the corporation. Then the storm broke. Temple Iron Company was denounced in the press as a monopoly, and the lonely abandoned furnace came into the fierce light of publicity.

In those days Baer maintained, on the west bank of Schuylkill, a summer house and bathing pavilion which he aptly named Bruin's Choice. Here he entertained many celebrities and men of high finance. On one occasion, during the height of the Temple Iron Company controversy, Thomas A. Edison stood upon the bank dubiously watching Baer floundering in midstream with the aid of a life preserver.

"Be careful, Baer," he warned.

"Yes," retorted Baer. "I am having trouble enough to keep my head above water."

Near Temple, at the point where the river attains its greatest depth (twenty-eight feet), the stream turns sharply to the west and passes under the limestone palisades from which the pioneer Leinbach family annually exported thousands of bushels of lime. This particular lime was known far and wide for its superior quality. The Leinbachs would load a scow with their product, light their pipes, and row leisurely down the canal, doling out bushel baskets of lime as they went. The thrifty German housewives would buy it for whitewashing. The farmers along the bank took some for fertilizing. The Brookes, wealthy ironmasters, would acquire a generous supply for their furnace at Birdsboro. Then when the scow was empty, the brothers Leinbach would paddle back for a fresh supply.

River and canal merge again below Tuckerton and pass by two monuments of the stone cutter's art of a century ago: the bridge of the Reading Railroad Company, and the finely chiseled Peacock (Felix's) Locks. If, as now suggested, one lock is to be preserved as a historical relic and model in the abandonment of the canal, Peacock's should certainly be chosen because of its marvelous workmanship. This lock was designed by the engineer Antes Snyder, son of Governor Simon Snyder of Pennsylvania and graduate of West Point in the class of 1829. As a boy in 1816 he had been kidnapped from the gubernatorial mansion at Harrisburg. A cause célèbre followed, and the attention of all America was focused upon the search until the kidnappers were apprehended and the boy restored to his parents.

With the approach to the suburban area of Reading comes the first hint of the business development which has transformed this length of once lovely watercourse. On the east bank, where graceful willows dipped into the stream, are now the chimneys and derricks of the extensive Carpenter plant whose fine-tooled steel is known throughout the world. Opposite the Carpenter plant rise the administration buildings of Reading Air Port, one of the best equipped in Pennsylvania. During the late war it was used as a prison camp, and forlorn prisoners of the once formidable Afrika Corps looked across the river to the slopes of Mount Penn, where during the Revolution an earlier generation of Germanic captives, the Hessians taken at the battle of Trenton, were imprisoned.

Opposite Reading, flowing down from the Blue Hills, appears Schuylkill's most important western tributary, the Tulpehocken Creek. The Tulpehocken, "Stream of Turtles" as the Indians called it, is pre-eminently the stream and watershed of the Palatines. Curiously enough, the first German settlers came into the Schulykill Valley from the west. These were Palatines whom Queen Anne of England had assisted in forming a settlement in the Mohawk Valley of New York. They remained there for some years but, becoming dissatisfied and hearing of the new lands in southeastern Pennsylvania which William Penn was opening to their countrymen, they resolved to move. Their toilsome descent of the Susquehanna in canoes and flatboats, driving their cattle along the banks, their ascent of the Swatara Creek, and their final settlement in the vales of Tulpehocken constitute an inadequately recorded epic.

Along the Tulpehocken is still to be traced the route of the Union Canal. Surveyed as early as 1762, this waterway was to join the Susquehanna with the Schuylkill. Such high hopes were entertained of it that when President Washington rode up the valley and stayed a night at the Ley farmhouse in the autumn of 1793, he inspected a half-built lock. Completed in 1828, the canal was never very prosperous, and it suffered a serious blow when the East Penn railroad was constructed in 1857 from Reading to Harrisburg, engrossing much of the cargo which had hitherto gone by canal. The Union waterway continued to function in a more or less desultory fashion until 1884 when, leaky and out of repair, it was sold at sheriff's sale.

From the confluence of the Tulpehocken, the Schuyl-kill, its culm-contaminated waters somewhat brightened by the clearer stream it has just received, pours southward along the industrial waterfront of Reading, the town planned and projected by the sons of William Penn.

CHAPTER 9

The Proprietary Town of Reading

WHEN the new town was laid out at the ford in the Schuylkill on the site of the Widow Finney's lonely farmhouse in 1748, it was inevitable that it should be called Reading. The ancient English borough of Reading on the Thames was the market town of the Penn family, who knew and loved it well. The provincial Pennsylvania courtiers, aware of this connection and being ever eager to pamper the vanity of their ruling family, suggested the name of Reading for the village which was to be the county seat of the "new Berkshire." It is surprising indeed that one of the earlier Pennsylvania towns—York or Lancaster or Carlisle—did not assume that name.

Thomas Penn, son of the Founder by his second marriage with Hannah Callowhill, might be termed the Patron of Reading Town. He came to America in 1739, and made a trip up the Schuylkill Valley. He stayed some days at the Finney cottage, and remarked that the site between the river and towering Mount Penn was ideal for a county seat. Thomas Penn probably was not an inspiring figure. It is recorded of him that when the settlers came to call upon their Proprietor, he had an invariable formula of greeting and farewell: "How dost do?" and then,

"Please, the other door." He was also reported to have yawned mightily as he asked Conrad Weiser whether he was really accomplishing anything in this beastly wilderness where there were neither good wines nor likely wenches. These, to be sure, were Thomas' salad days, when he was green in judgment. Later, when he returned to England, married and matured, he abounded in sage counsel for the welfare of the village which he had helped to found.

The river front of Reading, once so important, now lies abandoned as far as water trade and navigation are concerned, although great industries still line it. After the canal boats ceased to function, little pleasure steamers carried the townsfolk down to the sylvan dells of High's Woods and Poplar Neck, but these, too, have long since ceased to run. In the early days the wharves and warehouses by the ferry at the foot of Penn Street constituted a center of industry distinct from the village upon the hill. Here were the dwellings of the early ferrymen; and here were the great military storehouses, whose preservation was such a concern to the American Staff in the Revolution that, to threaten these magazines, Cornwallis made his advance up the right bank of the river after the battle of the Brandywine.

Our only Revolutionary-period plan of the river port has come down to us from a foreign source. One gloomy afternoon in 1777 a wretched convoy of Hessian prisoners waded through the ford on the way to their detention camp on Mount Penn. At the head of the detachment rode Captain Andreas Wiederhold in the green and gold frogged uniform of the regiment of Knyphausen. The Captain, an epicure at heart, looked dolefully at the drab

frontier village and wondered how he could while away
the months of his captivity. A man of resource, however,
with a talent for drawing, he used the measure of liberty
his captors allowed to make an elaborate diagram of the
streets and river front of Reading.

As a result of an exchange of prisoners, Wiederhold
was returned to Germany in 1781, when he deposited his
map in the archives of the University of Marburg on the
Lahn. When the victorious Americans irrupted into the
Lahn-thal in the spring of 1945, a Cornell professor,
serving in the Intelligence Corps, searched the archives
and found the map still intact.

One of the buildings shown on Weiderhold's chart, a
structure long since disappeared, was Continental Hall by
the riverside. As late as the spring of 1814 it housed
Captain Keim's militia company. Mobilized for the defense of Baltimore against the British fleet, the company
was awaiting high water to be floated down to Philadelphia. These paladins, well fed and housed and with a
liberal allowance of brandy sangaree, endured the delay
stoically. They employed their leisure hours (of which
they seem to have had plenty) in toasting the successes
of their naval compatriots:

> *John Bull he is a swagg'ring dog,*
> *As ever trod a deck, sir;*
> *But gun to gun, and man to man;*
> *We'll make him soon a wreck, sir.*

> *Yankee Doodle doodle doo*
> *Away your beer and cheery:*
> *We'll fill our glasses to the brim*
> *With Porter and with Perry.*

On the periodical Fair days, the river front and in particular the old Seitzinger Tavern at the bridge enjoyed a fair share of jubilation. In his diary a visitor in 1826 reported that "From every tavern was heard the Siren voice of the fiddle, while booths were erected in the streets, having for sale eatables and drinkables of all descriptions. The land might not have flowed with milk and honey, but it did flow with pies, cakes and beer. Sausages, Limburger, 'Kase Kucha' and 'Lepp Kucha' were there in great profusion. Pies of all descriptions showed their smiling faces. Horse cakes pranced over mountains of molasses candy, and gingerbread men cast amorous glances at the girls. Farm maidens came flocking from all directions, trudging for miles bare-footed to save their shoes for dancing, for shoes were somewhat scarce in those days."

Reading Dam, sometimes called Lotz's Dam, was located at about the site of present Spruce Street, and formed the junction of the Schuylkill with Union Canal. Holtzwart, the German artist who painted this part of the river in 1839, shows sailboats floating on the dam. An earlier, cruder sketch from *Portfolio Magazine* gives what is perhaps the earliest depiction of a Reading boat gliding under the bridge.

When the Schuylkill Canal was first pushed through Reading in 1824, its bed penetrated far into the town, crossing the main thoroughfare, Penn Street, at the eastern ramp of the present cement bridge which leads towards Harrisburg. This great moat, entailing as it did bridges over six streets, seriously inconvenienced traffic. The Duke of Saxe Weimar, who came from Germany in the spring of 1826, noted four locks in the Reading area, so the fall in the stream must have been considerable. It was not until 1834 that a bypass canal was built, connecting with the river at the foot of Franklin Street, thus eliminating an unsightly waterway through the town.

The stretch of the original canal through and just north of Reading presented a vexatious problem to the constructors. The terrain was of limestone and full of fissures. Each time the water was turned into the trench, it would vanish through the leaky bottom. The commissioners, summoned from Philadelphia in the emergency, rode up the valley for a consultation. In the group were Cadwallader Evans, president of the company, and Joseph S. Lewis, afterwards mayor of Philadelphia, who was to attain notoriety by wearing his high boots when he gave a reception for Lafayette. Also present were Ariel Cooley, who built the Fairmount Dam, and the ubiquitous Lewis Wernwag.

These dignitaries assembled and gazed down at the empty ditch with an air of futility. Then, realizing that a heroic gesture was called for, they summoned their best engineer, Thomas Oakes of Staffordshire in England. Oakes moved to Reading and took up the work. In August, 1823, a plague of the dread cholera swept the village and struck down both Oakes and his assistant Henry King. Such was Oakes' popularity and esteem in the community that the entire population walked behind his coffin to the graveyard of Trinity Church.

The plagues and epidemics which ravaged the valley of the Schuylkill during the years of canal construction make a tragic story as yet not fully told. The great, newly opened ditch engendered gases which took a fatal toll not only among the canal laborers (mostly Irish, newly arrived) but also among the villagers. Thomas

Oakes was the most illustrious victim but there were thousands of others.

During the spring of 1824 frequent announcements were made that the canal would be opened for traffic. Oakes had adopted the expedient of flooring it with wood for a distance of several miles north of Reading, and it was confidently expected that the trench would hold water. Accordingly, a mighty fleet of one hundred and five arks, laden with anthracite, were floated down from Port Carbon and massed above the town waiting for entry. However, not until the beginning of July could the commissioners pronounce the canal finished and navigable.

The great tidings were at once brought to Reading's leading citizen, ex-Governor Joseph Hiester, just out of office and back at his residence on Penn Square. When he had been elected three years before, his son Joseph, aged four, asked at the dinner table:

"Sag Mommi, simar nau al Governor?" ("Say Mama, are we all Governor?")

To which Mrs. Hiester replied: "Nay. Juscht ich und der Poppi." ("No. Only I and Papa.")

Duly impressed both with his own importance and that of the proposed dedication of the canal, Hiester gave orders that the great event should be celebrated in a manner befitting the occasion. It was resolved that an imposing naval pageant should be held.

The first boat, upon which Hiester and the Board of Managers embarked, was properly christened the *Thomas Oakes*, in memory of the devoted engineer. The second was named the *Stephen Girard*, and this particular stretch of the canal was to be named the Girard Canal in de-

ference to the Philadelphia merchant whose substantial
stock subscription had made construction possible. The
third was called the *DeWitt Clinton* after the patriarch
of the American canal system. The sentimental scribe of
the *Reading Gazette* who described the affair waxed enthusiastic over the "full weight of the youth and beauty
of the Borough of Reading" who lined the gunwales and
united in the chorus of a river ballad translated from the
German especially for the celebration.

All this took place in the late afternoon of a glorious
Fourth of July. The flotilla swept down the canal to the
strains of music and anchored in the dam below Reading.
Here the philanthropic lawyer Charles Evans, who afterwards donated a municipal cemetery to the town, made a
suitable address, and the steep mountainside reverberated
to the volleys of the Washington Guards. The enthusiastic
citizens were convinced that they were celebrating the
peak of transportation development for the entire valley.
Surely the clumsy Conestoga wagon, bumping laboriously
over the stony roads, could never compete with the
serene progress of the capacious canal boat! But even in
this hour of triumph a grim shadow of unsuspected competition was beginning to intrude itself. Far overseas in
Yorkshire George Stephenson was experimenting with his
iron horse. Already one of these new locomotives was on
its way to America, and surveyors were beginning to stake
out the projected railway which in the end was to strangle
canal navigation in the Schuylkill Valley.

The river families of one hundred years or more ago,
the Bells, Darlings, and Bensons, would scarcely recog-
nize the Reading waterfront of today. The extensive
Bushong distillery is only a memory, and the navigation

yards where so many boats were built lie neglected. Where are the gardens of the Quaker Samuel Griscom, superintendent of the canal, whose walks, hedges, and rose trees evoked the enthusiastic comment of every visitor? Somewhere under the rubble lie the foundations of the Griscom bird house, where the scarlet cockatoo, the admiration of all Reading, was housed. He had been brought to Griscom from Madeira by a sailor, and he could whistle "Mariners of England" without missing a note.

A section of lower Reading is still called Packerack. There is even a Packerack Tavern, although few of those who frequent it connect the name with Asa Packer, who played such an important part in the development of the Lehigh Valley and was the founder of Lehigh University.

Back in 1828 two young journeyman carpenters, Asa and Robert Packer, walked wearily into a Reading inn. They had trudged all the way from Connecticut, carrying their tools upon their backs. The advent of the canal gave them an opportunity, and by 1836 they were local magnates, owning a warehouse, docks, and a fleet of canal boats. These "Packer Boats," as they were called, were decked over and capable of being towed around Cape May and Cape Cod to deposit their loads of anthracite at Boston. Robert Packer died in Reading, comparatively obscure, but Asa removed to Mauch Chunk on the Lehigh River and became one of the outstanding financial figures of his period. His portrait adorns a wall of the impressive library on the campus of Lehigh University at Bethlehem. Above it sunlight streams through the great leaded window and illuminates the college seal with its proud motto *Homo Minister et Interpres Naturae*.

Founded by Asa Packer. But few persons in the University or in the Lehigh district associate Asa Packer with the town of Reading or with the Schuylkill River.

In 1836 William Henry Harrison, contestant for the Whig Presidential nomination, ferried over the Schuylkill on his way from New York to the West. He tarried for refreshment at the Ferry Tavern, and a band of Berks Democrats gathered outside to intone the gibing refrain:

> *The outlook is blue*
> *For Tippecanoe*
> *Van Buren's advancing*
> *His steed is a prancing*
> *We'll soon see the last of*
> *Old Tippecanoe.*

The refrain was prophetic. Three years later Harrison's successful opponent, the affable Martin Van Buren, "riding a noble cream-colored horse," crossed the river at Reading bridge. The span was bedecked with laurel arches for the occasion. Tippecanoe's hour of victory was to arrive, but not until 1840.

Just above the ford where the old Lancaster road once crossed the Schuylkill, Independence Island is located. Long neglected, it is enshrined with memories of picnics and political gatherings harangued by "Jimmy" Buchanan when he was an aspirant for the Presidential chair in 1856, and by the "Little Giant," Stephen A. Douglas, who opposed Lincoln in 1860. Douglas, wagging tongues aver, had imbibed so freely of Reading applejack that he had to be supported by two scions of the unterrified Democracy of Berks while delivering his address.

President Rutherford B. Hayes, Theodore Roosevelt,

and Woodrow Wilson included the river towns in their respective campaign tours. Then on a July day in 1914 when a frightened world hovered on the brink of a general cataclysm, a Spanish-American war monument was to be dedicated in Reading. Up the Schuylkill came the speaker, an Assistant Secretary of the Navy, a tall, self-assured young man in a white duck suit—Franklin Delano Roosevelt.

During the second great war there was a Democratic gathering at Reading which was addressed by a senator from Missouri—a rising man, men said. Some veterans from the Pacific who were in the audience commented upon his erect military carriage and were told that he had been an artillery officer in France in 1918, Captain Harry S. Truman.

Below Reading, the river flows by the deserted site of the Reading Iron Company, once the town's leading enterprise, and by the ruins of the furnace which the Eckert brothers, staunch Whigs, christened the "Henry Clay" during the mad, hard-cider campaign of 1840. Then it passes into the shadow of the steep *Navesink* (later corrupted into Neversink) hill. "Good fishing grounds," the Indians called the slope. Here, overlooking the Schuylkill, was the celebrated tavern White House, which Bayard Taylor loved so well and where he often used to come to drink his glass of beer and enjoy the view. It was on this veranda that he scribbled many pages of his fine novel *John Godfrey's Fortunes*.

Rippling down from the westward flows Wyomissing Creek with its reminiscence of the early Welsh settlers, although no trace remains of these pioneers except an old cemetery where some gravestones are engraved in Cymric characters and a corruption of the name of the township from *Cymri* to *Cumru*. Messersmith's mill, where flour was ground for Washington's army, was located at the mouth of this creek. Farther up the stream, in Revolutionary days, the water power was used in the boring and grinding of rifle barrels for the weapons inaccurately called "Kentucky rifles." Berks County folk take great pride in the fact that the "long rifle," which contributed so much to the success of the patriot cause, was constructed in the primitive forges of the Schuylkill Valley, and they resent the suggestion that it was made in Kentucky.

Wyomissing Creek, with its many glens and clearings where the colonial artisans toiled to make the guns which beat Burgoyne, is now incorporated into a well-ordered park. This park, with a model municipal hospital and art gallery, attests to the philanthropy of a group of enterprising Teutons who came to these shores eighty years ago and in this watershed built the Berkshire Knitting Mills and its affiliated branches, Reading's most important industry.

A mile to the southward and still on the western side of the Schuylkill appears Angelica Creek, so named by courtly General Mifflin, first and three times governor of Pennsylvania. His mansion, now the site of the Berks Poor House, stood near by. In the trying summer of 1777 a knot of disaffected military gentlemen made their trysting place here for hatching a mad project to unseat Washington as Commander in Chief and elevate General Horatio Gates to this post—a dimly comprehended conspiracy termed the Conway Cabal.

On a certain rainy evening, October 27, 1777, three officers of the patriot army sat down over a bottle of claret at the Bald Eagle tavern in the village of Reading. Two of these officers had been quartered in the hamlet for some months. One was General Lord Stirling and the other Major James Monroe of Virginia, who was to become the fifth President of the United States.

The third officer, Major James Wilkinson, had just arrived from the northern theater of war and was on his way to York to report to Congress the glorious news of the victory at Saratoga. "Wilkie" had made a leisurely and triumphant progress, stopping at all the taverns to report properly the great tidings which he bore. Indeed he had consumed so much time and brandy punch upon the road that, when he arrived at York and it was proposed to give him a testimonial, the cynical Scotchman James Witherspoon (late president at Nassau Hall and signer of the Declaration of Independence) suggested, "Why don't we gie the laddie a pair of spurs?"

Wilkinson's explanation for his delay at Reading is found in his own memoirs: "During the night the Schuylkill had over-flowed its banks and swept away all the scows from the neighboring ferries; I therefore found it impracticable to cross the river until the 30th, and arrived in York-town the seat of the Congress the next day."

One bottle succeeded another at the Bald Eagle. Wilkie ranted continuously about the decisive victory of Saratoga and about the superlative military talents of General Horatio Gates, which he claimed had achieved it. With these vaunts came his insistent deprecation of Washington, and his famous: "Heaven surely is determined to save the American cause, or a weak general and bad councils had long since lost it."

Monroe and Stirling listened attentively while the bibulous major revealed the full account of Gates' intrigues and ambitions, coupled with the details of the plot against Washington. Late that same evening a canoe made its way across the swollen Schuylkill with a messenger who rode down to Valley Forge. Washington, forewarned, was forearmed, and the cabal was broken. Our pious ancestors, ever alert to the suggestion of divine interposition, were convinced that a providential flood in upper Schuylkill had saved the patriot cause.

4

BELOW NEVERSINK

CHAPTER 10

Below Neversink

WHERE the palisades of Neversink still dominate the valley, a scenic railway once encircled the mountain. Delighted tourists gazed down at the horseshoe curve of Poplar Neck, at the big dam, and at the huge pavilion, the largest in Pennsylvania in its time, which the Reading Railroad built in the glen of Klapperthal. When the elaborate hotel which crowned the summit burned down, the mountain railway fell upon evil days and ceased to function. The dam is now partially breached and a blackened flood flows by the once beautiful Poplar Neck.

A century ago a wild district, still called "The Forest," extended up the western bank of the stream. The historian Morton Montgomery, who visited the site some eighty years ago, tells of the lordly chestnut groves and of the charcoal kilns which served the furnaces to the south.

Montgomery described the working of this forgotten industry: how the wood was laid in three layers, built up in the shape of a great bee hive, and then covered with clay for the ten days of burning required to properly char the chestnut logs. These kilns had to be watched solicitously, day and night, in order that the flame would be kept even and the wood not entirely consumed. He also described the bearded, swarthy charcoal burners, who invited him to inspect the conical, windowless wigwam in which they lived in much the same primitive fashion as the Lenape warriors who once roamed these same forests.

Schuylkill Valley ironmasters used charcoal as fuel until well into the nineteenth century, and long after the English furnaces had changed to coke and coal. However, the supply of wood, which in the early days seemed inexhaustible, eventually gave out, for the demand was enormous. It was estimated that in 1786 it would take an acre of trees thirty years to grow the amount of wood consumed in the Oley furnace in one day.

No one makes charcoal now. The foundations of some of the kilns can still be traced, but the chestnut blight destroyed most of the surviving trees and the last of the grimy charcoal burners has long since disappeared.

The district about the big bend of Schuylkill is rich in Indian relics, many of which were collected by the local scientist Levi W. Mengel, and can now be seen in the public museum at Reading. Just before the outbreak of the Second World War, some of the staff of the museum began to excavate in the glen called from time immemorial Indian Hollow. They penetrated to a rock shelter which may have been occupied two thousand years ago, when the Algonquins first came into the Schuylkill Valley, and which yielded a rich store of artifacts, stone axes, potsherds, pipes, and flint knives.

Northward from the east bank below Poplar Neck the landscape mounts to the range of hills which guard the Oley Valley—"O link, a kettle set in the mountains," as the Lenapes termed it. Here in this rich agricultural basin stand some of the best examples of the beautiful Pennsylvania limestone houses, dignified, well proportioned, and four square to the elements, like the sturdy race which built them.

One of these dwellings, only a mile back from the Schuylkill, was the comparatively unpretentious ancestral home of the Lincoln family. Here lived the great-uncle Abraham from whom the President took his name. Evidently he was not a very imposing character if we may judge from the description of him in a jury list of 1773:

> No. 3. Abraham Lincoln. A country-born Englishman. An illiterate man and apt to be influenced by the pleadings of Lawyers: apt to be Intoxicated with Drink.

Seated in the high-backed jury box of the old Court House in Reading, a trifle befuddled perhaps and not too fully comprehending the legal procedure before him, Uncle Abraham could scarcely have suspected that his was a name which would endure through the ages. The martyred President had always been vaguely curious about his forebears in the Schuylkill Valley, and only a few weeks before his tragic end spoke of a visit which he proposed to make to the old homestead.

At the beginning of the present century there was still living on the slope of Gibraltar Hill (so called from its likeness to the historic Rock) an old man named Lincoln, a third cousin of the President. He had served in the Civil War and had taken part in the last review of the Grand Army on Pennsylvania Avenue at Washington. That was the only occasion upon which he saw and heard his illustrious relative.

"I was with the Bucktails." he said later. "There wasn't much glamor to the review. We were all homesick; our uniforms and shoes were about worn out. The spectators were tired too and only when a band came along did they perk up. Our drummer boy was one of the tallest men in the army. When we came to the grandstand where the President and Sherman and old Stanton and other big-wigs were, we were halted and I seen the President eyeing our drummer boy. Soon an orderly comes over and talks to our Captain.

"The Captain says to me 'Sergeant Lincoln, your Cousin Abe wants to see Shaaber. Take him over.'

"When we got over to the stand the President says to our drummer: 'How tall are you?'

" 'Six feet four inches.'

" 'Just about my height. Who are you?'

" 'Mahlon Shaaber from Reading, Pennsylvania.'

" 'Reading! That's in Berks County where our old home is. When I get a little time I'm coming up to see it.'

"It wasn't many weeks later that I was down in Monocacy Railroad Station. The operator, Tommy Kline, was coding out a message.

" 'Holy Smoke!' says he. 'The President's been shot at Ford's theatre in Washington.'

" 'He shouldn't have gone to the theatre on Good Friday.' Says I, 'Now he'll never come up the Schuylkill Valley'."

For six miles the river runs past villages whose names as marked on the old maps are unknown now—Seidelville, Gickersville, Suckertown—and then it reaches the patrimonial estate and industrial plant of Birdsboro. For more than a century the Brooke family, the Seigneurs of the district, held patriarchal sway here much as the patroons did in the Mohawk Valley. Hither came William Bird in 1740 to establish his pioneer forge and to build his mansion, whose grounds and deer park ran down to the banks of the Schuylkill. The original building, although much altered, is now used as a community house. William's imperious son, Colonel Mark Bird of Revolutionary fame, swollen with prosperity and arrogance, boasted that he and his estate were immune to fire, flood, and pestilence. But within a year, it is said, the outraged river rose to inundate his farm, his house burned, smallpox ravaged the community.

In all the length of the Schuylkill there was no property more pretentious than the Bird estate. Contemporary descriptions dwell upon the glories of the box-wood, the yew walk, and the belvedere. They expatiate in particular upon the gaudy peacocks which strutted over the lawns. These birds were credited with occult powers, which enabled them to give warning of impending evil by shrill screeches. The belief in the supernatural powers of these glamorous fowl may explain why they were such favorite subjects of the neighborhood craftsmen who portrayed them in emblazoned manuscripts and baptismal certificates, on spatter ware and painted glass. Dwellers of the upper Schuylkill are prone to suggest a supernatural prescience in beasts and birds; it is a well-known and established fact in Berks County that on Christmas Eve the cows talk to each other in their chilly stalls.

Perhaps Mark Bird failed to heed the keening of his peacocks. At any rate, his disaster reduced him to bankruptcy. He went off to North Carolina, where he died, poor and forgotten. Such business as he had in Pennsylvania was managed by the young Scotch lawyer, James Wilson, who was later to become a justice of the Supreme Court of the United States.

When Wilson, as a shock-haired, penniless Caledonian fresh from the University of St. Andrew's, had come a-courting Rachel Bird, Mark's sister, the supercilious brother opposed the match. The young lawyer had his way and married Rachel. To complete the irony, when his arrogant brother-in-law's furnace tracts were put up for sale, Wilson took charge and sold the domain of Birdsboro to a Swiss military engineer named John Lewis Barde.

Barde was a colonial officer who had served with the British forces in the expedition against the Spaniards at Pensacola, and afterwards drifted into the Schuylkill Valley. He managed the property for some years and was succeeded by his son-in-law, Matthew Brooke. Later Matthew's sons George and Edward took over, thus founding a Brooke dynasty which has endured until the present. Brooke of Birdsboro has been for a century an honored name in the district.

Today the Bird estate is strangely transformed. Just south of the elaborate concrete bridge which now spans river and railroad stands the extended plant of the Birdsboro Steel and Iron Company, a war industry which furnished castings for the Navy. This development was built on the meadow which was once part of the Bird deer park. Indeed the only landmark which might be familiar to Mark Bird or Lewis Barde or Matthew Brooke would be Hay Creek, flowing down from the hills of Hopewell (Hopewell State Park) to join the Schuylkill.

Southeasterly past the islands of Mount Airy and the site of forgotten Campbell's Ford the volcanic cone of Monocacy Hill appears on the northern horizon. At the foot of this hill Daniel Boone was born, one of the most picturesque figures to emerge from the Schuylkill Valley. Boone's name is so identified with the development of Kentucky that few realize that his formative years were spent on the banks of the Schuylkill. Boone left the valley in April, 1750, when his family loaded their effects for the long journey to Virginia.

When the homely caravan took its way down the Schuylkill, Daniel Boone's boyhood in Berks County was concluded; his career as a world figure was just begun.

The Commonwealth of Pennsylvania acquired the Boone farm and homestead in 1939, transforming it into a wayside shelter and historic shrine with ample sleeping and recreational facilities. The Historical Commission, which administers the tract, claims that it received more visitors in the last year that any other rural historical monument in Pennsylvania.

Still gliding southeasterly over a shaly bottom and with the canal-bed paralleling the southern bank, the river passes Douglassville (Warrensburg on the old maps) with its graceful wooden bridge, soon to be supplanted by a concrete structure. Here, near the northern bank, was located the colonial hostelery called the White Horse, which gave its name to the ford in the river. The taverns on this particular stretch of the Great North Road were all dedicated to the animal kingdom; northward from Potts Grove were the Red Lion, the Black Horse, and the Black Bear.

Sometimes distinguished travelers alighted at the White Horse and walked down to look at the river while their horses were being fed and their supper prepared. On the evening of November 10, 1793, two horsemen arrived. The older and taller of the travelers was clad in civilian riding costume and rode a blooded Rappahannock mare. The hostlers along the road rubbed their eyes and asked if this could actually be the peerless Washington. It was indeed the President, and the young companion was his secretary and nephew, Bartholomew Dandridge.

At this time Philadelphia was still the nation's capital. The plague of yellow fever had made its dread appearance in the city the preceding August and was now so far advanced that the Cabinet and most of the government officials had fled. It became necessary for the government to choose some upland Pennsylvania town, far enough removed from Philadelphia, to serve as the temporary capital. The village of Reading had been mentioned as a possibility, and Washington with his usual thoroughness was journeying up to inspect the town and its accommodations. Also, as he was keenly interested in canal navigation, he proposed to take this occasion to view the Union Canal which was then being built.

The next year, 1794, Washington again passed the White Horse, this time in coach of state with military escort as became a Commander in Chief. It was his last expedition, and he was marching at the head of a militia army for the suppression of the insurrection in western Pennsylvania known as the Whiskey Rebellion. In testimony to the presidential liberality while on the journey there is the account of Sammy Dewees, who had played his fife in the Revolutionary Army. In the hamlet of Womelsdorf Captain Dewees assembled his men before the inn where the President was staying and made a complimentary speech with accompanying roll of drum, to which his Excellency graciously responded.

Then, according to Dewees, President Washington "requested me to march my men into the house. I did so. He then ordered different kinds of liquor to be set out, and invited us to partake with him, of whatever kinds of liquor we should choose to drink. I then asked my men to come forward and partake of the President's *treat*, and observed, that they should take a civil drink, and for each, to do so, in a quiet and respectful manner."

The General raised his hand in the formality of a parting salute, a punctilious gesture and, to the farmers of the Upper Schuylkill, a final one; for the veteran of a hundred battles was embarked upon his last campaign.

A year later the White Horse was visited by a French aristocrat, the courtly Duke of Rochefoucault de Liancourt, who had fled from his native land to save his neck from the guillotine during the Reign of Terror. Some of the Duke's titled compatriots, also fugitives, had established an asylum on the upper Susquehanna. Rochefoucault gives an account of stopping at the White Horse, four miles from Potts Grove, where "we again discovered the Schuylkill which we had left near Norris Town. Along its whole course its banks are delightful, and all the land through which it passes is good. I do not know

a finer river in point of water and views. If European
taste and magnificence adorned the banks of the Schuylkill with country-seats, it would not be excelled either by
the Seine or the Thames."

Three decades later on a spring day in 1830 a portly,
fair-complexioned visitor registered under the comparatively modest title of Comte de Survilliers. Had he
wished, he might have written after his name a succession
of imposing titles: Most Catholic King of Spain, Viceroy
of Aragon, King of Naples, for he was the exiled Joseph
Bonaparte, elder brother of Napoleon. Having recently
bought some stock in the Schuylkill Canal, he had come
to inspect his property.

On the river bank hard by Douglassville bridge stands
the oldest house in the upper valley, the dwelling which
the Swedish pioneer Mouns Jones built in 1716, as the
date stone still attests. The portholes with which it was
equipped during the French and Indian War have been
closed, but the structure must have been a sturdy one, for
it was one of the few river-bank houses to survive the
freshet of 1850.

Southward loom the crests of the Welsh Hills, whose
name affords another reminder of the Cymric immigration of two centuries ago. These hills sheltered the
notorious bandit Abe Buzzard, whose misdeeds gave un-
enviable publicity to a respectable neighborhood. In my
boyhood I read newspaper accounts of his exploits with
wonder and awe. Long afterwards, during criminal court
at Reading, it was announced that Abe Buzzard would
be tried—and for chicken stealing. The other young
lawyers and I were rather disappointed that the des-
perado had not been brought in for some higher crime,

but nevertheless we crowded into the Court room. Here sat a furtive, frightened man with shifty eyes, stooped shoulders, and a very bald head. As we looked at him in disillusionment we realized that idols of brass can have feet of clay.

Wilmer MacElree of West Chester, gentlest, kindest and most gossipy of local historians, loved to walk along this part of the towpath to the farm upon which the Navigation Company turned out its mules to pasture. The gambols of these animals always amused him and once he counted five hundred in the same meadow.

"Pope called the mules 'that strong, laborious race,'" he wrote, "but I love and admire them. With their scarlet plumes—colored cowtails on the bridles—bells hanging from a circle fitting over the hames or on the choke straps and shining brass buckles, these mules were pictures. You forgot their pedigree."

This same neighborhood was the site of the Swedish settlement called Morlatton. If William Penn really did come up the Schuylkill on his much debated canoe trip, it was for Morlatton that he was aiming. An amphibious race of fishermen and trappers, these Swedes were always upon the river.

Morlatton is also the site of St. Gabriels, one of the earliest Episcopal chapels in the Commonwealth. In 1767 the missionary Alexander Murray came from Aberdeen to this remote parish. From here, like St. Paul, he set out upon his adventurous canoe journeys up and down the Schuylkill to baptize and preach.

In the abandoned canal bed opposite Douglassville lie buried the remains of piers from which, a century ago, iron was exported. Some of this iron was brought from the charcoal furnaces at Joanna, the scene of Joseph Hergesheimer's colorful tale, *The Three Black Pennies*. Beyond lay the great forges whose names were household words in the Colonial era: Cornwall and Colebrook, Hopewell and Warwick. Here, in their stately homes, at their mahogany boards, the ironmasters filled their glasses with Madeira, port, or canary, to drink confusion to the Stamp Act. Their fox hounds ranged the hills just as did the packs of their contemporaries, the landed gentry of England. It is related of Bart Gable, foreman of Birdsboro, that if he were driving his load of ore on the Reading road and heard the baying of the hounds, he would unharness one horse, leave his wagon on the roadside, and join the hunt.

Colebrook was the scene of the "Legend of the Hound," put into dramatic verse by George H. Boker, which opens with the lines:

> *Colebrook Furnace in Cornwall stands*
> *Crouched at the foot of the iron lands*
> *The wondrous hill of iron ore*
> *That joins its wealth through the furnace door.*

Boker goes on to describe how the cruel ironmaster, enraged at the poor performance of his pack in a fox hunt and crazed with liquor, drove his favorite dog into the flame of the tunnel head. Ever after he was haunted by the specter of the dying dog and was finally found in bed, dead, his hunting whip in hand and his eyes set in terror.

> *The Squire and all his race are gone*
> *But this wild legend still lives on*

Christ save us from the wretched fate
Of him who dared his wrath to sate
On God's dumb creatures, as of old
Befell the Squire of whom I told.

All of the Schuylkill Canal locks were constructed with
care and toil. Special roads were built from the quarries
and, as modern explosives were unknown, each stone was
beautifully chiseled and matched by hand; the masonry
when completed ranked among the best in America. Since
the cessation of canal traffic, the locks have been looted
of their dressed stone, like the pyramids of Egypt and
the Colliseum at Rome. Their facings are to be observed
in the foundations of bridges, barns, and even churches
through the length of the valley.

South of the old settlement of Unionville and on the
west bank of Schuylkill are the abandoned Laurel Locks,
particularly admired for their excellent masonry. These
locks lay forlorn and weed-grown for many decades until Charles Marshall conceived the idea of incorporating
them in his estate and giving them a horticultural setting
so picturesque that it might well serve as an example to
owners of the other deserted portions of the canal bed.

Below Morlatton winds another of Schuylkill's tributaries, the lovely Manatawny, in whose valley were
located some of the earliest Pennsylvania forges, those
of Pine, Amity, Colebrookdale, and Poole. At Poole
forge, long conducted by Thomas Rutter and reputed to
be the first iron works in Pennsylvania, the first Indian
attack of this region occurred in 1728. From contemporary accounts it would appear that the skirmish was
more like an opera bouffe than an attack, although several

of Rutter's workmen were wounded. Rutter, more in sorrow than in anger, for he had always been kind and reasonable with the Indians and had set out bowls of milk for their consumption, sent a messenger post haste to the authorities in Philadelphia. He asserted that the usually peaceful Lenapes "had been incited by Indian Joe, a half-bred Spaniard of the Miami tribe."

The Governor, Patrick Gordon, was a fiery Scot from Lanarkshire. He rode up from Philadelphia, cursing the execrable roads, and spent the night at the Mouns Jones' house by the river. When he called a parley the next day Sassonnan, chief of the Lenapes, put in a contrite appearance. The Governor gave him "Six cambric handkerchiefs to wash away his tears." The chief looked doubtfully at the handkerchiefs and asked whether Onas (the patronymic title of the Proprietor) had not sent some rum as an additional present.

"Onas is grieved and troubled that you have invaded lands which you ceded in the days of our good Queen Anne and that you have attacked your good friend Thomas Rutter," the Governor said.

"I am grown old and vexed by seeing Christians on lands we Indians never ceded," Sassonnan replied. "As for Thomas Rutter, he is our friend and we will make a path of peace to his door if we must take out every bush and grub that stands in the way."

One of Rutter's partners, the engaging Robert Grace, boasted that he was descended from the earls of Pembroke. He must have been a person of tact, for he filled the dual role of close friend and landlord of Benjamin Franklin. Grace made the London voyage in 1737, a rare experience in those days, and studied the workings of

English and Scotch furnaces. When he came back to Philadelphia, he associated himself with Rutter in the operation of the forges in the Manatawny Valley. With them was another partner, Samuel Nutt from Coventry in England. The trio operated forges not only at Poole but at the Warwick and Coventry furnaces in the French Creek Valley ten miles downstream.

The tourist of today, rolling along on the concrete highway which parallels the river, looks across the placid stream to the hills and copses mounting to the western horizon. Hidden in those dales are the sites of other crude forges. The old ironmasters in their leather jerkins rode down this same road and crossed the Schuylkill at a forgotten ford west of Pottstown. The ironmasters survive only in the half-defaced legends on the tombstones in Morlatton churchyard, nearby.

Just here is the Montgomery county line. The ravaging mold of soot which so disfigures the upper river bed has become less apparent now; the banks have some of their original verdure. The Schuylkill glides imperceptibly out from Berks to form, for the ensuing twenty-five miles, the border between Montgomery County to the north and Chester County to the south.

CHAPTER 11

Boundary River

I N THE early days of the Schuylkill Valley, legal
writs did not always reach across county lines.
Sheriff Benjamin Davis of Chester County was hot
upon the trail of a horse thief one day in 1810, when
the culprit crossed the Schuylkill to Montgomery County
just in the nick of time. Safe on the opposite bank, he
raised his fingers derisively to his nose. Jake Yoder, one
of the Sheriff's deputies and a Pennsylvania Dutchman
from Oley, offered to "go over and get him."

"I can't arrest him on that side of Schuylkill," the
Sheriff replied, shaking his head despondently.

Outraged, the deputy broke into the vernacular
"Verdommte Schelmen's Fluss" (accursed rogue's river)
—and "rogue's river" it remained for many years.

Curiously enough, this stretch of the river has always
marked a political cleavage. A century ago it divided the
Democrats on the north from the Whigs on the south
bank. Today the north bank, upper Montgomery County,
largely peopled by German stock, is still apt to vote
Democratic, as are the neighboring German counties of
Berks and Lehigh; the south bank is staunchly Republican.

Here, in the vicinity of Pottstown, the Schuylkill

flows through the former domain of the Potts, pioneers of anthracite coal development in the upper river valley. Thomas Potts, usually styled "Junior" even though he was the patriarch of the family in Pennsylvania, was a hard-riding squire but withal a keen man of business. When he and his son John laid out Potts Grove, as the village was then called, they were still Loyalists and the streets were named King, Queen, Hanover, York, and Charlotte. Later, after the Stamp Act, they turned against the mother country but the street names persisted.

At the northern border of Pottstown, Manatawny Creek still ripples down to the Schuylkill, but through altered surroundings. On the height stands the stately mansion of Thomas Potts, occupied appropriately enough by the local historical society. This dwelling stood in the ancestral Potts estate of Stowe, later developed by the Richards family and now the site of an industrial town. While Thomas Potts lived, his dwelling ranked as one of the finest homes in all Pennsylvania. There were elaborate stables and slave quarters, and the gardens ran down to the river. The subsequent use of the river bank for railroad, canal, and highway played sad havoc with Thomas Potts' box-lined walks and flower beds.

The mansion itself was truly baronial. A visitor of the period relates that each day a cartload of wood was driven through the spacious rear door to feed one fireplace. Travelers who warmed themselves before the hospitable hearth included the Duke de la Rochefoucault and John Penn, Judge Richard Peters and the luxurious governor James Hamilton. Washington himself spread his campaign maps and held anxious consultations in the Potts parlor during the harassing weeks of October 1777

when it was thought that Cornwallis might march up
the Schuylkill.

The village of Stowe remained in the Potts entail until
it was temporarily lost during the American Revolution
by the ill-advised Toryism of John Potts. Like King
Charles the Second, he took refuge from his pursuers in
a tree. Later he escaped to Philadelphia, then held by
the British.

The Potts family were pre-eminently ironmasters, the
leading ironmasters of the land. It was natural that they
should have embraced this vocation, for the whole
Manatawny district was rich in minerals. William Penn,
back in England, was keenly aware of this hidden wealth.
Perhaps during his own canoe voyage up the Schuylkill
tales had been brought to him of mineral deposits under-
lying the soil. In any event he kept prodding James
Logan, his agent at Philadelphia, urging exploitation of
the upper valley.

Logan, not too anxious to entrust his precious person
to the rigors entailed by a ride into the back country,
replied evasively: "I have spoken to the Lenape Chiefs
since your departure concerning these alleged iron mines
but they say that they have not found any considerable
vein."

A more hardy, or at least more optimistic envoy appeared in the person of the German metallurgist Sproegel,
who went up the Schuylkill and waxed enthusiastic in
his report on the mineral wealth of the district: "I discovered asbestos, magnesites, amethysts, chorl and beryl,
besides copper, lead and iron."

Poor Sproegel lost his wife and infant son, victims
of the river fever, who lie in a forgotten cemetery by

the banks of the Manatawny. When he finally returned
to England, he discovered that William Penn had lost
his mind and was led about like a child. Penn died before
he could comprehend the report.

The Potts brothers had confidence in the industrial
future of the district. As early as 1724 they were operating the forge at Poole, and their relative Thomas Rutter
had established an iron works near the northern abutment
of present Pottstown bridge.

Were the Potts brothers to return to the site on the
northern river bank where they located their primitive
forge, they would find three miles of it occupied by
important industrial developments. At Bramcote is the
Stanley Flagg Foundry, with its slogan "Pipe Fitting
Since 1854." Lower down along the maze of railroad
yards are the foundations of the abandoned Pottstown
Iron Works, begun in 1863, and of the Warwick Iron
Company, begun in 1876. Below them runs a line of imposing plants extending to the Pottstown branch of the
Bethlehem Steel Company, formerly McClintock Marshall. Then the gigantic web of the Jacobs Aeroplane Factory appears, which during the Second Warld War rose,
as though by a magician's wand, on the meadows where
Thomas Potts once shot snipe. With the ending of the war
this Jacobs plant, turning from swords to plow-shares, has
been taken over by the Firestone Rubber Company.

The Schuylkill, as it flowed past the mansion of John
Potts, was a shallow stream full of reefs. "Our river
is navigable only in the freshes," David Potts once complained to the Provincial Assembly. It was swollen
enough on the October day of 1786 which is remembered
for the *Pumpkin Flood,* when so many pumpkins were

carried downstream. Usually, however, the Schuylkill was fordable in the summer months. During the winter "Potts' Ferry" operated as early as 1766. Later came "Pottstown Landing," a thriving river port when the Reading boats came downstream. At the foot of present Charlotte Street the citizens drew in nets filled with shad and rock fish, sometimes as many as three thousand in a season. River boats, the largest sixty feet long, were built by Mintzer & Reeder of Potts Grove and launched at this same spot.

Years ago a group of log cabins clustered about the northern end of Potts Grove Ferry. Their appearance gave little indication of romance or distinction, yet two of these cabins housed occupants worthy of note. One was a negro and the other a white man.

Black Sam, as he was called when he peddled fish through the village streets, had come over in a slave ship and had been bought by Thomas Potts at the slave mart by the dockside in Philadelphia. He went up into the Schuylkill wilderness with his master in the quest for anthracite, and afterwards boasted that he had carried the first surveyor's chain in the present county of Schuylkill. Also, this time in the capacity of a cook, he marched down the Philadelphia pike in 1777 with the detachment of Manatawny miners which Colonel Potts was leading to join Washington's army. Sam used to tell how, as they passed through the village of Trappe, Parson Muhlenberg looked doubtfully at their wretched equipment and muttered something about the shepherd David going out with his sling to meet Goliath of the Philistines.

The neighboring cabin sheltered Arthur St. Clair, who fought the Tories, the Indians, and the British, became

a brigadier general in the Revolution, and then returned
to a life of destitution in Potts Grove. "He looked more
like a beggar than a Military Chieftain; his worn-out
habiliments with ragged bridle and saddle made him an
object of interest to all the children and impressed on
their youthful minds the copy book lesson that republics
are usually ungrateful." When the new county subse-
quently named Schuylkill was established years later, the
name of St. Clair was suggested in belated recognition of
the general's services.

> *Seven cities strove for Homer dead*
> *Through which the living Homer begged his*
> *bread.*

Hard by the river bank stood the shed which served
as headquarters for the Philadelphia and Reading Railroad when the line was being constructed southward from
Pottstown. The stretch to Reading had already been
built. The first locomotive, shipped up to Reading on a
canal boat, was christened by some humorist *The Delaware*, because it had been allowed to slip into that river
at disembarkation in Philadelphia. The locomotive could
not run to Pottstown until the bridges along the route
had been raised; so at the jubilee dedication when the
Reading folk first came down over the new road, horses
provided the power. A second engine, *The Neversink*,
was brought up to Pottstown on a wagon. On frequent
trips from Reading it carried the iron rails with which
the section southward, from Pottstown to Sanatoga, was
constructed.

A destitute poet named Edgar Allan Poe arrived at the
railroad station in Pottstown one blustery March day in
1844. Poe had been up to Reading to deliver a lecture

for a desperately needed fee. He owed the doctor, the landlord—everybody. Poe had rich relatives in Pottstown; and on his return to Philadelphia he knew that the train was scheduled for a layover here that would give him enough time to call on the relatives to ask for funds. However, when he recalled that his father had come up the river on a similar mission some years before and had been rebuffed, Poe mounted the train without testing the generosity of his kinsfolk.

One of the Potts brothers, David, built the mansion called The Hill in present south Pottstown. So pretentious was this undertaking that the villagers dubbed it *Potts' Folly* and were not displeased when money ran out and construction was abandoned before the mansion had risen beyond the first floor. In 1851 a gentle and benevolent pedagogue, the Reverend Matthias Meigs, came and established a boys' school upon the site. Today the dormitories, class-halls, and athletic field of Hill School cover the eminence where *Potts' Folly* reared its head in the days of King George II.

At Pottstown the railroad and highway are on the north side of the stream. The canal was on the south side; and behind it, in the old days, the dense woodland stretched away, broken only by the clearings of the iron foundries. From his mansion, The Hill, Professor Meigs could descry the wisps of smoke which betokened the forges of Coventry and Warwick in the French Creek Valley. These were first conducted by old Sammy Nutt, who had come from Coventry in England. Later, when the district was laid out in townships, three new Coventries, East, West and South, appeared on the south bank of the Schuylkill.

Back of Pottstown Landing (Dog Town, they called

it a century ago) lies the district called Free Love Valley, once inhabited by the strange sect known as the Battle Axes. The valley was a curious place. A contingent of Dutch farmers peopled it, not too well educated and all too receptive for any new doctrine, whether it savored of Mormonism or of free love. With these there was a liberal sprinkling of rough furnace men from Coventry and Warwick, profane and quarrelsome. Rioting was common, and it was the current belief that Hell was only three feet under ground.

Then, fresh from New England, appeared bearded Theophilus Gates, foe of convention and apostle of nudism. Gates, professing to be shocked at the godless conditions which he encountered, called his disciples together for a miraculous demonstration that heaven was really close at hand. He had fastened crude wings made of light shingles to his arms, and with these jumped from a window. The experiment ended only in bruises, which the disappointed prophet ascribed to the fact that too many skeptics were present.

The Battle Axes were perfectly willing to follow Gates' leadership, but the harsh Pennsylvania laws intervened. In particular there was Constable Bill Rhoads, an intolerant martinet who had never danced to the pipes of Pan. If he came upon a group of naked Battle Axes bathing in the Schuylkill, he would lash them out with his wagon whip, a practice much resented by the aggrieved neophytes. Finally, in 1844, Gates was hauled up for trial in the courthouse of West Chester. The villagers crowded the courtroom to suffocation. The prosecuting attorney charged that the Battle Axes had gone about the country unclad, to the scandal of the neighbors.

"Is this true?" said the presiding judge to Lydia Williamson, a comely lass who was one of the deaconesses of the Battle Axes. "Why did you behave so scandalously?"

"The Lord by the voice of Theophilus Gates, commanded me to strip."

"Six months in prison at hard labor," retorted the judge.

A succession of islands dot the stream below Pottstown, where the Schuylkill begins a series of sharp loops, three of them in the next twenty miles. Below the islands the river still flows between fields and forests. The passenger on the Reading Railroad, which closely follows the north bank, can envisage the unspoiled water course of a century ago.

On the south bank lies Parkerford, once Lawrenceville, a long, attenuated hamlet jumbled at the base of Crab Hill. Below the village and looming up on the plateau are the buildings of the Pennhurst State School for the feeble minded. Here the perverse river turns due north in one of its bewildering curves, thus affording an observer from the Asylum a marvelous view which recalls that of the Thames from Windsor Hill. On a clear day one looks over the buildings of the Linfield Distillery to where the grain fields roll up to the Sanatoga hills, and to the picnic groves which shade the curious geological phenomenon known as the Ringing Rocks, or *Klinger Berg* as it was once called.

A roof emerging from the trees denotes the site of Crooked Hill Tavern, which for a few days in November, 1775, sheltered the amiable and unfortunate Major John André. Few realize that André was taken prisoner

twice, the first time when the Canadian garrison of St.
John's surrendered to the victorious Americans under
Montgomery. André and other captured British officers
were brought to Carlisle, in Pennsylvania, and were
lodged temporarily at Crooked Hill Tavern. Until recent times there lived in Pottstown an old woman whose
grandmother, Anna Deering, had worked in the tavern
during André's stay and remembered his spritely conversation and his performance on the flute.

Nearby, picturesque Sanatoga Creek, rippling into the
Schuylkill, suggests the boyhood of two lads who often
came here to fish and bathe, obscure louts at the time, but
each with the hand of destiny on his shoulder. One of
these lads lived in a farmhouse nearby, and the other
came to visit him from Norristown. At their respective
deaths each lay in state in the court house of the county
seat of Norristown, while Pennsylvania militia kept
watch and ward. At the outbreak of the Civil War both
boys had enlisted in the Federal armies, and both attained the rank of Major General. One, John C. Hartranft, became Governor of Pennsylvania and the other,
Winfield Scott Hancock, was the nominee of the Democratic party for President of the United States.

The Schuylkill panorama mounting to the eastern
horizon includes the village of Fagleysville and the
manor of twenty thousand acres which once belonged
to the Rhineland pioneer, Francis Daniel Pastorius, who
came to Pennsylvania in 1683 and founded the suburb
of Philadelphia called Germantown. His agent, Daniel
Falckner, gave his name to a part of the Fagleysville
district called, until the present day, Falckner's Swamp.
On September 23, 1777, George Washington, desperately

trying to out-maneuver Cornwallis who was somewhere
to the south, camped here. The General described the
place as "Forkner's Swamp."

Frick's Locks, once an important boating center, dozed
almost forgotten on the south bank until very recently,
when a treasure trove of Indian spears and artifacts was
turned up accidentally by a farmer who was plowing his
field. Between here and Black Rock to the south are the
traces of many Indian camps, but no foundations that
would betoken a permanent village. It is likely that the
Lenapes came up the river in summer, led a nomadic
existence, hunting and fishing, and then returned downstream to their permanent settlements to spend the
winter.

Linfield, nestling in the curve of the river and con-
spicuous because of its huge Kinsey whiskey distillery,
was formerly known as Limerick, or Limerick Station as
distinguished from the village still called Limerick
Square three miles to the north. The Kinsey plant has
brought prosperity to Linfield, but has destroyed all the
quaint characteristics of a riverside hamlet. The inland
Limerick, more fortunate, has preserved something of
its picturesque setting. The villagers still point out the
walls of Widow Lloyd's tavern at which John Penn,
a grandson of the Founder, praised the brown ale which
was the special pride of his hostess.

On the southern side of the Schuylkill begins the
former Manor of Vincent, once the domain of Sir Matthew Vincent, a rollicking cavalier who had drunk many
a rouse with merry King Charles and with his brother,
the Duke of York. French Creek was first called Vincent
Creek, and this entire district was developed by Sir

Matthew and by his Dutch collaborator, Andreas Vourazain from Breda. It included the sites of the prosperous twin-river towns of Spring City and Royersford, facing each other across the Schuylkill. Royersford was founded by the Huguenot emigrant Edward Royer, who maintained a ferry at this point.

Back from the south bank rises the steeple of old Zion's church, much frequented by worshipers from the entire countryside because of its melodious organ, one of three surviving organs built by Tannenberg of York, most celebrated of early American organ builders. The original edifice, with its wine glass pulpit, was destroyed when the church was remodeled in 1861. At that time the use of the *"Klingel Sacke"* was discontinued. This was a collection bag with an admonitory bell attached to a long pole. The bell was calculated to break the most profound slumber of any worshipper who attempted to doze through collection.

Below is Pikeland, named after Joseph Pike of Cork, who was accorded a large grant here in 1705 and gave his name to the tract. It is not clear whether he ever came to Pennsylvania to inspect his possessions. At a later period the township boundaries were run by a young surveyor named Anthony Wayne, better known as Mad Anthony Wayne of Revolutionary history. A century ago a passenger steamer, the General Taylor, puffed and wheezed along this stretch of the canal carrying passengers from Philadelphia up to Reading, a short-lived experiment because the waves from the side wheels impaired the banks.

The venerable village of Trappe stands on the heights opposite the south bank. The name is said to be derived

from the German word *treppe*, meaning a step. Here is
located the oldest rural Lutheran church in America,
bearing the inscription "Dedicated by the Society of the
Augsburg Confession, A.D. 1743," and here lies buried the
patriarch of Lutheranism in Pennsylvania, Henry Melchior Muhlenberg. The adjoining grave contains his distinguished son, Washington's trusted lieutenant, General
Peter Muhlenberg, known as "Devil Pete." In the old
stone school house the elder Muhlenberg conducted one
of the first "Charity Schools" in Pennsylvania. There is
no more appealing picture in all America than that of
the yellow octagonal chapel sleeping under the sycamores.
Small wonder that an almost continual pilgrimage of the
faithful streams up the Ridge to this shrine of Lutheranism.

The stretch of river below Spring City and west of
Trappe afforded many shallow fording places crossings
and "stations" for the clandestine Underground Railway,
which operated in the middle decades of the last century
and whose function was to smuggle slaves from the south
to the comparative safety of abolitionist New England.
The Quaker families of Chester County, the Coates,
Pennypackers, and Lewises, organized this "Schuylkill
Branch" of the Underground. One of the last survivors,
Elijah Pennypacker, who secured the first charter for the
Reading Railroad, loved to tell how mysterious lights
would gleam along the river bank and how as many as
ninety negroes would be smuggled across the Schuylkill
in one month. Elijah's daughter could remember how he
would return at dawn, having driven all night with ex-
slaves hidden under sacks of potatoes, and how a dozen
weary Negroes would sleep under the straw of the barn.

CHAPTER 12

Phoenixville and Perkiomen

JUST above the iron town of Phoenixville the river's waters used to foam over Black Rock, best preserved of all Schuylkill dams until its recent obliteration. Bayard Taylor would steal away from his office in Phoenixville to swim in these waters. Looming above is the mouth of the great tunnel, nineteen hundred feet long, which carries the tracks of the Reading Railroad through Tunnel Hill and into Phoenixville. Begun in 1835, this tunnel was the despair of contractors and took two years to complete. Curious geological specimens, fossils of birds and reptiles of the Jurassic Age, were found here and described in the scientific journals of the period.

The turbulent Irish laborers who built the tunnel settled themselves in a village on the summit and rioted regularly on Orange Day. One of the laborers of a somewhat later date was an emigrant from Galway, Bernard McKernan, who lived to be one of the last survivors of the Light Brigade, the ill-fated "Six Hundred" who charged at Balacklava. When a very old man, McKernan was called as a witness in the Court House at West Chester. Procedure was suspended while judges, lawyers, and spectators crowded around the gray-haired Irishman as he told about the Crimea and Lord Raglan and the great day of Balacklava.

Beyond the long curve, French Creek flows into the Schuylkill after passing through the yards and plant of the Phoenix Apollo Iron Company. A century ago, while beavers still lurked there, a young lawyer named Wayne McVeagh used to haunt the stream. Years afterwards, when he had become a famous advocate, President Grant appointed him Minister to Turkey. One wonders whether his thoughts ever reverted to his youthful expeditions on French Creek and to the ode which he composed, something about

> *Our Schuylkill's winding course through*
> *Autumn's haze.*

a poetical effort which, like so many others, has been relegated to the limbo of forgotten Schuylkill poems.

When David Reeves came in 1855 to organize the Phoenix Iron Works, he built the mansion of Reeves Park, termed by Governor Samuel Pennypacker, historian of Phoenixville, "the loveliest mansion in the Schuylkill Valley." His view comprised the mouth of French Creek, then a charming scene. Reeves prospered, made guns for the government in the Civil War, and sent his iron bridges far afield. His works expanded, but the charm of the river setting deteriorated amidst slag heaps and cinder banks.

Across the stream looms the village of Mont Clare, to which in the year 1754 came a certain Patrick Gordon, who squatted in a cave and assembled a harem of female slaves. He supported his strange household principally by fishing near Buckwalter's Island in the neighboring river, and crossed the stream by a ford which has survived under the name of Gordon's Ford. The cave has disappeared but Governor Pennypacker could point out its location. Pennypacker, in his boyhood, lived in Mont Clare, built in 1847 by his grandfather, the ironmaster Joseph Whitaker. The Mansion still overlooks the river from its setting in a beautiful park.

Phoenixville no longer is the village it was when wild turkeys still haunted Gordon's Ford and when Lewis Hammer, "a reputable citizen," crossing the Jacob's Hill on a winter day counted seventy wolves in a pack, "one of which he killed." Nevertheless it still boasts some quaint old houses and displays a memorial stone at the road intersection which marks the high water point of the British invasion during the Revolutionary War.

Through lower Phoenixville flows Pickering Creek, which in its upper courses pours through a hunting district suggestive of the shires and of the winter meets of Pychley or the Quorn. Here on crisp November mornings one may hear the bay of the fox hounds and see the red-coated riders cantering over the same hills which the army of Cornwallis traversed nearly two centuries ago.

Old Charles Pickering, for whom the creek was named, came over with Penn and is said to have been the first attorney to conduct a criminal case in present Chester County. Ultimately he himself came under the ban of the law. Wandering up Schuylkill in search of silver and finding none, he turned to the easier expedient of counterfeiting, for which he was convicted by the Pennsylvania Provincial Council in 1685. With his elk skin belt and silver buckles, Pickering was one of the glamorous figures of his day, being described by a local historian as "Miner, counterfeiter, attorney for ye King."

Moore Hall adjoins Pickering's former tract, with gardens which before the advent of the railroad ran to the river. It was built about 1735 by the Oxford graduate William Moore, descendant of the earls of Wemiss— "A gouty old aristocrat, haughty, domineering and avaricious, confined to a chair, waited on by slaves." When the British generals came up the Schuylkill in their victorious march from the Brandywine, they were delighted to find a dwelling which gave them such comfortable lodgings and recalled the country houses of their own land. By that time the elder Moore was dead. William Moore, junior, imbued it is to be supposed in the British traditions of his ancestors, was perhaps too gracious in his welcome to the invaders. At any rate, he was strongly suspected of Toryism and had great trouble clearing his name.

On the north bank, opposite Moore Hall, stands the reddish façade of the Protectory for Wayward Boys, which Cardinal Dougherty of the Archdiocese of Philadelphia established beside old Fatland Ford. Behind it rises the columned front of Fatland House, built before the Revolution by the Quaker James Vaux and afterwards occupied for a time by the young Proprietor, John Penn. In this dwelling during the second week of September, 1777, James Vaux had the unique distinction of entertaining General Washington for breakfast and then, later in the day when the British had crossed the river, of being an unwilling host to Lord Cornwallis.

The English exile William Bakewell came riding by this house sometime in the summer of 1798. Bakewell had once served a term as Sheriff of London. However, he had been guilty of an indiscreet criticism of the royal family, and it was deemed best that he take refuge overseas. When Bakewell first saw the Vaux house, it was not the classic structure of today. But with the view of the Schuylkill curving below the long slope, the site was incomparable, and Bakewell acquired the house. The Welsh traveler Sutcliffe, who sojourned there during the Bakewell occupancy, described the house: "The more I see of Fatland, the more I am convinced that it is one of the most healthful and beautiful locations that I've known either in England or America."

During the War of 1812 the Wetherill family, rich paint merchants from Philadelphia, purchased the estate. In their business the Wetherills needed lead, which was usually imported from Spain. With the advent of the war and the British blockade, the Wetherills had come up country prospecting for lead in the Perkiomen Valley, and they found it on the Vaux estate. This lead was of an inferior quality but the best that could be obtained, so the Wetherills bought Fatland and employed the architect John Haviland to erect the present mansion, abandoned now but even in its present plight one of the best examples of the Grecian revival in all of Pennsylvania.

Over the rolling slope to the north of Fatland lies Millgrove on the lower Perkiomen, now also in the possession of the Wetherill family. The present dwelling, built in 1765, served as a refuge for many of the fugitives who fled out of Philadelphia in 1793 to escape the ravages of yellow fever, some of whom lie buried near the house. About 1798 the farm passed into a family of mixed Spanish and French descent named Audubon, formerly

resident in San Domingo. So in 1798 the youthful John
James Audubon came to live in Millgrove.

On one of his rambles Audubon fell in with William
Bakewell, who invited him to visit Fatland, where the
young man met the engaging and beautiful Lucy Bakewell. What Audubon thought of his host we know from
his diary: "I was struck with his kind politeness and
found him to be an expert marksman."

What Bakewell thought of Audubon was not recorded,
but he must have had some misgivings over the appearance of the young emigrant, since Audubon tells us that:
"I was ridiculously fond of dress, would hunt in black
breeches, wear pumps when shooting, and dress in the
finest ruffled shirts I could obtain from France." An in-
congruous apparition this, for the backwoods of the
Schuylkill.

The visitor taught Lucy French and drawing. She
thrilled at his account of his trip to Philadelphia and his
interview with the scientist Humboldt, then visiting in
America. The couple rode about the country, to Schwenks-
ville to look at some egrets, to Norristown to buy drawing materials. In the end young Audubon married his
Lucy, and took her to the house at Millgrove.

Audubon made a half-hearted, ineffectual effort to farm
his estate and even to develop the lead mines. Then,
despairing of success in these ventures, he and his bride
removed to the West, where his activities gained him acclaim as the greatest ornithologist in the world. His
thoughts often reverted to Millgrove by the Perkiomen.
One June day, seated in a frontier tavern in Ohio Territory, he was drawing from memory some wild swans

which he had once observed in the Pennsylvania hills. Laying his work aside, he made this entry in his diary: "O happy river and golden time of youth. Would that I were again a carefree boy on the banks of my beloved Perkiomen."

In 1824, after the death of his wife, he came back to Millgrove and "stood motionless with a rush of memories." Two years later when, by another turn of the wheel of fate, he was wandering about London with his last few shillings in his pocket, his thoughts again reverted to Millgrove, "the house where I first took my sweet bride."

Upstream on the Perkiomen, past Indian Head Park at the confluence of the Perkiomen with Skippack Creek, the spires of Ursinus College break the northern skyline. Here is the well-known inn, dating from 1701, which purports to be the oldest tavern in Pennsylvania. Here also is the graceful stone arch bridge built in 1799 and still in use.

When the bridge was first projected in 1798, one of its staunch advocates was General Peter Muhlenberg, who lived nearby and was tired of fording the stream. Governor Tom Mifflin called the General to the state capital at Lancaster. "The only way I can see to get the funds" the governor said, "is to start a lottery. I know, General, that you are a Lutheran minister but will you sign the lottery tickets?"

"Devil Pete" scratched his head and then replied: "Well, we built our churches with lotteries so I guess we can have one for a bridge."

The lottery was successful and tolls were collected for many years until the structure was paid for.

There was much speculation as to the object of the

embrasures, two on each bridge wall, which extend out over the stream. When the trolley line came along, the delighted contractors placed their poles in these spaces and praised the wisdom of the bridge builders, who had anticipated the arrival of the trolley a century before it came into use. Only by an inspection of the plans of the original bridge, in Ireland, was it revealed that these embrasures were built as a refuge for foot passengers, crowded to the wall when "my Lord's coach and four" came splashing across the bridge, with scant regard for pedestrians.

South of the Perkiomen is the country of the Pawling family, whose memory is perpetuated in the nomenclature of the entire district: Pawling's Ford, Pawling's Bridge, Pawling's Mill. Old Henry Pawling, the patriarch of the family, came down in 1730 from Ulster County in New York and organized this domain. He lies buried in St. James Churchyard at Evansville.

In this same St. James, founded as early as 1721, the valley possesses another religious shrine almost equaling in interest the Augustus church at Trappe. During the reign of Queen Anne, the Episcopal Church decided that a missionary outpost must be established in the Pennsylvania wilderness. Many Welsh settlers then dwelt in the Perkiomen district, so a clergyman with the distinctively Cymric name of Evan Evans was sent out to build the original log church on the present site of St. James. The Welsh have disappeared from the countryside but their church remains.

In the churchyard is the tombstone of Captain Vachel D. Howard of the Maryland Light Dragoons, a mere boy who died at Valley Forge in the darkest hour of the encampment. When Washington rode up the valley in 1793, he digressed from his route and was found at the tombstone murmuring, "A brave man, a brave man. I knew him well."

5

NATION'S SHRINE

CHAPTER 13

Valley Forge

FROM the graveyard of St. James on a clear day one can see, beyond valley and ridge, the palisades of the south bank and the nation's shrine— the encampment of Valley Forge. Every river flows by one spot which for historic, aesthetic, or commercial reasons constitutes the zenith of its course. On the Schuylkill the spot is Valley Forge.

Valley Forge reservation looms above the site of General Sullivan's log bridge, thrown across the stream by the New Hampshire militia in the early weeks of 1778. The general decorated each pier with a memorial to a patriot leader (not forgetting himself), the middle one being dedicated to Washington. Sullivan boasted that the bridge would last until the wood rotted, but he had not reckoned with the devastating Schuylkill current. When the German Baron Riedesel, of Burgoyne's captured army, crossed the bridge on his way to his Virginia exile, it was already sagging; a few months later the ice floes demolished it. A full half century later, Irish laborers on the new canal, intrigued perhaps by the Celtic name of the bridge builder, erected a marker which has long since disappeared.

The original forge from which the shrine takes its

name was one of the possessions of the all-engrossing
Potts family and was conducted for a time by Isaac Potts.
Then, about three months before the arrival of the patriot
army, the Hessians raided up Schuylkill and burned the
forge. The existence of this forge had become almost a
myth until about twenty years ago, when Jerome J. Sheas,
then Park Superintendent, found the wheels and trip
hammer under twelve feet of creek silt.

The names of the two commanding peaks, Mount Joy
and Mount Misery, are usually attributed to the soldiers
of the encampment, but as a matter of fact the appela-
tions came from William Penn himself, upon the occasion of his trip up the river. It is alleged that the Founder
became lost on Mount Misery and picked up his trail on
Mount Joy. The original manor of Mount Joy, sometimes called Laetitia Penn Manor, was a tract of seventy-
eight hundred acres granted by Penn to his daughter
Laetitia Penn Aubrey in 1701, in spite of the fact that her
husband was the William Aubrey whom Penn detested so
cordially, and whom he described as "uncouth, ill-man-
nered, and avaricious. . . . A scraping varlet who will
count interest on a farthing."

The notoriety given in latter years to Washington's
encampment in Valley Forge has somewhat obscured the
stay of the British under Howe and Cornwallis, who were
encamped at the forge just before the American occupation.
While the British were here, in the third week of September, 1777, Washington with his tired army, sorely puzzled as to the enemy intentions, occupied the high ground
on the opposite bank of the Schuylkill near Fatland Ford.
His precarious position, with the swift Perkiomen between him and the precious stores at Reading, induced

Washington to cross the Perkiomen and march up the
Schuylkill to Limerick Square. This movement was just
what Cornwallis had hoped for; the way to Philadelphia
was now open. As soon as his scout master, Sir William
Erskine, had assured him that the American Army was
straggling up the Potts Grove road, Cornwallis made his
moonlit crossing of the Schuylkill at Fatland Ford. By
morning the chagrined Washington, still well to the
north, received news that the British were marching
southward to Philadelphia, which they occupied next day.
The fugitive Congress barely made its escape across
the Susquehanna to York. Washington, patently out-
maneuvered, retreated to the upper Perkiomen, advanced
again for the disappointing engagement of Germantown,
and eventually recrossed the Schuylkill with his discouraged troops to take up winter quarters on the heights
of Valley Forge.

The American forces remained at Valley Forge through
the trying winter until, on a June day in 1778, there
came the glorious news that the British, fearing to be
bottled up by the French fleet coming up the Delaware,
had abandoned Philadelphia. Then immediately the hunt
was in full cry; Washington was ready for the pursuit. It
was an inspired, rejuvenated, confident army that poured
over Sullivan's crude bridge to drive the British back to
New York, and most of the patriots were heartily glad
to be leaving the valley of the Schuylkill.

Sergeant Abijah Ford from Taunton had been assigned
to Conway's Brigade. On the day of the evacuation of the
camp, he led his squad to the bridge for the last time.
Looking down at the rushing waters, he saw them not in
their June radiance but in retrospect, ice bound and

sinister. Recalling anxious bivouacs in the snow while the British watch fires still glowed through the mist of the eastern bank, the sergeant barked out an order: "Single file, now, and only one caisson on the bridge at a time." Then he spat into the river. "I hope I may never see this pesky Schuylkill again."

Today the Reading railway runs between the river and the encampment, and just by the railroad station is the farmhouse which Washington used as his headquarters during the winter of 1777–1778. This modest stone edifice stands near the northern boundary of the encampment, by Valley Creek. South and west extend the lawns, groves, and monuments of the beautifully kept park. From the dominating point of the observatory of Mount Joy one may trace many miles of the course of the Schuylkill.

Washington Memorial Chapel (whose Gothic cloister seems somehow out of keeping with this very American setting) crowns the summit of the hill and is a popular place for weddings. Here in the museum is preserved Washington's tattered marquee, which the Custis family first deposited at Mt. Vernon. The Chapel dominates the Memorial Arch to the westward, upon which are inscribed the names of Washington's generals, and behind this is the stream with the picturesque wooden bridge leading to the former headquarters of Lafayette and Knox. The redoubts, redans, and cabins which were occupied by the frost-bitten colonial soldiers have been faithfully restored and are easily to be reached by well-constructed roads.

If the French engineer Louis L. Du Portail were to return, he would find the line of defence with the Star Redoubt, the Stirling Redoubt, Forts Huntingdon and Washington, and the flanking line of breastworks all sedulously and correctly reconstructed. Indeed, the original map which Du Portail stretched on the pommel of his saddle is still preserved. The accuracy of the restoration was assured in advance by a comparison of Du Portail's map with the "Spy Map" made by a Tory in British pay and submitted to Sir William Howe, the British Commander in Philadelphia.

Somehow the apparition of the debonair Du Portail, riding over the Schuylkill hills with his roll of maps and becoming a trifle tipsy when the news of the signing of the French alliance was announced, seems much more in accord with the real spirit of Valley Forge than the nostalgic, semi-apochryphal, and oft-repeated anecdote of the Commander-in-Chief praying in the snow.

So the American Army left Valley Forge and the woebegone Hessian captives moved in. On Christmas Eve of 1778, in the same huts which the troops of Wayne and Knox had occupied, the Germans lit their candles and sang their hymns. Then the place relapsed into obscurity, deserted and weed-grown. In 1824 a Utopian social organized by the English cotton manufacturer Robert Owen appeared on the scene. The Friendly Association of Valley Forge was established with the intention of founding a scheme of social readjustment. This experiment was short-lived, and Valley Forge became a site for political meetings, with accompanying ox-roasts. Daniel Webster spoke here and Henry Clay and Pennsylvania's favorite and darling son, Jimmy Buchanan.

As early as 1828, at a community picnic, the project of acquiring Valley Forge as a historical memorial had been broached. However, many decades were to elapse before steps were taken toward this end. Finally in 1877, at the

centennial of the camp, the eloquent lawyer Henry Arnitt
Brown of Philadelphia spoke in a driving rain to sixty
thousand bedraggled auditors on the subject of national
neglect. His impassioned plea had its effect. Washington's headquarters were acquired in 1879. The Commonwealth of Pennsylvania bought a large part of the former
campground in 1893, and formally took charge. Now the
shrine is visited annually by an average of one million,
two hundred and fifty thousand enthusiastic visitors. An
alumnus of the University of Pennsylvania even proposed moving the campus there.

And here at Valley Creek, the northern limit of the
park, the Schuylkill's function as a boundary river between Montgomery and Chester terminates. The Chester
hills recede toward the setting sun and the river flows
through Montgomery and Philadelphia counties, heading
for the Delaware and the open sea.

CHAPTER 14

Norriton

BEYOND the site of revolutionary Fort Huntington, most southerly outpost of the Valley Forge encampment, the Schuylkill passes through the industrial town of Port Kennedy, named for the pioneer Alexander Kennedy, who came to these parts in 1805. Here the river enters the ancient domain of Norriton, which includes the present borough of Norristown.

"Ours" proclaim the proud citizens, "is the largest borough in the United States."

Municipalities of this size usually become cities, but Norristown clings to its borough form of government. Both town and district take their name from an enterprising Quaker, Isaac Norris, who sailed from Jamaica two centuries ago to settle here.

This part of the valley was the former Manor of Williamstadt, granted by the Founder to his son William. When Penn's eldest son, the sickly Springett, died, it was the fond hope of the Founder that son William and his descendants would exercise a patriarchal sway at Williamstadt. But William Penn, Jr., turned out to be a wastrel and a spendthrift. He lived for a while in Philadelphia, where the provincial authorities found him a pretty handful. The scandalized father, back in England, was mortified to hear from his agent in Philadelphia that William, Jr., "In company with other extravagants engaged last night in a tavern brawl in Coombes Alley and beat up the watch." And again, "Being always in need of money he is now negotiating with Isaac Norris and William Trent to sell them his Manor on Schuylkill."

Sure enough the Manor was presently sold to Norris and Trent. The latter soon moved to the Delaware, and Trent of Schuylkill is better known as Trent of Trenton. Isaac Norris reigned in the manor on the Schuylkill; when Trent met Ben Franklin in London just before the Revolution, they chatted of Pennsylvania affairs and Trent described the development of Norriton.

William Penn, Jr., might have done better to have stayed by his river kingdom, for it was a lovely spot. The stream bed was studded with charming little islets which supported oaks and flowering laurel. Unfortunately, the building of the dam near old Swede's Ford has obliterated most of these islets, together with the memory of the picnics and Fourth of July gatherings and municipal celebrations which used to be held upon them.

A century ago the south bank of the Schuylkill, all the way from Port Kennedy to Norristown, must have been a floral paradise. The historian Buck, who often walked along the stream, spoke of the flowering fruit orchards and of the excellent fertility of the soil. He always maintained that the view from the twin locks of Catfish Dam was more beautiful than that of the Potomac at Harper's Ferry. Perhaps this was true in Buck's time, but the pyramids of coal which the Reading Company has piled at the river landing of Abrams have not tended to preserve the original charm of the landscape; and Catfish Dam, beloved of artists, is gone.

In the neighboring and ancient Manor of Mt. Joy, one of the many limestone beds so typical of the Schuylkill Valley can be found. The Pennsylvania Germans are sometimes termed "the limestone race," since most of their settlements, whether in Pennsylvania, Maryland, or Virginia, followed the calcium deposits from which they built their houses and barns. As early as 1708 Oldmixon in his *British Empire in America* spoke of the excellent lime ore found at Mt. Joy. Alexander Kennedy first exploited the deposit, and he soon found that the limestone on the north bank of Schuylkill was of a higher quality and more extensive than that of the south bank.

However, the south bank has its own riches, for the limestone, extending westward, blends into the marble deposit of the King of Prussia quarry, whose stone adorns the front of Girard College in Philadelphia and other structures built during the Grecian revival in Ameria. The names of this quarry and of the adjoining tavern testify to the admiration once felt for Frederick the Great. In the early days of Pennsylvania many of the settlers had served in the armies of Frederick, and some had charged with him on the victorious field of Rossbach. Consequently, they were prone to commemorate his features on slip-ware, china, and glass.

King of Prussia was a secluded corner until the advent of the automobile brought its rushing tide of holiday travel. Now this erstwhile quiet hamlet will be further projected into the light of publicity when the new Pennsylvania Turnpike is extended through it from the west.

This same turnpike, intended eventually to follow the western bank of the lower Schuylkill into the very center of Philadephia, will give future tourists a succession of lovely views on the Hidden River.

Just above the site of Catfish Dam, where the highway bridge crosses the Schuylkill, is Betzwood, an unassuming hamlet and yet one which housed one of the modest beginnings of the cineomatic industry. The country estate of the Betz family, rich brewers from Philadelphia, was located here. In the meadow by the river where their percherons once grazed stand some commercial buildings, in which about 1913 Sigmond Lubin, pioneer of the "movies" in Philadelphia, established a studio called Betzwood, which ranked as an earlier and eastern Hollywood. Travelers who crossed the bridge (many of them still driving a spanking pair of bay geldings in that era) were astounded to see cowboys dashing along the river bank or yelling Indians chasing a mail stage. The pictures made at Betzwood were all "silent," and in their development only sunlight was used. The actors who appeared in them and whose autographs were then so eagerly sought—Ethel Clayton, Arthur Johnson, Marie Dressler—are shadowy figures out of the past.

In a stone dwelling east of Betzwood, many decades before "movies" were ever thought of, lived a boy who was to be acclaimed as one of the greatest scientists of his day. He came up to the lonely farmhouse by Germantown turnpike in 1740 at the age of eight. Already hailed as an infant prodigy, he could discourse fluently in Latin and was experimenting with a water mill. Sometimes, on summer afternoons, he bathed in the Schuylkill, the same stream of which he was later to be chosen the official surveyor. His name was David Rittenhouse. When he had become world famous and had taken his seat with Franklin as one of the very few American members of the Royal Society of London, he came back to the Norriton house where he had made his first diagram of the stars, the model of the renowned orrery, which was once the pride of Princeton College but is now mislaid or lost.

When the German settlers first came to Norriton, they found the Swedes already established there, approximately on the site of present Bridgeport on the south bank. Mats Holstein, Mounce Rambo, and Peter Yocum, bearded Scandinavian pioneers, worshipped at the old church at Swedesburg. The later stone structure was not built until 1760; but the missionary Wrangel, from Stockholm, harangued to a mixed audience of settlers and Lenapes (dragged in for the service of which they did not comprehend one word) in a log edifice which has long since disappeared. "Mattsung" they called the district in those days.

Bridgeport was at one time expected to have a brighter future than the village of Norris across the river, but when the bridge was thrown across the Schuylkill in 1829, the population gravitated to Norristown. Chevalier du Portail, the French volunteer officer and engineer at Valley Forge, settled in Bridgeport at the close of the Revolution.

The broad expanse of river between Bridgeport and Norristown is the site of Old Swedes' Ford of colonial days. Here on a somber December day in 1777 General Washington, who had just broken up his camp at Whitpain, was seeking to cross the river and reach a temporary refuge at Valley Forge. The General first proposed marching his troops up the Egypt Road (so called, it is said, because it lead to the fertile district of Fatland), but in the end decided to cross at Swedes' Ford, on a shaky bridge of wagons with a flooring of fence rails. This lugubrious crossing marks the lowest ebb of morale for the patriot forces during the entire war. Du Portail, wrapped in a military coat in which he had once crossed the Rhine, sat shivering in the drizzle, watching the bedraggled Continentals straggling over the wavering bridge and shook his head. That night, writing to Du Choiseul at Paris, he said, "There is more enthusiasm in a single coffee house in Paris than in the whole thirteen colonies."

The power plant of the Philadelphia Electric Company marks Barbadoes Island to the north of the trolley bridge. The name recalls Isaac Norris' West Indian background, when he lived some years in Barbadoes. After Norris' time the island became part of the countryseat of Colonel John Bull (a stout Whig despite his Tory name), who raised luscious catawba grapes and sent a bunch to President Jefferson at Philadelphia with his compliments. Still later comes a curious connection with the University of Pennsylvania, when Barbadoes was conveyed to Provost William Smith "for the uses of the college." There were even alumni to suggest that the college would do well to remove from its setting on Fourth Street in Philadelphia to this lovely isle.

This utopian idea was not taken very seriously by the college authorities, and presently the Philadelphia newspapers were full of announcements that Barbadoes Island had been transformed into a race course, that a two-mile tract had been laid out, and that a purse of Four Hundred Dollars was to be offered for a race between the gray gelding *Governor Mifflin* and the sorrel mare *Pride of Schuylkill*. Afterwards, bathing establishments were installed, with picnic grounds under the beautiful oak trees.

The real beginnings of the settlement of Norristown were located on the high ground on the mainland north of Barbadoes. Here where the Ridge Road, now Main Street, crossed Stony Creek, the first houses were erected. Here, too, was the well-known tavern, Norrington House, marked in Nicholas Scull's map of 1775. Nevertheless, when a meeting was held to consider the incorporation of the village of Norristown, it was convened not at Norrington House but at the Jeffersonville Tavern, two miles up the road.

Norristown, dominated by the graceful copper spire of the Presbyterian Church built in 1854, has not grown northward from Stony Creek as much as once predicted. Instead it has extended south and east. Even the house where General Hancock once lived as a schoolboy is now by-passed in the march of progress. Until recently men were still living who could remember the road which ran up the river from Swede's Ford to Stony Creek, and the beech trees which lined it. In those days Colonel Bull maintained a picturesque series of small dams and mills, and farmers brought their grain all the way from Doylestown to be ground there. These mills disappeared when the canal was built and the water rose, and the river front is nearly lost in a maze of railroad tracks.

CHAPTER 15

Downstream to Flat Rock

BEYOND the long curve at Swedeland below Norristown, the Schuylkill passes a succession of smoking industrial plants on both banks. These give little indication of the peace and beauty of the valley when the Quaker, James Wood, came upstream more than a century ago to found the mill near Ivy Rock, a modest undertaking which was to be the progenitor of the Alan Wood Steel Company.

It was John Wood, son of James, who in 1842 made the accidental discovery of the process for polishing, or "russianizing," which had hitherto been monopolized by the Russian iron mills. Passing through his works one day, Wood casually left the imprint of his oily hand upon a pile of cooled billets. When the billets were converted into iron sheets, the lustrous imprint of the hand remained. Wood perfected the process and sent an example to the Crystal Exhibition of 1857 at London, where it attracted the attention of Prince Albert and won a prize.

Near the present Alan Wood works were recently to be observed some remnants of the locks built for the first canal, projected at the end of the eighteenth century. It must have been a promising enterprise in its day, for the governor himself, General Tom Mifflin, rode over from

Lancaster to view the operation. Even DeWitt Clinton, father of the New York canal system, professed interest in the Schuylkill venture, and wrote for details. But the ill-starred venture ended in bankruptcy.

To the north lies Plymouth Meeting of the Society of Friends, a quaint landward shrine dozing under the maples. Near here the most beloved artist in all the Schuylkill Valley, Thomas J. Hovenden, lived and died. Few American artists have excelled Hovenden in popular appeal; and most of us, at one time or another, have possessed a lithograph of *Breaking Home Ties* or of *John Brown at Harper's Ferry*. Hovenden gave up his life in an endeavor to save a child who had strayed into the path of an advancing train.

Downstream little save the name remains of the reef at Ivy Rock, once the terror of boatmen. Below here the south bank mounts sharply and takes on the precipitous wooded character which continues for eight miles. Back of those cliffs lies the gloomy defile of the Gulph, where Washington faced the British General Grant during some tense December days in 1777 before he marched up to Valley Forge. Beyond are the estates, country homes, and clubs of the aristocratic "Main Line" district, a title which has become an American synonym for elegant leisure.

The original scenic charm has been well preserved here; Gulph Creek ripples down to the Schuylkill in its pristine beauty. Matson Ford Road, leading to where the Conshohockens face each other across the river, is bordered by pretentious manors suggestive of Hampshire or the Cotswolds. Winston Churchill is reputed to have said that if he wished to show a visitor the best of American country life, he would take him not to Lenox or Long Island, but to the "Main Line" of Philadelphia.

Beneath these cliffs of Conshohocken Peter Matson erected his log cabin in 1741, his grant of land having been signed by a third William Penn, grandson of the Founder. Matson, an enterprising pioneer, soon noted that the Friends coming from Gwynned and Plymouth on the east side of the Schuylkill were accustomed to ford the river just below his house on their way to the Merion and Radnor Meetings on the west side. He improved the crossing, and some say he exacted a fording fee. In any event the name Matson's Ford soon came into general use.

It was so named on a May morning in 1778 when a debonair French volunteer, who was introduced to Matson as General Lafayette, crossed the river to reconnoiter the British in the direction of Philadelphia. Matson, an old soldier himself, had his doubts about this rash exploit; and these doubts turned into confirmed apprehensions when he learned next day that the Marquis was encamped at Barren Hill, two miles to the east, and that the British were encircling him. Lafayette was too adroit however, and presently the escaping Americans came wading back through the stream. One of the Matson descendants used to tell of the ludicrous appearance of the Oneida Indian auxiliaries, who formed part of the American party, as they swam through the current with only their bald heads and scalp locks protruding. When General Lafayette was making his triumphal tour of America in 1824, he drove out from Philadelphia to the ford, moralized upon his narrow escape, and muttered something

about *l'insouciance de la jeunesse*—the audacity of his
youthful campaign.

Some months after the Lafayette escapade and while
the Revolution was still running its course, the Matsons
acquired a distinguished neighbor in the person of Edward Shippen, Chief Justice of the State of Pennsylvania.
While the Shippen family were spending the summer
months at the Ford, they were often visited by General
Benedict Arnold, military Governor of Philadelphia, who
came courting pretty Peggy Shippen. Tradition has it
that the elderly suitor was morose and distracted, as he
may well have been, for he appears even then to have
been contemplating his later treason.

Long after the Matsons and Shippens had disappeared
from this locality, and when a permanent name was being considered for the bustling manufacturing villages
which had grown up on either side of the stream, the
name of Shippenville was suggested. But by that time the
Shippen family was out of favor because of the taint of
Toryism, and the name "Conshohocken," or "Pleasant
Valley," was chosen.

The career of the proprietary family of Pennsylvania
may be traced in the manors which William Penn strewed
along his favorite stream. Williamstadt was granted to
William Penn Jr.; Mt. Joy, to his sister Laetitia Aubrey.
Below Conshohocken lies the former Manor of Springett
with its memories of Gulielma Maria Springett, first wife
of the Founder, although Mrs. Penn never saw the villa
which it was planned she should occupy on the heights
above Spring Mill.

Somewhat later a stone, gable-ended house arose over

the river bank, built by a Gallic adventurer, Peter Legaux, who came into these parts from Loraine just after
the American Revolution. From his eyrie above the river,
Legaux observed the traffic wending its way down the
shallow stream, and immediately conceived the idea of
blasting the river bed so as to admit boats of deeper
draught, a conception which was the genesis of the subsequent canal. Also, as he was the owner of both river
banks, including a tavern on the farther side, he asked
and received from the Pennsylvania legislature the right
to maintain a ferry. In Legaux's time there were no
bridges spanning the river—the first Flat Rock bridge was
not erected until 1810, and the bridge at Swedes' ford
not until 1829.

This indefatigable Frenchman had many irons in the
fire, but his most startling proposition involved establish-
ing a vineyard. It was his dream that the steep banks of
the Schuylkill would one day be lined with rows of vines
similar to those on his native Moselle. The traveler Brissot de Warville, who visited Spring Mill in 1788 just as
the delegates for the Constitutional Convention were as-
sembling in Philadelphia, was not too convinced as to the
success of the experiment: "It will be a long time, before
the wine can be cultivated to profit in America; first, because labor is dear and the vine requires vast labor; secondly, because the wines of Europe will be for a long time
cheap in America."

The Quaker missionary Robert Sutcliffe, prejudiced
like most Englishmen of the period against any foreigner,
particularly a Frenchman, passed Spring Mill in 1804 and
also regarded the vineyard with deprecatory eye: "As Le-

gaux's vines are not suffered to grow more than three feet in height, they have the appearance of a field of raspberries."

In the end, Legaux's schemes brought him only tribulation and ruin. The subscription list to the vineyard company embraced such names as Robert Morris, Stephen Girard, Aaron Burr, Peter Muhlenberg, and Alexander Hamilton, but the company soon found itself in bankruptcy. The moldering foundations of the ferry-house can still be traced, but not the vineyards, the sawmills, or the joinershop which the optimistic Frenchman established, two centuries ago.

At Spring Mill the Schuylkill turns sharply to the right at the point where the cottage of Colonel Samuel Miles once stood, the farm to which this veteran returned, broken in health and spirit, after he had been taken prisoner by the British in the battle of Long Island and had spent two years on the prison ship *Jersey* in New York harbor.

A naval veteran, Judge Richard B. Jones, who could boast that he was the last survivor of the ill-fated frigate *Philadelphia,* all of whose crew were taken prisoners in the harbor of Tripolis in 1801, came here to pass his years of retirement. He wrote a treatise on the subject of the curious boiling springs which gave Spring Mill its name, the same springs which attracted the all-seeing eye of Franklin when he was examining the Schuylkill as a possible water supply for Philadelphia. Judge Jones, in his walks about the country, explored the possibilities of the marble deposits at present Marble Hall, just back from the river, and predicted the development which that industry afterwards attained. The exact method by which this marble was cut is not clear. Mease in his *Picture of Philadelphia* (1801) speaks of "The saws, operated by water power which cut the marble at Marble Hall."

Beyond Spring Mill the Schuylkill enters upon its longest tangent in its race for the sea, a straight course for the Falls six miles below. Railroads occupy either bank, and the old line of the Reading passes through Flat Rock tunnel on the west bank, piercing the picturesque cliff called Mt. Ararat. The construction of this tunnel was almost as much of an engineering problem as the building of the long tunnel above Phoenixville. During the year 1839 the work was under the supervision of Moncure Robinson, who had so much to do with the original layout of the Reading Railroad. Here on a winter morning stood Robinson, one eye upon the operation and the other reading the contents of an official letter in which he was being invited to leave America and build railroads for Czar Nicholas I of Russia. Happily for the future of the railroad, Robinson stuck to the Reading and in the end achieved the splendidly leveled roadbed from the coal regions to tide water.

Flat Rock Dam, still intact, backs up the longest stretch of "slack water" now remaining on the Schuylkill and gives the river width and dignity. Between the riverside manufacturing area at Conshohocken and the similar industrial district on the "island" below Flat Rock Dam flows a stream as yet unspoiled by commerce and dotted with the boat houses, not too tastefully planned, of the Philadelphia folk who come here in the summer. Near the former railroad station of Lafayette swimming races were once held, which attracted notable swimmers from all parts of the country. Lafayette has reverted to its old

Indian name *Miquon,* one of the affectionate titles by
which the Lenapes sometimes addressed William Penn,
although he was usually called *Onas.*

Miquon is best known today for the fine paper produced in the Hamilton plant, which operates, appropriately enough, not far from the site where the first paper-
mill in America was established by William Rittenhouse
in Monshone, or Paper Mill Run. Here, at or just below
Miquon, was the western terminus of the long abandoned
highway over which the Penns journeyed from their
dwelling at Pennsbury on the Delaware to their manors
on the Schuylkill. And below this, where Holgate's full-
ing mill stood in pioneer times, the road from Baltimore
to New York once crossed the Schuylkill.

In the centennial year 1876, a New England bard
walked along the heights at Rose Glen on the opposite
side, near the mouth of Mill Creek. The townsfolk whispered that Mr. Longfellow was composing a river poem
and, sure enough, some weeks after the poet's return to
Cambridge there were published the lines:

> *O River of tomorrow, I uplift*
> *Mine eyes and thee I follow as the night*
> *Wanes into morning and the dawning light.*

On the slope, in the suburb now called Shawmont in
his honor, lived the inventor Thomas Shaw, the genius of
the hydraulic pump and of the railroad binder. Like
Moncure Robinson he refused opportunities for foreign
employment, one from the Emperor Napoleon III, who
offered Shaw a high position in the direction of French
railways. The inventor, however, preferred to spend his

years of retirement walking over the Roxborough hills,
where one of his descendants found him one June day in
1888 sitting on the cliff by the river, watching a boat race
between the University of Pennsylvania and Cornell.

Thomas Shaw had many visitors in his Schuylkill dwelling. One was a young scientist from New Jersey named
Thomas Edison, who was experimenting with a crude
talking machine, which was regarded by his friends with
amused tolerance. Shaw presided at a lecture which Edison gave in Temperance Hall at Roxborough. A concert
was to be given in the same hall some days later, and
Edison arranged that his machine should announce this
event and repeat the words "tickets fifty cents." One of
the amazed auditors cried out, "Why, it's just like a human voice!"

Looming imposingly on Roxborough height and dominating the Schuylkill, the apse of the unfinished cathedral
of the Episcopal Diocese of Pennsylvania stands rather
forlornly. This district is part of the ill-defined tract
known as Port Royal, a name also given to an island and
fishery in the river below. It was at Port Royal that
Madam Farmer, widow of Major Jasper Farmer, made
her discovery of the excellent limestone, equaling in
quality the Port Kennedy deposit, which was to contribute so much to the prosperity of the neighborhood.
Chief Justice Nicholas Moore, writing to Penn on September 13, 1690, jubilantly proclaimed: "Madam Farmer
has found out as good limestone on Schuylkill as any in
the world."

A provincial bard, quoted by John Holme in his *The
Relation of the Flourishing State of Pennsylvania*, commemorated the discovery in verse:

A few years since it's known full well.
Here lime was burned of oyster shell.
No lime-stone in these parts was found
But now by searching in the ground
Great store was seen in a short time,
Of which some now make good stone lime.

The shafts from which the limestone was hauled in ox carts now lie deserted, half hidden in shrubbery. And exactly where, we wonder, was the "soap stone quarry near Spring Mill" which the *Picture of Philadelphia* recommends as the goal of a Sunday promenade from the city, an excursion far too long for the pedestrians of this age.

6

GORGE OF
SCHUYLKILL

CHAPTER 16

Manayunk

FROM the window of a Reading railroad train one can see the masonry of the locks at Flat Rock Dam as trim and well pointed as when the canal was in its zenith, although boats no longer pass through. Above the dam the hill town of Manayunk mounts steeply. Manayunk, "while we drink," was one of the Indian names for the Schuylkill.

When the pioneer Levering brothers came to the site of Manayunk, while William Penn still lived, they established a sawmill at the foot of present Levering Street, where the shad lurked under the bank of Wood's Island. The Founder himself had paid an early visit to the place, after he had concluded his treaty with the Indians under the elm of Kensington. Some of the Lenape chiefs offered to guide him "a days journey toward Susquehanna." It was a toilsome journey but Penn, then thirty-eight years old, was trim and fit, not the portly dotard pictured in Benjamin West's much lithographed and misleading painting. The trail took Penn to the heights commanding what was later Hagy's Ford, and he stood looking across the rushing Schuylkill.

One of the Leverings, who was with the Founder on that day, afterwards described how the "hills of the west

bank mimicked mountains in their disordered masses of
mighty rocks, flung by nature's hand in wild confusion.
The deep ravines, cleaving these hills, suggested cruel
scars, long healed, and now made health-giving in their
clear streams, singing gayly as they leaped to the river in
myriads of fairy cascades."

The present broad expanse of Flat Rock Dam hides the
former site of dangerous Rummel Falls, a much-feared
rapids whose ominous voice reverberated among the hills
of Lower Merion during the Spring freshets. "Wind N.,"
wrote Joseph Price in May 1805, "could hear Rummel
Falls Roare plain." In 1818 another visitor wrote about
"This very spot where *Rumhill Falls* endangered the
lives of the boatmen."

Below Rummels came a succession of reefs and another
fall below Mount Ararat. Some islands, which were once
the resort of wild fowl and gave pastorage for hogs, have
entirely disappeared. As all islands in the province were
rigorously reserved by the Proprietary, no warrants were
issued for their survey until 1760. In fact, many islands in
Schuylkill lie unpatented until the present day.

The highway leading south from Reading followed
the river bank in the old days. Later it was moved up to
the ridge, the present route. Old residents tell of wagon
trains half a mile long, laden with up-river corn, wheat,
and rye. Over this same road testy John Crawford, who
had been an Indian fighter in Ohio, drove the stage from
Manayunk to Philadelphia. Passengers who rode only
when it rained were severely discriminated against by the
captain.

"No. You don't ride in good weather and you can't
ride now. Damn you, walk!"

When Manayunk celebrated its centennial, a local
newspaper editor described his cliff town: "The houses
on the steep hills are so thick that no more can be built.
Some are perched up on rocks, others in holes. Some are
so high as to have twenty-three steps up to the first floor,
others so far down that two stories are below the street
level. Many have the old out-houses; some the old
pumps."

The scribe might well have noted the similarity of location between Manayunk and the lower town of Quebec, Sunnycliffe corresponding to Dufferin Terrace in the
Canadian city. And Manayunk, like Quebec, has seen
banners wave and has heard the fanfare of trumpets and
the tread of marching feet. Washington came here after
his defeat at the Brandywine, but tarried only long
enough to get his army across the Schuylkill. He came
again some weeks later, marching down the Ridge Road
for his attack on Germantown. Joe Stains, who lived to
see the Civil War, used to tell his children about "the
Americans coming down the Ridge. There was General
Armstrong with the Pennsylvania Line, our best troops.
They came past Green Lane each man wearing a piece of
dirty white paper in his hat for identification. Not much
of uniforms. Looked like a lot of tramps."

In contrast to the appearance of the Americans is the
appearance of the British army marching down the same
Ridge Road, as seen and described by Mary Levering:
"First came three horsemen, the most splendid looking
men on noble prancing steeds, one of them, they said was
Lord Cornwallis. Then followed the artillery and light
horse and the German soldiers. The sight was splendid."

Manayunk's days of pageantry are long gone. The

spirit of the river town of today is best expressed in the
commercial island between canal and river. There the Con-
tainer Corporation has its plant where the Dobsons
once set up their whirring looms. The industrial development of Manayunk began with the advent of water power
furnished by the dam, although the practicability of this
service was at first regarded with some scepticism. When
Captain John Towers erected two mills in 1816 and
leased "the right to use one hundred inches of water from
Schuylkill Navigation Company at Flat Rock," there
were many doubting Thomases to predict that the Captain would go broke. However, he prospered until his un-
timely death. The Hagners, the Ripkas, the Bories who
followed him made Manayunk a prosperous village and
founded an industry for Philadelphia.

This length of the river was formerly a great shad fishing center. A cluster of forgotten islands, Duck Island,
Jones Island, and Rummel's Island, were once so important because of their fishing facilities that acreage upon
them brought a higher price than river frontage on the
steep southern bank. Some of the islets were submerged
by the dam, others lie long deserted. But in the days of
their glory the fishing rights in this section were so prized
that each angler was allowed only one casting of his hoop-
net in twenty-four hours, and residents on opposite banks
must fish on alternate days. Andrew Anderson, who
owned the location of present West Laurel Cemetery,
seems to have been the piscine czar of the river, for he
leased out most of the fishing rights.

The precipitous terrain of the south bank discouraged
agricultural development, but Mill Creek tumbling down
from the west was once studded with mills for the manu-

facture of paper and gunpowder—a curious combination
of production. The paper industry of the district must
have been important, for the Quaker evangelist Robert
Sutcliffe, pushing his canoe up against the rushing current
of the Schuylkill, records a visit to "a respectable paper-
making friend of mine from Metz in Loraine, a former
Redemptioner. His mill would be considered an extensive one in England and is employed in making paper."

From Harriton, the seat of the Harrison family back
in the Merion Hills, down to the Schuylkill, Mill Creek
falls two hundred and fifty feet in four miles, an ideal
setting for mill dams. Here in this narrow valley much
of the gunpowder for Washington's army was made, the
labor provided largely by German indentured servants.
There were sawmills along the creek, the largest, directly
at the mouth, having been conducted by Christopher Robbins. This was the same Robbins who later became landlord of the Three Tuns Tavern in Whitemarsh, and
whose name and fame spread over the countryside because of his celebrated recipe for brandy punch. The
timber sawed at the Mill Creek sawmills was floated down
the Schuylkill. So execrable were the roads in this wooded
section that the hogsheads of tobacco from "Harriton"
plantation were moved to market by inserting an axle
through each cask and rolling it along the narrow trail.

On this same south bank where the chimneys of Pen-
coyd once belched forth their eddying clouds of black
smoke stood the stone fishing house of Melchior Meng.
Meng was so ill advised as to take the wrong side in the
Revolution, and his lands (including a part of the present
West Laurel Hill tract) were confiscated by the vengeful
Whigs at the end of the war. The list of his personal

property, taken by the public Escheator, is interesting and includes an item of singular appeal to the culinary taste of the gourmets of our time, "one half barrel of choice Schuylkill shad."

Access to the river from the rocky south bank could be attained only by following the water courses. Thomas Penn, after an inspection of the marble quarries in upper Merion, crossed the Schuylkill at the end of a trail which led down the valley from Merion Meeting and met the river north of West Laurel Hill Cemetery. Travelers from Philadelphia usually came up the north bank and crossed in canoes. The colonial merchant Paul Jones was far more enterprising. Scorning ordinary methods of transit, he took advantage of a heavy frost to turn his sleigh on to the surface of the ice-bound Schuylkill at Market Street and placidly drive all the way to his farm at Pencoyd, "while the guest who accompanied him marveled at the wonderful meadow through which they sped like the wind." The real marvel seems to have been that the adventurous driver did not run foul of one of the many rocks protruding from the river.

All this was long ago. There are no fisheries now, and the Pennsylvania Railroad viaduct swings across the former ford and past the cemetery where Charles Brockden Brown, first American novelist, lies buried. Behind this is the Welsh tract where the memories of the Cymric pioneers are perpetuated in the names of Gladwyn, Bryn Mawr, Cynwyd, and Bala. The Gorge of Schuylkill, as the early chroniclers termed it, ends with the granite reefs of Pencoyd. Thence the river glides southward to the boundary of Fairmont Park at the Wissahickon, and thereafter through Penn's "Greene Country Towne."

CHAPTER 17

Wissahickon and Falls of Schuylkill

ELOW the site of the old Robeson mill is the mouth of the charming Wissahickon, the Catfish Creek of the Lenapes. What a fabric of retrospect this euphonious title evokes: suggestions of happy-tired picknickers tramping downstream after a day of pleasure, of canoe trips, bicycle excursions, and all the holiday round of the great city to the south!

Young printer Franklin, who sometimes trudged out to the creek in the long summer evenings, regarded it with a more practical eye and calculated its flow as a possible water supply for Philadelphia. Indeed, only a century ago, when the stream bed was studded with dams and paper mills, Wissahickon seemed destined for a work-a-day future. The glen was seriously considered as the road bed for a railway connection to Chestnut Hill and Germantown, a project which, if completed, would have effectually ruined the landscape. Then, in a happy hour the city of Philadelphia acquired the Wissahickon watershed and annexed it to Fairmount Park.

Some localities seem destined for mystic associations. Just as the wild Brocken superinduced the legend of Faust, so this vale of Wissahickon has its occult tradition in the sojourn of the German hermit, Kelpius, of whom Whittier sang:

> *Painful Kelpius from his hermit den*
> *By Wissahickon, maddest of good men.*

Kelpius lived in a cabin, in several cabins it would appear, for no one seems to agree upon the exact location of his dwelling. His picture, done by the primitive artist Witt and said to be the first portrait painted in America, survives in the collection of the Historical Society of Pennsylvania. When Kelpius came to Philadelphia from Wurtemberg, he assured his followers that he would never die. Nevertheless, in 1708, when he felt a misgiving that death was creeping upon him, he called his disciple Geissler to his side and entrusted to him the famous box containing the Philosopher's Stone, or Rock of Wisdom. This stone must have had remarkable properties, because when Geissler attempted to throw it into the Schuylkill, it exploded with a detonation that shook all the hills of Merion.

The career of Kelpius is sometimes erroneously associated with the building called the Monastery, still standing in the valley. This Monastery, however, was the home of still another group of German pietists, who practiced the strange rites described by the historian, Julius F. Sachse: "In this almost inaccessible glen of Wissahickon the Elders advanced through the icy waters leading the candidates. Then each was immersed and the Segenspruch (blessing) was pronounced. In the evening a love feast was held and the rite of foot washing practiced."

But to the rollicking picknickers who swarm each Sunday over the moldering foundation of the venerable Monastery, the place is associated with sunshine and revelry rather than with mystical ceremonials of long ago.

A peak dominating the Monastery is alleged to have been the assemblage place of the Delawares, when they held their last mournful council before leaving their beloved Wissahickon to go into exile in the Wyoming Valley of Pennsylvania. The statue of their chieftain Tedyuscung emerges imposingly above the foliage of Indian Rock, and only an unromantic cynic would suggest that the chief was really a cowardly braggart who eventually burned to death in a drunken frolic.

Wissahickon has its martial tradition, and some imaginative dreamers assert that the blare of Revolutionary bugles still reverberates along the northern slopes where a lively skirmish was fought. General Armstrong, who was handled rather roughly in the engagement, records that he left one of his field pieces "in the horrendous hills of Wissahickon near the Rittenhouse Paper Mills."

Many writers have sounded the praises of this happy valley, among them the eccentric Philadelphia novelist George Lippard, who used it as a setting for his fine novel, *Monks of Monks' Hall*. When Lippard decided to take an Indian wife, he selected a corner of Wissahickon glen near the present "Mom Rinker's Rock" and was married there with appropriate pageantry.

Poor harried Edgar Allan Poe, always in debt and grappling with the possibilities for placating his long suffering landlord, was accustomed to stroll out to the Wissahickon from his home in Spring Garden. A point is still shown where he is supposed to have written parts of his story "The Elk of Wissahickon." And once he recorded: "Our Wissahickon is of so remarkable a loveliness that were it in England it would be the theme of every bard." Poe was evidently not aware of the fact that an appreciative English visitor had already appeared in the person of the distinguished William Cobbett, who showed his admiration in certain laudatory passages in his *Rural Rides*, a work published in 1830 during his Philadelphia exile.

Presently another overseas visitor arrived in the person of the winsome English actress Fanny Kemble, married to Pierce Butler of Philadelphia, who rode out almost daily to the Wissahickon. This was no ordinary tourist. Born to the Thespian tradition of a distinguished family, she was early inured to plaudits and to blandishment. Sir Walter Scott himself had shown her about Abbotsford, the naughty Lord Byron had begged for an introduction, and the victor of Waterloo had invited her to Apsley House. Washington Irving, secretary to the American Embassy at London, wrote to arrange for her reception at New York. And on a certain memorable occasion at Frossard's Riding School in London, six years before the American visit, she had the honor of a presentation to a slight, shrinking, brown-haired girl, the Princess Victoria, daughter of her Grace the Duchess of Kent, a lassie who, men said, might one day be Queen of England.

Whether Fanny ever evoked any of these reminiscences during her rides up Wissahickon glen we do not know, but on a golden spring Sunday she stood at her horse's side by the old stone bridge and descanted upon "Wissahickon's waters deep and bright radiant with the softest light I ever beheld."

The Wissahickon still does not lack devotees. Cornelius Weygand has commemorated it in a graceful treatise; and Christopher Morley tells how "in his salad days" he would take a hansom, drive out to the Lotus tavern in Shur's Lane, and be served with the good cheer which the place afforded:

> *Ho! away for the Wissahickon*
> *For the dance and good stewed chicken.*
> *Catfish and waffles! good hot toddy.*
> *Cheers the heart and warms the body.*

It was Kit Morley, too, who enthused over the charm of the Walnut Lane bridge, once hailed as the longest concrete arch in the world, "Curving in a sheer, smooth, superb span that catches the last western light on its lovely flanks, it flashes across the darkened valley like an old Roman viaduct in southern France."

Farther down the Wissahickon, almost at its mouth, the tracks of the Reading Railroad are carried over the ravine by a stone bridge, almost equaling the Walnut Lane bridge in beauty of design and excellence of execution. There had been a crude wooden bridge here; and when the first train to Norristown ran across it, the cars were stopped directly over the gorge so that the distinguished passengers could gape down at the stream far beneath. Then came a hasty belated decision to erect the present stone span in a working period of three months. The Nolan brothers, recently arrived from Ireland, were the only contractors who would essay the task in the limited time allotted. Their old mother, Anna Bennett, who lived to be a centenarian, installed herself in an armchair by the glen and spurred on the laggard workmen.

Thanks to her efforts the arches were completed in the required period.

Just below the mouth of the Wissahickon, in colonial days, stood a log fishing house called Fort St. David, frequented by a group of wealthy gentlemen from Philadelphia, mostly of Welsh extraction as the name implies, who paid an annual rental in catfish. This association had semimilitary functions which they did not take too seriously, stressing rather the culinary side and eating their fried fish from pewter platters which had been presented to them by the Penn family. During the Revolution some Hessian soldiers were quartered in the "Fort" and used it so uncouthly that the St. David's group never went back. Eventually they merged with another body of fishermen who called themselves at first *Colony in Schuylkill,* later *State in Schuylkill,* and whose career intertwines itself with the lower Schuylkill.

Here at the mouth begin the broad park driveways following both banks of the stream. At dusk as the long line of cars creeps out from Philadelphia, the suburbanites returning to their homes see the river at its best. The rays of the setting sun sinking over George's Hill gild and glorify the river. Gone for the moment are the culm deposits so disfiguring by day. The proud, broad river pours seaward.

Just south of Fort St. David's is the site of the Falls of Schuylkill, so prominent in colonial archives but now almost a legend. Tourists who pass the inn on the river bank and read the name *Falls Tavern* are puzzled to see no evidence of a cataract. And yet, in the early history of the province of Pennsylvania, Falls of Schuylkill was a location frequently referred to. For a long time this was the limit of navigation from the south, the northern boundary of the tide and a disconcerting barrier for the shad and sturgeon that came leaping upstream to spawn. The erection of Fairmount Dam three miles below and the subsequent backing up of the waters has so submerged the former cascade that only a few rocks remain protruding from the river. It is hard to believe that in the times of high freshets this Schuylkill Falls made a noise so great as to be plainly heard in Philadelphia, four miles away.

The Lenapes loved the Falls of Schuylkill, and after the advent of the white man they lingered last on this very spot. From their wigwams on either bank they could view the perilous black reefs over and about which whirled the rapids. Hagner, the historian of the Falls, writing a century ago, described them as "swift rapids, rising to a height of twenty feet when the stream was in flood. The huge 'Reading Boats' carrying fifteen hundred pounds each, were then tossed so high that at times crew and cargo both failed to re-appear."

And the *Portfolio* of 1802 has a metrical description beginning:

When Schuylkill o'er his rocky bed
Roars like a bull in battle.

To the early projectors of Schuylkill navigation, the Falls presented an almost unsurmountable barrier. In those days, before the advent of the dams, the ice freshets brought down great bergs which could and did shatter a mill-wall three feet thick. Men said that so turbulent a river could never be dammed. However, there was one early pioneer, a man of scope and vision, who first saw the possibility of utilization of the Falls of Schuylkill for water power and who devised a plan for piercing the reef. This was Josiah White, justly acclaimed as the father of Schuylkill navigation.

About the year 1810 White observed the following advertisement in a Philadelphia newspaper:

> For sale by Joseph Kennedy, the Falls of Schuylkill, the buyer to have water-power, on condition he build locks for accomodation of boats plying the River Schuylkill he to dig, continue, support, keep in repair, a millrace on and contiguous to the tract. . . . If the owner constructs a lock for navigation of the Schuylkill, at the Rapids, he will be entitled to collect a toll of 50 cents, from every passing boat coming from Reading to Philadelphia.

This advertisement was a confession of failure; Kennedy had been unable to harness the Schuylkill and was eager to sell out. Nevertheless, Josiah White remained undaunted and bought the Falls. Already he had evolved the principal of the "Bear Trap Lock" from a faded sketch made by his grandfather in 1728. "Brest high in the icy waters," as he tells us in his day book, he labored and finally his canal and raceway were completed. His enthusiastic biographer said of the feat that "A major river was made navigable over dangerous rapids even during flood or drought and when White's Dam stood fast against the great flood of 1816, he knew that he had succeeded."

Now Josiah leased out part of his water power and impatiently waited for the Pennsylvania public to take up his plan for a Schuylkill canal. Meanwhile, as he had

to live, he established a nail factory in partnership with
Joseph Gillingham. One day as White was drawing with
chalk in his barn, tracing the course of the proposed
canal, a bespectacled youth appeared named Erskine
Hazard, who had entered Princeton at the age of thirteen
and afterwards had gone off to explore the wilderness of
Niagara. He offered himself as an additional partner and
was accepted. Then the city of Philadelphia began to
cast envious eyes upon the new dam as a source of water
power for the city. This would have been the end of the
nail factory.

"Everything Erskine and I do, succeeds in so far as
perfecting the invention but not as to making a living,"
was Josiah White's plaintive observation.

The negotiations with the city fathers dragged their
tedious course. Presently another visitor appeared at the
Falls in the person of a distinguished German baron,
Frederick Augustus Hauto, who had original ideas, first,
for throwing a wire bridge, the first of its kind in the
world, over the Schuylkill and, secondly, exploiting anthracite coal in the Lehigh Valley. The young partners
entered eagerly into both plans, although still hopeful
that their pet project, the Schuylkill canal, would not be
too long postponed.

The figure of Judge James Finley from Fayette
County in Pennsylvania, who may be regarded as the
progenitor of the wire bridge in America, enters here.
The two successive bridges at the Falls were built under
his supervision, and the second is familiar to us in the
many lithographs made after the original painting by
William Birch. The original bridge was the talk of
Philadelphia while it lasted, and excursionists flocked

out from the city to pay a penny for the privilege of crossing. It could not have been too durable, for it was suspended from wires winding from the mill windows on the east bank to some large trees on the west bank. In the end, as might have been expected, it fell into the river.

By this time the partners had begun to tire of the Falls of Schuylkill and were planning to transfer their activities to the mining of coal. Accordingly, Baron Hauto donned what he called his "Mauch Chunk costume," fox-skin hat, red-flannel shirt, and leather breeches, and went off to Harrisburg in an endeavor to get some financial aid from the Pennsylvania legislature. The solons at the capital regarded him with amused indifference, and the Baron moved on to the Lehigh coal fields, where he was presently joined by White and Hazzard. All this was a century ago. Josiah White sleeps in his tomb in the old Friends' cemetery; of his once famous dam there remains only some crumbling masonry built into the eastern abutment of the present Falls railroad bridge. However, he was the first to demonstrate the feasibility of Schuylkill navigation.

7

FAIRMOUNT

CHAPTER 18

The Fair Mount, East Drive

ALONG the entire course of the Schuylkill the four-mile stretch from Falls of Schuylkill to Fairmount Dam is richest in architectural grace. Many of the splendid mansions built along the river have happily survived. Since nearly all of these houses were drawn or painted in years past, a comparison of the present with the original is possible. Frequently the artist seized the opportunity to introduce the river as a background. Consequently, some of the most charming and descriptive glimpses of the stream and of the boats which floated upon it a century and more ago have been preserved.

The Schuylkill never stamped its name upon a definite conception of landscape painting like the Hudson school or the Dusseldorf school of the lower Rhine, but it has not been neglected. Sully, who worked longer and more productively than any other American painter, has used the Schuylkill as a setting for some of his most pleasing portraits and groups. Charles Willson Peale made sketches of the river banks. Thomas Birch did the three river views which now adorn the walls of the Historical Society of Pennsylvania. The old waterworks at Fairmount Dam is said to have been more often depicted in oil, water color, gouache, and pastel than any other American scene. The prints and engraving of this scene, beginning with the fine *Ansicht Auf den Schuylkill bei Philadelphia,* produced at Dresden, are countless. The tourist of today who strolls down Shaftesbury Avenue in London or along the book stalls by the Seine cannot go far without being confronted by some Schuylkill view, usually of Fairmount Dam.

The somewhat uninspiring environment of the present Falls of Schuylkill district gives little hint of pomp or fashion, and yet a century ago this neighborhood was studded with aristocratic dwellings. Perhaps the most imposing of these was Font Hill, home of General Thomas Mifflin, Pennsylvania's first governor.

> *Above the highway rising bold*
> *The pillared Mifflin house behold*
> *Where once a score of fountains played*
> *And acres spread of lovely shade.*

Here the governor dispensed the hospitality for which he was famous, and to this house he was carried when stricken in the yellow fever plague of 1793.

A curious mineralogical formation was noted by the English traveler Wansey, who visited Font Hill in 1796: "The ground here by Falls of Schuylkill is full of pieces of mica which glitters in the sun. The first settlers, knowing little of minerals took it for flakes of silver and freighted a ship for England with it, concluding their fortunes made at once."

This deposit probably covered a part of Mifflin's deer park, in which he took such pride and which was bisected by present Midvale Avenue. The park was kept up as late

as 1855, although the estate had passed out of the
Mifflin family, for the Governor was far too generous
a host to have well-ordered finances. When he died at
Lancaster in 1800, he had lost most of his property.
In this same locality, high above the river, stands
Smith's Folly, formerly the home of William Smith,
Provost of the University of Pennsylvania. Here on a
rainy spring evening in the year 1790, Doctor Smith was
dining with Thomas McKean, Thomas Willing, and
David Rittenhouse when an agitated messenger arrived
from Philadelphia to announce the passing of Benjamin
Franklin. Doctor Smith, profoundly moved, bowed to
Rittenhouse and then retired to compose an appropriate
elegy:

> *Cease, cease ye clouds your elemental strife*
> *Why rage ye thus as if to threaten life?*
> *Seek, seek no more to shape our souls in dread*
> *What busy mortal told you "Franklin's dead."*
> *What though he yields to Jove's imperial nod*
> *With Rittenhouse he left his magic rod.*

The Smith mansion lay abandoned for some centuries
after the Provost's death, until it came to be occupied by
an odd pedagogue named Joseph Neef from Bern in
Switzerland, who established a school wherein he aimed
to teach "by observation rather than by study." The
school had a great vogue until Peter Du Ponceau, president of the American Philosophical Society, rode out
from Philadelphia to inspect it. Du Ponceau's judgment
was that the idea was "ridiculous nonsense," after which
drastic pronouncement the popularity of the institution
declined.

Another eminent resident of Falls of Schuylkill was Doctor Joseph Carson, long Professor of Materia Medica at the University of Pennsylvania. Carson in his youth had journeyed to Madras and studied oriental epidemics. In 1832 the Falls district was afflicted by an insidious disease, which no doctor could diagnose. Dr. Carson, from his Indian experience, was able to pronounce it yellow fever and to render invaluable service in combatting the plague. It is interesting to recall that the doctor's grandson, another Joseph Carson, is president of the Fairmount Park Commission.

Falls of Schuylkill is not without its Revolutionary background. At the farm house of Henry Hill, near present School Lane, General Washington established his headquarters during the first week of August, 1777, while the British invading force was groping its way up the Chesapeake. Some of the staff lodged with him at the Hill house; and Lafayette, just arrived in Philadelphia after his long journey from South Carolina, rode out for a visit. The Marquis recorded that the camp contained "About eleven thousand men, ill armed and still worse clothed, many of them almost naked. The best clad wore hunting shirts and large gray linen coats which were much used in Carolina."

On the spot where some of the reefs still protrude to indicate the location of the former rapids, the tracks of the Reading Railroad are carried across the Schuylkill by six stone arches, erected in 1853 and greatly admired for the scientific exactitude of the masonry. These arches, designed by the engineer Osborn, were erected by the master mason Christian Schwartz, who helped design the famous askew bridge at Reading (first modeled in soap, it is said) and who was killed far up the river near the south slope of Neversink Mountain while signaling a train.

Below the railroad bridge the river and the east Schuylkill Parkway pass under cliffs crowded with the mortuary monuments of three world-renowned cemeteries, known as North, Central, and South Laurel Hill. The present cemetery represents parts of three estates which formerly fronted upon the stream. Of these the most northerly was The Laurels, belonging to the rich linen merchant Joseph Sims.

Joe Sims who dined from golden plate
The wealthy lord of broad estate.

Then came George Pepper's Fairy Hill. The southerly area of the cemetery formed from "Edgley," still standing, was once the patrimony of the Rawle family. Doctor Phillip Physick, standing on this same eminence one summer day in 1780, rhapsodized over "the fine view of Schuylkill, up and down the river, a veritable vale of Tempe worthy of the pen of a classic poet."

When the architect John Notman designed the elaborate cemetery entrance, still admired after a hundred years, he could scarcely conceive that so many notabilities were to be borne to their last rest through these portals— General Hugh Mercer of Revolutionary fame, General Meade of Gettysburg, Commodore Isaac Hull of the frigate *Constitution*—the list is endless. In Laurel Hill, too, the Scotchman James Thom executed his matchless group of figures taken from Scott's novel *Old Mortality*. This, it is said, was the first time that Sir Walter was depicted in modern costume.

Mendenhall Ferry, so often referred to in colonial correspondence, operated on the river below the cliffs of Laurel Hill. Hard by was the ford adjoining land of the Hood family. The ford and neighboring tavern took the name of Robin Hood. In the *Pennsylvania Gazette* of March 1, 1775, we read that James Hood offers at Public Sale "the Robin Hood Tavern with about three and a quarter acres of orchard and garden ground near the river Schuylkill. Suitable for a gentleman's country seat and having an excellent prospect over the river aforesaid."

The advantages of this ford were so manifest that on September 11, 1777, while the battle of Brandywine was being fought, the Supreme Executive Council detached a guard of militiamen to encamp by and watch the crossing. It was near the ford at a forgotten location called "Robin Hood Ferry Wharff" that the hero of so many river anecdotes, Sheriff James Coultas, demonstrated the navigability of the Schuylkill by taking up "from the lower part of the Big Falls two flat boats laden with 4323 pounds of hay in twenty-one minutes" —a notable feat performed in the autumn of 1770 and much exploited in the newspapers of the day.

The name Robin Hood has attained publicity in recent years because of the out-of-door summer concerts given in the picturesque glen on the east bank. These concerts, a new conception in municipal entertainment, are given under the auspices of the Robin Hood Dell concert group and have attracted hearers from all over America. They have served as a model for similar undertakings in the parks of many of our eastern cities.

Near Laurel Hill is the bridge upon which trolley

cars, when trolley cars still ran, crossed the river for a scenic tour of the west park. Here, if one were out upon the broad bosom of the river and were to glance up at the cliffs of the east bank, he might perceive above the foliage the roofs of two historic dwellings, both operated by the Park Commission as public museums. These are Strawberry Mansion and Woodford House.

Strawberry Mansion, long known as the estate of Somerton, was built about 1800 by Judge William Lewis, who is quaintly described as "country bred and always smelling a little of the barnyard." From an architectural standpoint, the mansion owes more to Lewis' successor, another jurist named Joseph Hemphill, who enlarged it during the first decades of the last century. Judge Hemphill was a prodigal builder, much on the order of his neighbor Governor Mifflin. When he heard that his son Coleman proposed to entertain the members of the City Troop, he grandiloquently commanded that his music room be doubled in size for the event. This lavish hospitality led inevitably to a financial crisis, and the estate was bought in by a practical businesswoman named Mrs. Grimes.

Mrs. Grimes, to the horror of her sport-minded neighbors, promptly plowed up the racecourse and proceeded to raise strawberries in the formal gardens which Barbé de Marbois once said reminded him of Versailles. When the fine "carriage-folk" rode out on their Sunday excursions from Philadelphia, Mrs. Grimes regaled them with strawberries and with her famous thick cream. So the place came to be known as Strawberry Mansion. From the quaint box-bordered garden in the rear of Strawberry, one gets a delightful unspoiled glimpse of the river

shimmering below. Indeed it is one of the all too rare
vantage points from which to reconstruct the beauty of
the Schuylkill's banks in the era when the great river
houses were in their hey-day.

A stone's throw to the south stands dignified Woodford, now housing the Naomi Wood collection of furni-
ture and antiques, one of the most important assemblages
of its kind in America. This graceful dwelling was once
the country home of William Coleman, a member of
Franklin's famous Junto. Coleman is described by the
Sage in his *Autobiography* as having "The coolest, clear-
est head, the best heart and the exactest morals of any
man I ever met."

Woodford's story is intertwined with that curious suggestion of Toryism, or at least of a passive distrust of
the patriot cause, which marked the occupants of so many
of the aristocratic Schuylkill mansions. In Woodford
the Tory tenant was witty and spirited Rebecca Franks.
So obdurate was Mrs. Franks in her attachment to the
Crown, that she put Woodford in mourning when
the British evacuated Philadelphia. Afterwards, when the
Americans had reoccupied the city, Mrs. Washington was
holding a dignified reception in honor of the French
minister, and all good Whigs were wearing cockades in
honor of the event. This mischievous Tory lady seized
the occasion to tie a cockade to her dog's tail and bribed
a servant to introduce him into the reception.

Long afterwards when Mrs. Franks had left America
and was living at Bath in England, a young American
officer, Winfield Scott, fresh from West Point, was making the European tour and called upon her. He found her
in a wheelchair, very old, very deaf, and very repentant.

"Would to God that I too had been a patriot," she muttered.

Below Woodford are the northern limits of that district of Philadelphia which was formerly called the Northern Liberties and which extended eastward from the Schuylkill to the Delaware. Here on the cliffs stands Randolph House, sometimes called Laurel Hill, the name afterwards adopted by the adjoining cemetery. Randolph House is now under the supervision of the Park Commission.

About the time that the white flag of the Bourbons was being hauled down from the ramparts of Quebec, this part of the river, from Fairy Hill on the north to Ormiston House on the south, belonged to a cultured and engaging young aristocrat named Francis Rawle. He had made the grand tour in Europe, a rare privilege in those days. He was married to the beautiful Rebecca Warner. A long and happy life seemed to loom before young Rawle. Then, one summer day in 1761 as he roamed the river bank, fowling piece in hand, the gun exploded with fatal result.

Sam Shoemaker, Francis Rawle's most intimate friend, came to settle the estate and eventually married the widow. Here again misfortune marked the career of a landlord of Laurel Hill. Shoemaker had been Royalist Mayor of Philadelphia, was a close friend of the notorious Tory Joseph Galloway, and had aided the British during their occupation of Philadelphia. He had to flee with the retiring British forces, leaving his widow disconsolate in the Laurel Hill dwelling. That she herself had marked Tory proclivities is shown by her diary:

October 22, 1781. The first thing I hear this morning
is that Lord Cornwallis has surrendered to the French
and Americans. Intelligence as surprising as it is vexatious.
October 23, We still flatter ourselves that the astounding news is not true.

The Shoemakers, like their neighbors the Franks
family of Woodford, went into exile in England at the
close of the Revolution. The Randolph family, which
succeeded in ownership, gave their name to the house on
the heights.

Below, not far from where Frederic Remington's
bronze cowboy dominates the cliff, bubbles one of the
many sparkling springs on both banks of the river still in
active use. Even today, in good weather, groups of people equipped with jug and pitcher form lines, awaiting
their turn.

In midstream lies Peters Island, trysting place for
canoers and lovers, temporarily a peninsula because the
soot has filled up the channel formerly separating it from
the west bank. Happily it is to be restored as an island,
for in its present state it is far from inspiring except on
regatta days when the college crews sweep by and the
banks are lined with enthusiastic spectators.

Columbia Bridge crosses the Schuylkill just south of
the island, and this span carried the tracks of the first
railroad leading from Philadelphia to the west. When
the road was laid out in 1832, the state of Pennsylvania,
which sponsored it, ignored the direct route out Market
Street and chose to convey its westbound passengers far
to the north and to ferry them across the river at the
point where Columbia Bridge was afterwards built. This

diversion provoked a gibe from a writer in the *Casket* of the period: "A traveler may leave the banks of Delaware and go to Pittsburgh without even entering the city of Brotherly Love—that is, if he is such a Goth as to wish to do so."

Looking down upon Peters Island from the heights of the east bank is Ormiston House, whose traditions are intertwined with those of the Scottish family of Burd, although the mansion was originally built by the Tory Joseph Galloway. Ormiston was the name of the original Burd seat near Edinburgh. Hampton Carson, once a Park Commissioner and well steeped in Fairmount lore, always protested that one summer evening he heard the shrill wailing of a ghostly bagpipe floating down from Ormiston Hill. It was appropriate that "Neddy" Burd, the colonial jurist, should come to live by this river which he knew so well. As a young lawyer he had lived up the valley in Reading and had marched out gallantly to join General Washington, leading a company of Berks militiamen, which he had raised through his own efforts. Taken prisoner at Long Island, he beguiled his captivity by making sketches of a house which he would one day own by the banks of the Schuylkill. Long afterwards, in 1793, when he heard that Ormiston was on the market, it seemed to represent the fulfillment of his dream and he promptly acquired the property.

Since all of the Fairmount houses have such interesting traditions, it would be a matter of difficulty to say which of them should be accorded first rank. It is probable, however, that the mansion of Mount Pleasant, below Ormiston, is the best known; indeed, it has been described as "the finest historic seat in Pennsylvania."

THE FAIR MOUNT, EAST DRIVE

Mount Pleasant was built in 1762 by that one-armed sea-dog and privateersman, Captain John McPherson, a figure who might have stepped out of the pages of Smollett. He it was who proposed to the Continental Congress that he be allowed to head a nondescript flotilla of galleys and schooners and sally out from the Delaware to attack the British fleet wherever he could find it on the high seas. Congress, startled by this audacious proposal, hesitated and temporized, whereat the disappointed McPherson sulked in Mount Pleasant and turned to the making of a city directory. In this volume it was his humor to list all the "cross women" in Philadelphia, the names of these viragos occupying three pages.

Baron Steuben, who lived in Mount Pleasant during the Revolution, always said that it suggested the location of the castle of Prague looking down upon the Moldau. But the mansion's most striking Revolutionary association is not with Steuben but with Benedict Arnold, who purchased the estate while military Governor of Philadelphia, although he probably never dwelt there. One thing is certain; the mortgage which he gave remains unsatisfied to the present day.

A path led down the cliff in those days, meeting the Schuylkill very near to the bank where the statue of General Grant now stands. Down this trail on summer mornings, while Philadelphia was still the national capital, came a swarthy undersized man to bathe in the river. This was his excellency, Juan de Mirailles, a Spanish grandee of the great house of Alba and the first minister accredited by Spain to the American Congress. Mirailles would have liked to stay in Mount Pleasant, but the estate was escheated by Arnold's treason and bought in by Justice Edward Shippen, whose daughter, Peggy, was Arnold's wife. Still later it was acquired by General Jonathan Williams, member of Congress and first superintendent of West Point Military Academy.

Beyond the cliffs of Mount Pleasant the Northern Liberties district rolls to the eastward, up to the eminence which Stephen Girard chose for the erection of the Grecian façade of his new Trade School and to Bush Hill, the Hamilton Estate. Somewhere here, probably on the site of the present East Park reservoir, stood the rows of vines which William Penn had had planted by his steward, James Harrison. The Founder had high hopes for this venture. "The wine industry will be worth many thousands of pounds a year for our province," he wrote hopefully to Logan. However, the French viniculturist imported for the care of the vineyard died, and the neglected grapes rotted on their stalks.

Nearer the river still stands the house called "The Cliffs," built by Joshua Fisher, whose grandfather had come over with Penn in the ship *Welcome*. When the young Yorkshireman Richard Bache married Franklin's daughter Sarah, he carried her over the threshold of the same dwelling; and the delighted bride wrote to her father in France describing her induction into "this small charming house."

The stately framework of Girard Avenue Bridge, once ranked as the broadest bridge in the world, crosses the Schuylkill at about the northern limit of the "Faire Mounte" (a name first recorded in the Holme map of 1687), in the district which formed the modest nucleus of the present extensive park. There are really two "mounts," the one of Lemon Hill and the other now occupied by the marvelous Philadelphia Art Gallery, erected upon the site of the gardens and waterworks of the municipality. For Philadelphia, down as late as the year 1900, got most of its water from the Schuylkill, pumped to Center Square from the old waterworks at the foot of Chestnut Street, and later from the Fairmount plant.

Sedgley was located east of the bridge. It functioned lately as a Park Guard Station. In its prime Sedgley was the seat of the rich and elegant William Crammond, and had the double distinction of having been designed by the great architect Strickland and of having been painted by William Birch.

On Lemon Hill lived Robert Morris, financier of the American Revolution. Morris planned the original mansion (burned down and replaced by the present house) on an extensive scale and installed the first icehouse in Philadelphia. In his greenhouse the first lemon tree in Philadelphia could be observed, a circumstance which gave the estate its name, although Morris could not foresee that he was founding a cultural monument for the city which he loved so well and which treated him so thanklessly. When the banker fell upon evil days and had served a term in the debtor's prison, he was fearful of being recommitted to a cell. So he lurked for weary months in this same mansion. Washington came out to see him, spoke of the value of his services to the patriot cause, but apparently did nothing practical to ameliorate his distress. Poor Morris took furtive walks along the Schuylkill and could scarcely leave his house by day without fear of arrest or worse fate "Good heavens what vultures men are in regard to each other! There is a

Frenchman outside who threatens to shoot me at the window if I do not pay his note."

Henry Pratt, who succeeded Morris, became equally embarrassed financially, and the estate was opened as a pleasure ground known as Pratt's Gardens. Then the city of Philadelphia acquired the gardens to protect the water supply of its hydraulic works below, and this purchase was the foundation of the present Fairmount. The mansion of Lemon Hill, still gracious and well ordered, is now the home of the custodian of the neighboring art museum. Whoever stands upon the museum terrace just where the bronze statue of John Marshall looks benignly down upon the Schuylkill will be rewarded by a charming view of Lemon Hill, enshrouded in its foliage just as it looked in the days of Robert Morris.

By the Schuylkill basin and under the brow of Lemon Hill stands the line of ornate boat houses, the Bachelors, the Undine, the Schuylkill Navy, the University Barge, and others, representing a sporting tradition. Boat racing on the Schuylkill, today the scene of so many college regattas, began on a modest scale in 1835 over a three-mile course opposite Belmont. On a summer day in that year the towpaths, platforms before the icehouses, and runways of the boat houses (simple structures then, not the elaborate buildings of today) were crowded with enthusiastic spectators. The Blue Devils, gaudily arrayed in sky-blue jersies, rowed against the Imps, attired in red and orange.

This contest was one of the earliest exhibitions of eight-oar rowing; and it may be claimed that the forming of the University Rowing Club, about the time of the Crimean War, represents the beginning of organized athletics at the University of Pennsylvania. The college at the period was still on Ninth Street between Chestnut and Market, where the Federal Court Building now stands. The students took their recreation in a boxing gymnasium kept by the Englishman Tom Barrett, or in the billiard parlors of Jimmy Hughes in Sansom Street above Sixth. Sometimes the boys, tiring of these amusements and longing for fresh air, would take an omnibus out to the Fairmount Water Works, where they would hire a boat and row up to Peters Island or the mouth of the Wissahickon. Here the college crew of 1859 was organized.

Most of the members of this crew were destined for tragic careers. Nearly all of them entered the Federal Army when war broke out two years later. Johnny Markoe, bow-oar, was wounded at Balls Bluff and lay weary weeks in Libby prison. James Starr, No. 2, was wounded at Brandy Station. Penrose Buckley, No. 5, fell at Savage's Ordinary. The stroke, Hamilton Kuhn, died at Gaine's Mill.

When the boathouses were first projected, Fairmount Park was restricted to the Water Works and to the part of Lemon Hill which the city had acquired from the Sedgely estate. There was no road of any kind along the east bank up to the Falls; many icehouses stood between the site of the present river drive and the river. There was only a grass-grown path up which pedestrians walked on a Sunday afternoon and admired the fine trees on South Laurel Hill, still in the possession of the Pepper family. Opposite, on the west bank, the foliage was so dense and beautiful as to evoke the attention of Thackeray, who visited Philadelphia during his American tour and walked out by the Schuylkill. The canal and towpath were on the west bank, although in 1835 there was much debate on a proposal for erecting an aqueduct bridge over the river and sailing the canal boats directly into Philadelphia.

What has become of the important puffing little steamboats which once plied upstream from Fairmount, crowded to the gunwales with eager pleasure seekers? The combined time table and prospectus is still to be read wherein the passengers are advised to:

> Look at the ten boat houses to your right not forgetting the Skating Club. Observe the old mansion of Lemon Hill, once home of Robert Morris. Look across at the water tower, 130 feet high on west bank. See the Zoo; a number of animals have already arrived. At Girard Avenue bridge observe the bronze statues, vases of flowers and fountains. Observe the delicate Iron Bridge on which trains on the Air Line from New York to Washington cross Schuylkill. Note the flag showing ground proposed for the Centennial. Observe the canal boats which pass us. Note the ridge of rocks which was once Schuylkill Falls. Land there for catfish and waffles. Look up stream at covered wooden bridge and at Powers and Weightman chemical works.

The riverfront has improved with the advent of parks and highways, and yet one must regret the passing of the scene of long ago, as described by John B. Thayer, when "instead of the Park being a thronged pleasure ground it was in comparative solitude except for the teams of canal mules with the tinkling of their bells. No bathing suits and we could swim *in puris naturalibus* at any point. In those days Atlantic City was a barren waste and Cape

May could only be reached by a boat after a days journey.
So our only resort to escape the city heat was to go out
to Bobby Arnolds Tavern at Falls of Schuylkill, enjoy
catfish and waffles and replenish the inner man with
libations of rum punches and mint juleps."

The sportsmen of the Schuylkill are best depicted in
the canvasses of the incomparable Thomas Eakins. William Rush's woodcarvings of the Schuylkill tritons and
the famous allegorical painting in which Nancy Vanuxem,
the reigning toast of her day, modeled the river have
not the spontaneity or sincerity of Eakin's oarsmen floating
under the railroad arches. A recent apostrophe to the
Schuylkill boatmen ends:

> *You should know that Eakins*
> *Painted you*
> *He put you in a single shell*
> *In the middle of the river.*
> *Against a soft West Philadelphia sky.*

The Philadelphia Museum of Art, one of the outstanding institutions of our time, crowns the hill where
the Water Works once stood, although of the thousands
of visitors to the site, very few picture the gardens and
reservoirs which occupied this same eminence for more
than a century. Down by the stream's edge the architectural setting of other days is unchanged. The Grecian
façade of the old waterworks and the columned pavilion,
copied from Le Notre's *Temple d' Amour* at Chantilly,
are still reflected in the Schuylkill.

Philadelphia owes the plans of the Water Works to a
conscientious public servant named Frederick Graff, with
whose name and career few citizens are acquainted even

though he has his monument in the museum garden near the present aquarium. This memorial, done by Graff's sculptor son, depicts him seated, drawingbook in hand, just as he sketched out the proposed Water Works in the year 1815.

The city drew its first water supply from a station, a crude one it appears, near the banks of the Schuylkill by Chestnut Street, from which water was pumped into the central square. Graff, who was a butcher boy and son of a German emigrant, became interested in municipal hydraulics and conceived the idea that he could make some improvements in the existing system. One day on Market Street he met the architect Benjamin Latrobe, who had his own ideas about Philadelphia's water supply. Pointing up to the summit of Fairmount, Latrobe said: "The top of this hill is 50 feet above any point in the city. If we can force the water up by the pressure of a dam in Schuylkill the service charge to our citizens will be sensibly reduced."

The eager planners began to discuss the building of the dam and agreed that Ariel Cooley, fresh from his engineering triumphs at Flat Rock, would be the ideal choice as supervisor. Cooley was employed, but even his enthusiastic hopes did not envisage the actual economies effected. The expense of lifting four million gallons of water a day was lessened 90 per cent.

Charles Dickens on his American tour arrived in Philadelphia after the completion of the water works, and was proudly escorted to Fairmount. "Philadelphia is most beautifully provided with fresh water," he wrote later, "which is showered and jerked about, and turned on, and poured off, everywhere. The Waterworks, which are on a height near the city, are no less ornamental than useful, being tastefully laid out as a public garden, and kept in the best and neatest order."

Acropolis of Philadelphia! This suggestion often made for the Hill of Fairmount is the more plausible because the columns and pediment of the Parthenon are duplicated in the façade of the art gallery. However, the hill is so far removed from the center of the town that only a very partial citizen would claim that Fairmount could ever play the part which the Acropolis did in the city of Themosticles. But there can be no dispute as to the advantage of the broad dignified Mall and the Schuylkill drive which continues it, giving direct entry to the heart of the city.

CHAPTER 19

The Fair Mount, West Drive

ACROSS Fairmount Dam and slightly to the north, in the midst of the present Zoological Gardens, still stands John Penn's mansion, Solitude on Schuylkill, now used as executive offices for the Zoo. Penn, who dabbled in poetry, might well be exasperated, if he were to return today, to find lion houses and buffalo pens in the gardens where once he walked, notebook in hand.

John was the son of Thomas Penn and grandson of the Founder. He made a most inauspicious entrance to America. Shipwrecked off the Jersey coast, he landed, wet and bedraggled, at Egg Harbor. Once arrived in Philadelphia, he rambled about the countryside, visited this knoll by Schuylkill, and finally bought it. The record of his purchase still survives in his day-book: "Early in the year of 1784 I made a dear purchase of 15 acres costing 600£ sterling on the banks of Schuylkill. I named it from the Duke of Würtenburg's house, 'Solitude.'"

Half a century later, when Pennsylvania had almost forgotten its erstwhile proprietors and their Schuylkill estates and when "Solitude on Schuylkill" had lain neglected and forlorn for a long period, a bustling, quizzical old gentleman named Granville Penn, John

Penn's younger brother, arrived in Philadelphia. Presently, society was electrified by the arrival through the mail of engraved missives reading: "Mr. Penn requests the pleasure of your company at Solitude on Schuylkill Tuesday, June 29th between one and five o'clock. Steam boats ply from Fairmount every hour."

Granville Penn, snuffbox in hand, received his guests under a striped marquee erected for the occasion. All the elite of Philadelphia attended. As the guests clasped Granville's hand and drank his punch, they must have been vaguely aware that they were officiating at the passing of an era, that the Penn connection with their once loyal province of Pennsylvania, begun when the Founder had paddled upstream on that radiant morning so long ago, was now concluded.

Northward along the river front and across Girard Avenue is the Letitia Street House, one of the oldest brick dwellings in Pennsylvania, brought from its original location near the waterfront of Philadelphia and set up in the park. The inscription claims that it was built and lived in by William Penn, but this theory has somewhat weakened under modern research. Nevertheless, this Letitia Street House with its period furnishings and lovely garden is a fine example of an old Philadelphia mansion in the period of the early settlements.

Below Letitia House, pedestrians on the West River Drive often pause before a plaque marking the point once occupied by the "Castle," or fishing house, of that aristocratic and gastronomic club called *State in Schuylkill*, founded in 1732, one of the oldest social organizations in the entire English speaking world. The Castle, of which many pictures survive, was a rather ornate wooden structure erected upon a tract of about one acre, leased from a certain "Baron" Warner for a rental of a tray full of perch caught in the nearby river.

The head of this august assemblage—"citizens" they called themselves—has always been known as the Governor. In the long and illustrious line of governors probably the best remembered is Sam Morris, who commanded the City Troop in the Revolution and who entertained Washington at the Castle. The tradition is that Washington was served with the proverbial menu of fish and barbecued pig, washed down by the club's redstring Madeira and insidious fish-house punch. The exact date of this visit has never been verified, but the club members aver that the President's diary, kept at the period in careful detail, has one page inexplicably blank. It is maliciously insinuated that the empty page follows the date of Washington's visit to the Castle.

For ninety years State in Schuylkill remained on the west bank. Then in 1822, after the building of the Fairmount dam, the fishing (for oddly enough the members did occasionally fish) deteriorated. So, regretfully, on May Day of 1822, the "citizens" loaded their Castle on a scow and poled it to a new site, Rambo's Rock, four miles down the river.

Charming Sweetbriar stands upon the high ground above the site of the former Castle, the house and grounds restored and well maintained by the Modern Club. This was the estate developed by Samuel Breck, prominent in city affairs a century and a half ago, who, by curious anomaly, was born in puritan Boston and educated in a Benedictine monastery in France. An old print shows the gardens of Sweetbriar running down to the river, with

horses disporting on the lawns. If the artist who made
this print were to return to the sketching point, he would
see no horses but would view the lawn sloping back
to where two tall memorial columns surmounted by
statues of Pennsylvania's Civil War heroes, Generals
Meade and Reynolds, dominate the west bank of the
Schuylkill.

When Sam Breck came back to Philadelphia after his
sojourn abroad, the fastidious homecomer, always con-
servative, was shocked by the rising tide of democracy.
From his river retreat of Sweetbriar, Breck registered
uncompromising protest against the decline in manners
and formality which he so profoundly deplored, complaining that "General Washington, when president, rode
out to take the air in a coach drawn by six horses with
two postillions on the box but now that levelling philosopher, Jefferson, rides out on his pacing nag without even
a body servant."

While in France, Breck had witnessed the tragic
scenes which ushered in the French Revolution. Afterwards in Philadelphia it was his privilege to extend the
courtesies of Sweetbriar to many of the refugees whom he
had visited in Paris prisons and who had been fortunate
enough to escape to the new world. Notable among these
were Talleyrand, late Bishop of Autun (although little
of his clerical background survived); Noailles, brother-
in-law of Lafayette; Louis Philippe, afterwards King of
France; and the two royal brothers, the Ducs de Montpensier and Beaujolais. These titled exiles and many
others were entertained at Breck's hospitable board. No
house in all of Fairmount exceeded Sweetbriar in its
tradition of gracious hospitality.

West of Sweetbriar one of the few surviving relics of
the Centennial Exposition of 1876 still stands, the present
Horticultural Hall. This site was long occupied by fire-
seared ruins, the remains of Lansdowne House, another venture of Governor John Penn; but a dwelling
more intimately associated with the name of a succeeding occupant, the important and wealthy William
Bingham. Landsdowne was much frequented by Philadelphia society; but its popularity was due not so much
to Bingham, a dull man intent upon making money, as
to his wife, the beautiful Nancy Willing. Nancy was the
toast of the town, and the "Republican Court" which she
conducted at her city house and in Lansdowne was on
the scale of royalty. Her levees set so high a standard
that a Miss Franks, writing from New York, said that
the ladies of Philadelphia "have more cleverness in the
turn of their eye than those of New York in their whole
composition," and again: "With what ease have I seen a
Chew, a Penn, an Oswald or an Allen entertain a large
circle of both sexes without the aid of cards, never flag-
ging nor seeming in the least strained or stupid."

Amid all this elegance, however, detractors were not
wanting to hint that William Bingham had amassed his
fortune in the West Indies by methods not too creditable,
that he was a Schuylkill nabob. Peter Marco, the colonial
wit, expressed this feeling in satirical lines:

> *Tho' to Lansdowne wits and fops repair*
> *To game, to feast, to flatter and to stare*
> *But say, from what bright deeds doth thou derive*
> *The wealth that bids thee rival British Clive?*
> *Wrung from the hardy sons of toil and war*
> *By arts which petty scoundrels would abhor.*

But whatever might have been whispered about the background of the host, nothing could detract from the popularity of the entrancing hostess. In all the annals of Fairmount there is no more moving picture than that of the crowds which lined the lane down which Nancy Willing Bingham was carried in her palanquin for her last voyage to Bermuda. Stricken with a lingering disease, she died at Hamilton in her island refuge and never came back to Lansdowne.

At the time of its destruction, by accidental conflagration, Lansdowne was unoccupied and belonged to English Lord Ashburton, one of whose ancestors, Alexander Baring, had married a daughter of the Bingham family. This titled owner, however, lived overseas in Hampshire and evinced little interest in Philadelphia or his mansion by the Schuylkill.

Beyond Memorial Hall rises Cedar Grove, like the Letitia Street House not an original Fairmount structure. It was brought stone by stone from its original location near Frankford, now a section of eastern Philadelphia. This mansion of the important Crammond family was being engulfed in the commercial development of its original section. It might have disappeared altogether like so many colonial edifices had not the descendants of the original occupants intervened to save it and set it up in its present location.

Horticultural Hall and Memorial Hall, amid the elms, recall the Centennial of 1876, the Schuylkill's golden exposition summer when all the slope from Girard Avenue westward to George's Hill and northward to Belmont was crowded with a bewildering array of towers, minarets, and pagodas. On the morning of May 10 of that year an observer on the cliffs of the east bank, looking across the river, would have seen Belmont Hill white with the tents of the West Point Cadets. The exposition buildings were festooned with bunting; strains of music were wafted over Schuylkill. This was the day chosen for the formal opening of the Centennial Commemoration by President Ulysses S. Grant.

At the long train platform (fifteen hundred feet long, the proud citizens boasted) which the Reading Railroad had erected for the reception of its Centennial trains from up the valley, a thousand choristers were descending. These were shepherded and directed by the peerless concertmaster Theodore Thomas. For weeks they had been drilling in the rendition of the "Centennial Hymn," written by John Greenleaf Whittier for the auspicious opening. The choir arranged itself in three rows, and presently the toll of bells and the booming of cannon proclaimed that the President with his escort of militia cavalry had left the Walnut Street residence of his host, George W. Childs, and was driving out to the Schuylkill.

Grant had always been the particular darling of the City of Brotherly Love. His imposing equestrian statue adorns the East Drive; the cabin, formerly at City Point, from which he had conducted the siege of Petersburg has been brought up, log by log, and set up near Lemon Hill. So the President's visit to the exposition was eagerly awaited. And yet, on that drizzly May morning, there was some uncertainty as to whether the veteran would be at his best, after enjoying the well-known Childs hospitality; even Grant's admirers had to admit that occasionally he took a drop too much. However, as this dedication was scheduled for early in the morning, it was

hoped that the speaker would be in good form, especially
since royalty was to be represented amid the distinguished
gathering on the tribune.

In those days the flow of kings, emperors, and maha-
rajahs to our shores had not yet begun. Prince Edward
of England had made his tour two decades before under
the modest title of Baron Renfrew, but he was merely
an heir apparent. Our only truly regal visitor had been
King Kalakaua of the Sandwich Islands, who smelled of
onions and was obese. Now the Schuylkill Centennial was
to be graced by a real emperor, Dom Pedro of Brazil.
To greet the emperor properly, the Philadelphia band-
masters had been struggling with the cadence of the
Brazilian national anthem.

At last the brilliant cavalcade passed before the ros-
trum, and Grant mounted to his place of honor. He
discarded the cigar which he had been chewing all
through the ovation in the streets and buttoned the top
buttons of his frock coat, until now negligently open. The
distinguished guests took their places and Theodore
Thomas raised his baton. Then from a thousand throats
rolled the strains of Whittier's anthem:

> *Our father's God from out whose hand*
> *The centuries fall like grains of sand.*

> *Be with us while the New World greets*
> *The Old World thronging all its streets*
> *Unveiling all the triumphs won*
> *By art or toil beneath the sun.*

The President arose. The great throng, reaching almost down to the banks of the river along which William

Penn had once pushed his lonely canoe, stood in expectant silence. Grant fumbled with the address which lawyer Carrol Brewster had written for him and began monotonously to declaim. At one point he paused after stating: "One hundred years ago our country was new and but partially settled."

Dom Pedro to the right, Governor Hartranft of Pennsylvania to the left, looked up inquiringly. General Joseph R. Hawley, Chairman of the Centennial, bent forward. Here was a suggestion of Lincolnian eloquence. Was the veteran of the Wilderness about to surprise them with a second Gettysburg Address? But no miracle ensued. The General merely adjusted his glasses and reverted to the realm of platitude: "I invoke your generous co-operation to secure a brilliant success for this exposition."

The sloping lawns of George Hill are vacant now. The Schuylkill still flows placidly between the river drives. Of all the elaborate exposition buildings which dominated it in that summer of 1876, only Memorial Hall and Horticultural Hall remain.

North of George Hill, which the two gentle Quakers, Jesse George and his sister Rebecca, gave to Philadelphia for park purposes "in the hope that the simple rural elements of our homestead will give pleasure and helpful exhilaration to people of all ages and conditions," stands Belmont, objective and delight of Schuylkill excursionists for over a century.

William Penn's land agent, the Reverend William Peters, built Belmont and developed the grounds which boasted the finest avenue of hemlocks in America. When Peters left Pennsylvania and returned to England to die, he gave the estate to his son, Judge Richard Peters, Secre-

tary to the Board of War in the Revolution. Judge
Peters' hospitality was a tradition in the land, and Colonel
John Forney (no mean authority, for he was himself regarded as the leading raconteur of his time in Pennsylvania) said of the Judge that "he could write the best
song, tell the best story and was the best wit of his time."

Judge Peters, like his neighbor Sam Breck, opened his
house to the forlorn French refugees and had as his particular guest the Vicomte de Noailles, brother-in-law of
Lafayette. Noailles, whose resources in his exile were at
first pitiably small, profited by his enforced stay in Philadelphia to embark in commerce; and apparently he was a
shrewd trader. "Every day at the High Street Exchange
this ex-nobleman was the busiest of the busy, holding his
bank book in one hand and the sleeve of a merchant in
the other while he drove his hard bargain."

Whatever his business success in America, the Vicomte
could not have been too punctilious in the payment of his
personal debts. A quarter of a century later, when Lafayette visited Philadelphia, he was dunned by a local tailor
for the payment of a bill for a coat made for his brother-
in-law while still living at Belmont.

The Mansion was a charming place until the state of
Pennsylvania built its inclined plane for the West Chester
Railway in 1832. After that the privacy of the surroundings was terminated, for passengers entraining for the
west were brought up from the river level and put into
their cars directly on Belmont terrace. The tourists had
an unpleasant habit of stealing flowers and breaking
shrubbery. As for the train crews, when the stock of fuel
for their engines was low they would appropriate the
Belmont fence rails. Among those who felt the desecration
most keenly was the Irish actor Tyrone Power, grand-

father of the cinema star, who rode up the west bank on horseback, saw the piers of the new railroad bridge in the stream, and protested that all the beauty of the Schuylkill had vanished.

In the centennial year Belmont was renovated as a public restaurant and for a brief period attained some measure of its former popularity. Every evening Proskaucr's Hungarian orchestra played Strauss waltzes, and the dancers looked down upon the curving river glistening below in the moonlight. The marvelous ceilings and paneling remain today, but Belmont is only a shadow of its former state.

Beyond Belmont is the mansion of Mount Prospect, built by the Johnson family while Jefferson was President. The Walns, who came later, changed the name to Ridgeland. In their time arose the tradition of "Tom Moore's Cottage," this cottage being a one-story hut with a "pig's eye" window standing by the bank not far from the neighboring river mansion, "The Lilacs," another house of legendary charm.

Voltaire's statement that "if there were no deity it would behoove mankind to create one" also can be applied to the human tendency to perpetuate legends. So the good folk of Philadelphia resent any doubt thrown upon Tom Moore's Cottage, and in support of the claim for his occupancy quote the well-known "Lines Written on Leaving Philadelphia":

> *Alone by the Schuylkill a wanderer roved,*
> *And bright were its flowery banks to his eye;*
> *But far, very far were the friends that he*
>   *loved,*
> *And he gazed on its flowery banks with a sigh.*

And there is Moore's dedication to his friend, W. R. Spencer, beginning:

> *Believe me, Spencer, while I wing'd the hours*
> *Where Schuylkill winds his way through*
> *banks of flowers,* . . .

How the Irish poet who was in Philadelphia for only ten days, in 1804, could have found time to occupy this hut is difficult to comprehend, but the tradition persists as does the "cottage."

In the days when both banks of Schuylkill near Philadelphia were dotted with dignified mansions, the merchant George Plumstead, a rival of Stephen Girard, sent his tall tea ships to Calcutta and Hong Kong and amassed a fortune. With his profits he built a pretentious house on Mount Prospect which he called Montpellier. When Fairmount Dam was built in 1821, the cleansing ebb and flow of the tide ceased in the Schuylkill and odors accumulated, so that most of the great houses in this section were neglected or abandoned. Fanny Kemble remarked that at the time of her visit to Philadelphia the stately Schuylkill river houses were "either deserted or leased out for taverns." Among the mansions so neglected was Montpellier, which finally came into the hands of a law publisher named Topliff Johnson. The publisher greatly improved the estate and hoped to live and die there. Unfortunately for him, just after the Civil War the Fairmount Park Commission, reaching out for more land, threatened to take over Montpellier. Johnson protested that this condemnation would break his heart. Finally, in 1868, the Commission took over the estate and changed the name, no one knew exactly why, to Chamounix. Nemesis and a proper solicitude for adding one more

legend to the annals of a storied river prompted Johnson
to die.

At City Line, northernmost limit of Fairmount Park,
are the golf links and clubhouse of the Philadelphia
Country Club, which before the days of the automobile
was considered a fair goal for an afternoon drive. Each
May Day a brilliant defile of coaches and four-in-hands
started at the old Bellevue Hotel in mid-Philadelphia and
wound out along the river to be reviewed and judged on
the terraces of the country club. Those were the days
when Colonel Edward Morrell boasted that he could
turn his four roan horses in the space of fifty feet, when
Anthony Biddle's well-matched bays were so much admired, and when Judge Willis Martin guided his yellow
and black drag with grace and dignity. The spans of
blooded horses are no more, but the long lines of frame
stables which housed them still survive, as do the country-
club greenhouses once renowned for their horticultural
glories.

Strolling out under the maples which adorn the coun-
try-club terrace, one can look across to the mouth of the
Wissahickon and far down the winding Schuylkill. The
line of the broad Mall leading out from the city to the art
gallery and river can plainly be discerned, with the
spires and skyscrapers of the Quaker metropolis rising in
the background. Standing here, one feels that the Schuylkill has lost its rural character. Above Fairmount it is
still a landward stream; below Fairmount it is an urban
river.

8

URBAN RIVER

CHAPTER 20

Urban River

THE eighteenth-century Irish tourist, Arthur Young, complained that the river Liffey at Dublin, so rich in historical reminiscence, was spoiled by commercial development. The same statement might be made of the Schuylkill in its course through lower Philadelphia. The comparison is the more apt in that the width of the Liffey at Dublin is just about the same as that of the Schuylkill at Market Street Bridge.

Standing upon the broad terrace of the Art Gallery and looking downstream, one sees below Market Street a succession of piers, chimneys, and derricks. Even the classic front of the Pennsylvania Railroad station loses its architectural effect because of lack of perspective; the structures which surround the station detract from the dignified proportions of a stately building. The post office on the west bank, a graceful building in itself, seems precariously poised upon concrete stilts. However, the completion of the new Schuylkill boulevard, now projected southward on the west bank of the river, will remove this impression of unsolidity and give the post office a proper setting. Indeed, the entire character of this district may materially change for the better. The present far-reaching plan for municipal adornment includes the great triangle bounded by the Schuylkill, Market Street, and the Mall. This plot, it is hoped, will be a civic center, properly landscaped and retaining something of the romantic aspect of a century ago.

Certainly, the Schuylkill is scarcely an inviting spectacle. A different scene presented itself a century and a half ago, when the artist Birch leaned over the parapet of the Permanent Bridge (the forerunner of the present Market Street Bridge) and looked curiously down at a half circle of men, waist deep in the water, drawing in a huge seine of shad. As Birch gazed downstream on that summer morning, there was little to obstruct his view. The meadows sloped gently down to the line of willows on the river bank. Minnow Creek, long since disappeared underground, still flowed from its source behind present Logan Square and debouched into the Schuylkill through a morass at the foot of present Arch Street.

The setting which Birch admired was distinctly rural. Most of the buildings which later featured the locality, such as the River Tavern on Race Street, much frequented by the members of the political society of St. Tammany, the octagonal penitentiary which Trollope ridiculed, and the pleasure gardens and pagodas of the pleasure park *Sans Souci*, so popular in the 1830's, were not yet in existence. Strickland's Labyrinth abutting on Arch Street, usually thronged with Sunday visitors, was laid out in 1827.

The Wigwam Tavern with its river baths was at the foot of present Race Street. Here, in Washington's first administration, John Coyle, a broth of a boy from Galway in Ireland, dispensed good cheer. The British traveler Priest compared it to Vauxhall and reported that

"one evening at six our party of pleasure went out to a
tea garden conducted by one Coyle and remarkably situ-
ated on the bank of Schuylkill. Excellent coffee served in
style."

Downstream the only important structure to break the
skyline, as artist Birch saw it, was Sam Breck's high shot
tower near the foot of present Arch Street. The tower
was located on Schuylkill Fourth Street. In those days
there was a double classification, one sequence of streets
beginning with First Street along the Schuylkill and then
named numerically from west to east, while another
sequence began with First Street along the Delaware with
succeeding streets named numerically to the west. Broad
Street was the dividing line.

This same Sam Breck, a scholar as well as a man of
affairs (his fine address at the dedication of the Philadelphia Athenaeum in 1814 is good evidence), has been
mentioned earlier as the proud owner of Sweetbriar Mansion. He was still prouder of his shot tower, which arose
to the stupendous height of one hundred and sixty-six
feet. When Lafayette rode out to view the tower, Breck
boasted that in full operation he "dropped" five tons of
lead bullets in a single day and that he could manufacture
shot "suitable to kill racoons, Indians or Englishmen."

Often, in a setting much transformed, one can reconstruct the long ago by the aid of contemporary fiction.
In one of Charles Brockden Brown's novels the hero,
Arthur Mervyn, walked along Minnow Creek towards
the Schuylkill about the year 1793, and noted the grass-
grown ramparts of the abatis which the British had constructed during their occupation of Philadelphia and the
moldering huts in which the yellow fever refugees lived

in that same summer. He observed that there was no road as yet leading along the east bank of the Schuylkill, although on the west bank a well-defined highway led up to Mendenhall Ferry and beyond.

Over the Wernwag Bridge on the west bank rose the graceful church spire which dominated the forgotten village of Mantua. Through the foliage one could glimpse the white front of Powelton, seat of John Hare Powel, a luxurious gentleman, we are told, but one who did not disdain to conduct a very profitable ferry at Callowhill Street. It was at Powelton that the jubilant Whigs, victorious in the state election of 1834, held a barbecue which was long a convivial tradition in the neighborhood.

The River Tavern with its broad porches, shown in the many drawings of the eastern end of Wernwag's Bridge, had a fair patronage. So did the Schuylkill (Howland's) Tavern at the western end, which was much frequented by the Philadelphia swains who drove their fair ones out to sip juleps and enjoy the river view. In 1806, on the bitter cold night when the tavern burned down, the bridge was threatened by sparks and was saved only by a bucket brigade of swaying tavern guests ("more or less inebriated" as the *Gazette* records, rather in sorrow than in anger).

Two interesting experiments with far-reaching results occurred along this stretch of the river. Here took place one of the earliest launchings of the steamboat, and here was staged the original experimental trial of a machine-driven vehicle, the progenitor of the modern automobile.

On a rainy spring day in 1785 the artist Rembrandt Peale strolled, pallet in hand, along the Schuylkill just

above the pontoon bridge at High Street. A crowd was
assembled, and from a passer-by he received the intelligence of strange doings in the stream. It appeared that
the half-demented engineer John Fitch, of whose experiments with a boat driven by steam all Philadelphia was
talking, was out with a new venture. Then, as Peale recorded, "Hearing there was something curious to be seen
at the floating bridge, I eagerly ran to see a strange shal-
lop with twenty men on board. On deck was a small
furnace with a complex crank over the stern giving mo-
tion to three or four paddles like snow shovels. It presently backed off and proceeded down to Gray's Ferry."

Artist Peale, more amused than impressed, stated that
he had no confidence in John Fitch or his steam-driven
craft. The Philadelphians remained sceptical, even deri-
sive, whereat the aggrieved inventor announced that he
would await the arrival of Doctor Franklin (then being
buffeted on the north Atlantic on his last homeward
voyage from France) to have a second and convincing
trial upon the Schuylkill. This trial was postponed, as
Doctor Franklin did not show the expected interest in experiments on steam navigation.

Two decades passed; Philadelphia had gained and lost
its distinction as a national capital; Jefferson was inaugurated at the new White House by the Potomac; then the
Schuylkill again became the scene of a mechanical experiment. This was in mid-summer of 1805. Another Philadelphia inventor, Oliver Evans, announced in the columns
of the contemporary press that he had perfected an auto-
matic, steam-driven contraption which would proceed under its own power over land and water. The Philadelphia
public were invited to come out to Central Square and

see this device, which had been pompously named the Oruktor Amphibobolus.

The inventor made the further startling statement that the Oruktor would roll out Market Street to the Schuylkill and there embark upon the surface of the river. To the amazement of many sceptics this program was faithfully carried out. Amidst the plaudits of the assembled multitude, the smoking Oruktor propelled itself out Market Street, slid into the river, and paddled off downstream. After so impressive a demonstration, one marvels that a long century was to elapse before the development of a practical automobile.

The advantages of the comparatively level terrain west of the Schuylkill at Market Street became evident as early as 1700, when a plan of streets and lots was temporarily laid out. This development, which never materialized, would seem to have been a bold venture, since Philadelphia itself still hugged the western bank of the Delaware. Southward from the bridge, in the colonial period, the present site of the University of Pennsylvania was pasture land sloping gently to the east. The Alms House, designed in 1828 by the architect Strickland and now partly preserved as the Pennsylvania General Hospital, had not been begun yet. The fields and vineyards of the Hamilton estate, seat of the younger branch of that aristocratic family, mounted the slope to Woodland Mansion with its stables and greenhouses, its liveried lackeys, and furnishings brought over from London.

Barbé-Marbois, who visited the Hamilton estate during Washington's administration, wrote: "The banks of the Schuylkill are adorned with a great many dwellings which belong to the richest citizens of Philadelphia. It is on the right bank of this river that there lies the house of Mr. William Hamilton. If ever Pennsylvania had a king, a prince, a doge, or a master, whatever he might be, it is there that he will live if he wishes to occupy the most beautiful site which exists in the surroundings of Philadelphia."

When a scion of Woodlands, young William Hamilton, matriculated as a member of the class of 1762 at the College of Philadelphia, the institution was still located on Fourth Street. "Billy" Hamilton was accustomed to ferry his horse across at the Middle Ferry and then ride east on High Street to the College. At graduation, when he was chosen as valedictorian, he entertained the members of his class at Woodlands. The banquet, we are told, was elaborate, featured by countless toasts pledged with fiery Jamaica and heady Madeira. At the end, as the roistering revelers straggled down the long slope on their homeward path to the ferry, they were traversing the future campus of their college. However, almost a century was to intervene before the College of Philadelphia (by that time the University of Pennsylvania) removed from its central Philadelphia location to this part of the Hamilton estate.

The mansion of Woodlands still looks down upon the stream, much as it did when its Tory owner planned the enlistment of the aristocratic youth of Philadelphia into a Loyal Legion to fight against General Washington and when the enraged patriots threatened to burn his house; but the estate is strangely transformed. The southern part is now Woodlands Cemetery, in which the columned Hamilton dwelling serves as the executive office; the northern part of the tract is absorbed in the campus of the University.

Stately old William Hamilton the elder, former student at Christchurch, Oxford, who was accustomed to promenade upon his terrace and enjoy the view over the river below, would have been startled by the apparition of academic halls and dormitories covering the bank. He might have been equally puzzled by a vision of the huge stadium named Franklin Field, colorfully bedecked with flags on the days of football contests, and by the ornate façade of the University Museum, and by the mass of huge Convention Hall where our national destinies have so often been shaped.

And certainly he would have been put to it to comprehend the transformation of his river meadow, where the playing fields of the University are now established. There on the slope where the squire's prize Merino sheep once grazed, young athletes run and jump, hurl the discus, and throw the javelin, a joyous Spartan decathlon re-enacted on the banks of the Schuylkill.

CHAPTER 21

Down Through Kingsessing

SOUTH of the academic, box-lined avenues of the University, the cattle bellow in the stockyards just above Bartram's Gardens and the derricks creak in the Atlantic Refining yard below. The ramified tracks of the Baltimore and Ohio extend over the site of the lovely Baptisterion. The sidings of the Pennsylvania Railroad at Girard Point obliterate all trace of the Dutch Fort which once stood there.

Here the Schuylkill is flowing through the locale of its earliest settlements. Above University Bridge its background is largely eighteenth century and Georgian. The lower river gropes back through the centuries to the era when Gustavus Adolphus of Sweden was leading the Protestant forces in the Thirty Years War, and when the house of Nassau held sway in the Low Countries. Not that the Swedish or Dutch dignitaries, embroiled in the complex statecraft of Europe, ever found much time for consideration of the struggling settlements on the Schuylkill; but the colonists took themselves very seriously, toiled at their ridiculous forts, and conducted the *opéra bouffe* warfare immortalized in the satire of Washington Irving.

New Sweden! What memories the appellation con-

jures up. And what might have been the destiny of the
Schuylkill Valley had Sweden been able to maintain the
commanding position which it had occupied in Europe under Charles XII, and so have retained its ability to protect its colonies in Pennslyvania? Would the state capital
be called New Stockholm and the Constitution be modeled
upon Chancellor Oxensteirn's Compendium? Would Gustavus Adolphus instead of William Penn look down upon
us from the tower of City Hall?

The temptation to transgress beyond the limits of the
river is nearly irresistible in this storied district of landmarks that may cause a vagrant fancy to ramble far afield.
What indeed constitutes a watershed? And with so many
points of appeal presenting themselves on either bank,
there is an exasperating tendency to leap back and forth,
from one side of the stream to the other, thereby creating
only confusion. For the sake of clarity this chapter will
deal with the west bank only, as far south as the Penrose
Ferry Bridge.

South of Woodlands the elaborate span of Gray's Ferry
Bridge swings over the Schuylkill, just where the Yorkshireman George Gray maintained his colonial ferry,
serving a road once regarded as the most important leading into the city. It was at this ferry, it will be remembered, that the unfortunate volunteer French officer Du
Coudray was drowned in the second year of the Revolution. This rash cavalier, against the advice of the ferrymen, insisted upon keeping a seat in the saddle while the
boat was crossing the stream. Near the opposite bank the
horse became frightened and jumped over the gunwhale,
drowning his rider.

At Gray's was the crossing of the old King's Path,

which led up from Chester and the southern country.
Gray had acquired the ferry rights from Benjamin Chambers, an inveterate litigant in the early history of New
Sweden. A truculent rogue, this Chambers! He made
sure that no traveler would cross the ferry without paying the proper fee by the simple expedient of building his
house in the middle of the road, an obstruction which
provoked the ire of the early tourists.

This stretch of the west bank must have been a lovely
sylvan retreat. Gone, now, is the *Sanger Halle* in which
members of Philadelphia's German societies assembled
during the Franco-Prussian war to hear the triumphant
bulletins from Metz and Sedan and to sing *"Die Wacht
am Rhein."* Vanished also is the mansion of Doctor
Benjamin Lay, once a gathering place for Philadelphia
aristocracy, the house which Kennedy sketched in 1856.

The apogee in the history of Gray's ferry and bridge
came on April 20, 1789, on which occasion the bridge was
festooned with laurel and crowned with arches. On the
Philadelphia side an expectant group of dignitaries was
gathered, headed by Governor Tom Mifflin and Richard
Peters, speaker of the Assembly. Presently the acclaim of
the multitude on the west bank and the sound of trumpets
announced the approach of the first President on his way
to his inauguration in New York. Washington, with his
usual affability, descended from his carriage, mounted a
white horse, and led his escort up upon the bridge "where
a child clad in white lowered a laurel wreath upon Washington's brow as he passed under one of the huge laurel
arches which formed a feature of the decorations."

The *Columbian Magazine* for May 1789 carried a fine
copper plate engraving, from a drawing by Charles Will-

son Peale, showing the decorations and in particular the eleven flags planted on the eastern side of the bridge. These standards were emblematic of the eleven states which had ratified the federal constitution. Pennsylvania's flag was the one which Captain Bell carried out to China, the first American state flag hoisted in the antipodes.

A few weeks later Mrs. Washington came over the bridge on her way to rejoin her husband in New York. Again the trumpets blared and cannon boomed at Gray's Ferry. The City Troop, in gala array, escorted Mrs. Washington to the adjoining Gray's Garden for a banquet at which, as a matter of historical record, forty-five bowls of fish house punch were consumed.

This mention of Gray's Gardens recalls the pleasure grounds at the west approach to the ferry, with the greenhouses, box-wood maze, graveled walks, and pavilions, long the goal of summer excursions. Washington went there frequently during his residence in Philadelphia, and at a later date the place became so popular that horse-drawn cars ran out from Philadelphia. The tavern was at one time conducted by that famous fisherman Curtis Grubb, "who would bring home a basket of perch when no one else could get a nibble."

The garrulous colonial gossip Jacob Hiltzheimer, writing in 1787 while the delegates to the Constitutional Convention were dragging out an interminable debate in the State House, said: "Drove my wife and Mr. and Mrs. Barge out to see the walks, fountains and woodland retreats which George Gray has arranged at his ferry. In the afternoon Mr. Washington came out with some gentleman from the Convention."

Gray's Ferry dropped out of the limelight with the

advent of the nineteenth century. Only once, during the War of 1812, was public attention again focussed upon it, after the news came that the British fleet had entered the Chesapeake. There was apprehension that the enemy might march northward and cross at Gray's for an attack on Philadelphia. The city fathers, in feverish alarm, projected a line of earthworks at the ferry and hit upon the idea of having each segment of the citizens contribute one day's work. So there was an Irish trench and a German trench and one constructed by the colored people. These bastions were never manned, but their grass-grown slopes were long used upon successive Easter days by the children of Philadelphia for the rolling of eggs.

This part of the river has been immortalized by Doctor Weir Mitchell, second to none among our Pennsylvania writers in his love for the Schuylkill Valley. It was at this point that Hugh Wynne, hero of the novel which bears his name, made his escape across the stream from the British lines: "The town was all asleep, and I saw no one until I passed the Bettering-house, and the Grenadiers cleaning their guns, and powdering their queues and hair, and thence pushed on to the river. The lower ferry, known also as Gray's, lay just a little south of where the Woodlands, Mr. James Hamilton's house, stood among trees high above the quiet Schuylkill. I paddled swiftly downstream. Not a hundred yards from the ferry I saw ducks on the east shore, and, having loaded, paddled over to Rambo's Rock, and was lucky enough to get two ducks at a shot. As I passed Bartram's famous garden, I saw his son near the river, busy, as usual, with his innocent flowers."

A succession of warehouses and refineries looms to the

south, interrupted only by the house and garden of the colonial botanist John Bartram, preserved as a municipal park under the Fairmount Park Commission.

Bartram acquired the tract in 1728; long afterward he wrote, "I was set up in the wilderness when I started building this house in 1730."

In 1770 when he had been hailed by the great Carolus Linnaeus of Stockholm (himself the father of systematic zoology and botany) as "the greatest of natural botanists," Bartram chiseled over the front window of his study the inscription which hundreds of visitors read each day:

> 'Tis God alone, almighty Lord,
> The holy One by me adored.
>
> John Bartram, 1770

In the interval Bartram had been appointed Royal Botanist to his Majesty George the Third, had become a member of the American Philosophical Society, and was the proud recipient of a congratulatory letter from the Queen of Sweden. The delighted addressee wrote to his friend, the poet naturalist Hector St. John Crevecoeur: "As I make no doubt that thee understandeth the Latin tongue, read this kind epistle which the good Queen of Sweden, Ulrica, sent me a few years ago. Good woman! that she should think in her palace at Stockholm of poor John Bartram on the banks of the Schuylkill appeareth to me very strange."

Surely, in all the length of the winding Schuylkill there is no more appealing shrine than this garden tract of seven acres! Many of the trees and shrubs which bloom there now have sprung from rare seedlings which Bartram and his son William collected in their journeys to Lake

Ontario and to Florida. The quaint old stone house with its out-buildings, watering trough, and cider mill remains much as Bartram left it. Its visitors' roster shows a line of distinguished names, including that of Peter Kalm, the Finnish botanist who made the house his headquarters in 1748. Franklin visited here, and Logan, and David Rittenhouse, and Crevecoeur, who has left us an account of the sojourn in his *Letters from an American Farmer*. The only visitor who seems to have been at all deprecatory was President Washington, who "Breakfasted at Mr. Powel's, and in company with him rid to see the Botanical Garden of Mr. Bartram, which, tho' stored with many curious plants, shrubs and trees, many of which are exotics, was not laid off with much taste, nor was it large."

John Bartram sat on the terrace facing the river on the twenty-second of September, 1777. He was a dying man and his condition was not improved by the disquieting rumors which clustered thick and fast. The patriot army had been defeated at Brandywine; Cornwallis was marching northward towards Chester; the Hessians were at Naaman's Tavern; Lord Howe was expected momentarily on the banks of the Schuylkill. As the dying scientist listened to these baneful announcements and looked down upon his beautiful garden, he murmured the foreboding that the work of a lifetime was to be destroyed by the ruthless invader. He died before nightfall.

During his visit to Philadelphia in 1787 the Yankee surgeon Doctor Manasseh Cutler made a trip down to Gray's. Perhaps his curiosity had been piqued when he visited Doctor Franklin in his house back of High Street a few weeks before, upon which occasion the Sage exhibited a two-headed snake "Found near the confluence

of the Schuylkill and Delaware." Anyhow Doctor Cutler
rode down the river and found William Bartram at work
on his plantation and apparently not expecting visitors.
"He was attired in a short jacket and trousers, without
shoes or stockings, hoeing his garden."

West of Bartram's gardens lies the ancient district of
Kingsessing, studded with landmarks of the first Swedish
occupation. Here was the site of luckless Fort Elfsport,
which the Swedish garrison abandoned because of the
ferocity of the mosquitoes which infested the site. Hard
by, probably in the vicinity of the old Swede's mill built
by Governor John Printz, was "ye Towne of Kingsessing
in ye Schuylkills." This latter "towne" must have been a
place of some importance in its day, for in 1680 the local
court transferred their sittings from upland, now Chester,
to Kingsessing. The historic church St. James of Kingsessing, with its old horse-block and interesting mosaic pointing (*galleting* is the technical term), founded in 1760 and
rebuilt in 1854, stands on this tract. South of St. James is
the Blue Bell Tavern, with its reminiscences of Lord
Howe, of the Hessian General Knyphausen, and of
Washington. It was at Blue Bell that Washington, escorted out from the city by a committee of citizens, voiced
his farewell to Philadelphia.

Perhaps the most attractive of the older dwellings in
this neighborhood was Whitby Hall, now bodily removed
to Haverford. The Hall was erected by Captain (Sheriff)
James Coultas. In 1740 Captain Coultas came courting
one of the comely Gray girls, daughter of George Gray
the ferry man. The suitor was accepted with the stipulation that when married he would live near his father-in-
law. Accordingly, in the next year, Coultas propitiated

his bride by settling in Kingsessing, where he built Whitby Hall.

Now great tankers churn up to Point Breeze where the Indian conference with Governor Printz assembled. What would be the thoughts of the ten sachems who paddled down the Schuylkill on that June day in 1654 if they were to view the transformed stream of today: the rows of oil tanks, and the piers of the unfinished Penrose Ferry Bridge ranging over stream and meadow like the imaginary war machines of the Martians in H. G. Wells' tale. Penrose's Ferry, sometimes called the Rope Ferry and the most southern of the many Schuylkill ferries, dates from a fairly early period. Why there should have been a crossing planned at this point is not quite clear, since originally the ferry served no important role and was surrounded by marsh land.

If the sachems drifted past the bridge site, they would search in vain for any vestige of Fort Manayunk, or Fort Schuylkill as it was sometimes called, which Printz built to command the approaches to the Hidden River. Fort Schuylkill was on the west bank of the river, somewhere above the present Penrose Ferry Bridge. It was designed to control and protect the all important beaver trade. The Swedish missionary Campanius called the fort *Manaijung, Skorkilen* (Manayunk, Schuylkill), and gave a fairly accurate contemporary description: "Manayunk on Schuylkill is a handsome little fort built of logs filled up with sand and stone and surrounded with palisades cut very sharp at the top. It is mounted with great guns as well as the other forts."

When Sammy Penrose first stretched the ropes for his ferry, the neighborhood was lonely enough and Sir Francis Loveland, the colonial governor of New York who owned it, gave leases which carried with them "the right to hunt, hawk and hound." Later, when this part of the valley became more settled, the inevitable ferry tavern reared its head on the western bank. The foundations of this tavern, still to be seen, mark the end of the tour down the western side of the Schuylkill. Across the river lie the historic districts of Passyunk and Moyamensing and Wicaco, the heart of New Sweden.

CHAPTER 22

Up Through Passyunk

TWO of the original Swedish farmhouses are still standing upon what was once Lasse Cocke Plantation on the lower east bank. Passyunk, or "the level meadow," is built up now and rolls eastward over the farm where the blind pastor Fabricius of the Swedish church of Wicaco on the Delaware once had his summerhouse. The pastor would have been scandalized to know that the site of his prize orchard, where he raised the Lombardy pippins which were the talk of Philadelphia, would be desecrated in the later years by Point Breeze Race Course.

Here on Magazine Lane, the former Beggartown Road, are to be seen the low stone buttresses of the old powder magazine abandoned since 1874. The powder magazine lay to the northward in a more central location, but it engendered so much apprehension among the neighboring residents that in 1808 it was removed to the present location, where it was last used in the War of 1812.

East of the docks and warehouses of Girard Point lies the site of the Sesquicentennial of 1926. The new Naval Hospital arises from the park marking the site of the commemoration, but of the exposition buildings only the stadium survives. In this immense arena Gene Tunney won the fistic crown from Jack Dempsey in the famous long-count bout of 1929. It stands deserted for most of the year and is filled only for an occasional pageant and for the annual Army-Navy football game.

Above Girard Point (the name commemorates Stephen Girard's lower Philadelphia farm, upon which the Board of City Trust later erected model houses) stood the old Swedish Fort Korsholm. Commander Swen Shute, so prominent in the development of the lower Schuylkill territory, built the fort on what he described as "a reedy island in Schuylkill." All trace of the island has disappeared. It must long ago have been absorbed into the eastern bank. Commander Shute's fortification was built on the foundation of an earlier blockhouse which Lieutenant Mans Kling had equipped with iron cannons, which were designed to throw stone balls at any invader—French, Spanish, Dutch, or English—who might rashly venture to dispute the sovereign sway of Sweden over the Schuylkill. The hamlets or farmhouses mentioned in some of the early Swedish chronicles, such as Olaf Stille's estate at Techoressi, Gripsolm, and Nya Wassa, have so completely disappeared that their very sites are conjectural.

The bluff known to the early chroniclers as Passyunk Bank runs for two miles on the eastern bank. Just back of this lies the Shetzline House, better known as the old Swedish Glebe House, or parsonage, a structure remarkably little changed in the two hundred years of its existence.

Near this point was located the important Dutch fort of Beversreede (or was it *Beeversrode?*), "the road of

the beaver," which is so often referred to in the history
of the lower Schuylkill. The corner where Gallows Lane
now meets the River Road has been claimed as the exact
site of Beversreede, and a commemorative bronze plaque
has been erected between the establishments of the Atlantic Refining Company and the Philadelphia Gas Company. However, the evidence as to the exact location is
not too conclusive.

Just which colonial strategist first located a fort at this
place is not clear, but it is claimed that Captain Cornelius
Mey, who explored the lower Delaware for the Dutch
East India Company in 1624, made a report upon the
advantages of the site. At that early period the threat of
Swedish rivalry upon the Schuylkill was not taken too
seriously by the complacent and somnolent authorities at
New Amsterdam. Nevertheless, by 1648 the Scandinavian
irruption had begun in earnest, and the enterprising Swedish governor, Johann Printz, had erected his Fort Manayunk on Schuylkill. This post, advantageously constructed
to command the Minquas trail from the south, by which
the Indian beaver trade reached the Schuylkill and Delaware, was a distinct threat to the waning Dutch interests.
When the news was brought to Governor Stuyvestant at
New Amsterdam, he bestirred himself and hastily directed Commissary Andries Hudde to build a stronghold
on the Schuylkill which might rival the Swedish fortification and restore Dutch prestige. Hudde explored the
lower river and chose the site on Passyunk Bank which
Captain May had visited thirty years before.

As soon as Commissary Hudde began to cut his palisades, the tidings spread like wildfire up and down the
river. Earlier, there would have been no opposition, but
the period when the Dutch held undisputed sway over

the lower Schuylkill was gone. The Swedes were becoming restless rivals as ship after ship came into the Delaware from Gotenburg and Malmo. The boundaries of New Sweden were extending despite the feverish protests in Amsterdam and the tirades of the governor at New Amsterdam. Indeed, more Scandinavian immigrants were presenting themselves at the Swedish ports of embarkation than could be crowded into the available vessels. Worst of all, the Swedes were depleting the Schuylkill beaver market, so that by 1642 the supply was short thirty thousand skins.

In his mansion at Printz Hall on Tinicum Island, some miles below Schuylkill's western bank, sat the grotesque Swedish Governor John Printz, weighing over four hundred pounds, we are told, and washing down each copious meal with a gallon of liquor. But for all his portliness there was nothing lethargic in Governor Printz's composition. He knew his colony well. In his ketch *Christina* he had sailed up the Schuylkill and surveyed the military advantages of the "Passyunk bank" with the eye of a soldier who had fought under the great Gustavus Adolphus. So, comprehending the threat entailed to the Swedish interests by the building of Fort Beversreede, he decided that some action must be taken.

Not too certain of his own authority, for the interlocking claims of Sweden and Holland on the lower Schuylkill had never been clarified, Governor Printz nevertheless sent a messenger to Hudde and boldly demanded that work on Fort Beversreede should cease. The theatrical Hudde at once assembled his armed guard of six able-bodied men, the imposing force which New Amsterdam had detailed as a garrison to protect the workmen. He harangued upon the importance of the crisis and directed the devoted garrison to die at their post if necessary. Whereupon the wily Swedes, avoiding actual hostilities, removed all the trees in the neighborhood and "twice destroyed the palisades surrounding the fort." When, despite all obstacles, the intrepid Hudde had somehow completed his fort, Governor Printz countered with a measure unique in military annals. He built a stockade of his own directly in front of Beversreede and between it and the river.

"The gable of the Swedish house is only twelve feet from the gate of our fort and vessels in the river Schuylkill can discover our fort only with difficulty," wrote the discomfited Hudde to his superiors at New Amsterdam. This ridiculous rivalry lasted until 1655, when Swedish rule in Pennsylvania definitely terminated and the Dutch again took over until they were in turn superseded by the English in 1664.

Northward through Passyunk, past the extensive gas works, is the site of the dwelling known as Harmar's Castle, where the redoubtable Indian fighter General Josiah Harmar, once Commander in Chief of the Army of the United States, resided. Thomas Jefferson, then Secretary of State in Washington's first cabinet, moved into this house in the spring of 1793, just before the yellow fever plague. On the last day of March Jefferson wrote to Madison: "I shall in the course of the week get on the banks of Schuylkill."

As the season advanced he wrote again: "We are in sight of Bartram's and Gray's gardens but have the river between them and us. My house is entirely embosomed in high plane trees and under them I breakfast, dine, write and receive my company."

Among these callers was President Washington, who rode down disturbed by rumors that Jefferson intended to resign from the cabinet, which as a matter of fact he did before the end of the year. As the dread announcements of yellow fever began to come from the stricken city to the northward, the secretary prepared to abandon his river dwelling. He explained that he would have moved sooner but did not wish "to exhibit the appearance of any apprehension." Jefferson finally departed for Monticello in October.

Near the Harmar house stood the Golden Swan, a favored goal of sleighing parties and the center for good cheer. Nearby is Gray's and here, still protruding from the river bed in low water, is Rambo's Rock, Serval's Rock as it was first called when the Swedes dried fish upon it. This tiny islet was once a well-marked point in the topography of the district, although its very existence is hardly realized today.

It was to this same Rambo's Rock, or rather to the adjacent tract called Millmont, on that May day of 1822 that the cumbersome "castle" of the State in Schuylkill came floating downstream, poled by the perspiring "citizens." One of the mariners, James Barkett, took time out from his arduous duties to indite a couplet commemorative of the occasion:

> *The San Marino of the west*
> *Secure with guardian Castle blest*
> *And fixed on Rambo's Rock.*

State in Schuylkill had been installed at Rambo's for three years when the rock was honored by the arrival of a distinguished visitor, a lively old gentleman in a preposterous wig who was introduced to the members as the Nation's guest, General Lafayette. With the General was his secretary, Mr. Levasseur, and his eldest son George Washington Lafayette. The neighborhood was not strange to either of the Lafayettes. The General, wounded at the Brandywine, had been ferried across the river at Gray's Ferry just below. His son, during the time that he was in America as Washington's guest at Mount Vernon, had frequently visited Philadelphia and taken fishing trips down the river.

The occasion was a notable one, and a hint of impending hilarity is contained in the minutes of the Society appropriating a special allowance for crockery expected to be broken. Rail birds, shot on near-by League Island, and steaks were served. The Marquis donned a cap and apron and superintended the cuisine. The Society's best Maderia was served with many toasts, and Lafayette enunciated his *bon-mot* referring to his having visited every state in the Union and being now admitted as a citizen of the State in Schuylkill.

On St. Valentine's Day of 1856 the Schuylkill was solidly frozen over, and the citizens drove out Chestnut Street and then down the surface of the river to the Castle. Luther Eichorn, the baker from Bainbridge Street, stood on the bank and watched the spectacle which he recorded in his diary: "Such a feat is not remembered by any of the inhabitants of Passyunk."

For sixty-five years, winter and summer, the citizens of State in Schuylkill rode, walked, or skated down to Rambo's Rock. Then in 1887 they moved once more, this time to Essington on the Delaware, quitting the Schuylkill permanently.

In this built-up portion of modern Philadelphia, the

boundaries of the holdings of the early settlers, the Rambos, the Cocks, the Penroses, as indicated in the Scull and Heap Map of 1760, are scarcely discernible. The greater part of the many watercourses and creeks, Jones Creek, Hay Creek, and Bow Creek, which formerly flowed down through Moyamensing and Passyunk to join Schuylkill, have gone underground.

The most important surviving building of the post-colonial era is the Naval Asylum on Gray's Ferry Road, designed by Strickland in 1830. On this property the Quaker Abolitionist James Pemberton, father of the Pennsylvania Abolition Society, had his plantation, the Evergreens. At an earlier period, Chief Justice John Kinsey had his summer dwelling here, which he called Plantation House. One morning in 1778 during the British occupation, a lad with Pemberton connections perceived some soldiers in strange outlandish uniforms, speaking a gutteral dialect, sneaking up to the chicken house. "These rascally Hessians took all the hay and most of the potatoes which belonged to the tenants to the great distress of the family. I went a little further and see a number of Hessians crossing over the bridge of boats lately made for that purpose."

The hospital, in its time a training school, has had a long and useful career, functioning as long ago as the War of 1812. As one wanders under the shade of the great trees which surround the present hospital, he pauses to read the names on the memorial plaque: Bainbridge, Hull, Decatur, and Farragut. These captions evoke visions of epic sea fights and of dejected English commanders proffering their swords in embarrassed surrender.

It is somewhat surprising that in 1844, when the Congressional committee was seeking a site for a Naval Academy, they did not locate on the Schuylkill rather than at Annapolis. James Biddle, who was Commandant in that year, was a native Philadelphian and would presumably strive to keep the Academy in Philadelphia, particularly as classes were already in training there. However, the cadets complained so bitterly of the rats, the damp walls, and the horrible food that the change of location was deemed better in the interests of the service.

Nearby upstream is Chestnut Street, beside the tract embraced in the ancient patent of the Society of Traders dating back to 1684, the not too well-defined district known to colonial chroniclers as Moyamensing. Moyamensing and part of Passyunk were granted by Queen Christina of Sweden to the military pioneer Swen Schute, who had fought in the Thirty Years War. Schute's grant was conditioned upon the annual payment of ten bushels of wheat, a picturesque custom which might well be revived like the pageant of the tribute of the rose in the old church at Mannheim.

Near the present Baltimore and Ohio Railroad Station is the site of that curious building known as the Baptisterion, parts of whose foundation could be seen as late as 1877. This Baptisterion represented the fulfillment of the aspirations of the Welsh-born Baptists of Philadelphia. One of the pioneers of this faith was the Reverend Morgan Evans, who crossed the seas to Pennsylvania in 1761. Mr. Evans, in the course of his rambles along the Schuylkill, discovered this location and hailed it as ideal for the rites of immersion as prescribed by his church. Long afterwards he gave an enthusiastic description of his beloved baptistry:

"In this beautiful spot on the banks of Schuylkill I have baptised thousands. The fine oaks afforded a grateful shade and underfoot, in season, were wild flowers and aromatic herbs."

Trees and flowers have long since disappeared from this work-a-day district. Only a quaint woodcut survives to recall the vanished splendor of the Baptisterion on the Schuylkill.

CHAPTER 23

The Mouth

THE Hidden River covers one hundred and twenty-eight miles from its natal spring high up in the thickets of the Tuscarora Hills, through the fertile champaigns of Berks and Montgomery, under the palisades of Valley Forge, and past the parks and wharves of Philadelphia to the point of junction with the Delaware.

Mouths of rivers seldom attain the prominence of their middle courses. Whether it be the Rhine dividing in the alluvial delta of Holland, the Seine melting into the estuary of Le Havre, or the Mississippi lost in the lower Louisiana bayous, the ending of a majestic stream is often disappointing. A like fate might have befallen the Schuylkill had not man intervened to establish an important naval station at League Island, just where its waters mix with those of the broad Delaware. This installation gives the mouth of the Schuylkill individuality and importance, a marked transition from reed-covered meadows which suggested to Arendt Corson, first white navigator in the valley, the name of Hidden River.

League Island is a peninsula now. Broad Street no longer passes over a bridge spanning Hollander Creek—the eastern end of the creek has been filled up. When it was still an island, the area totaled about nine hundred acres, and some early Swedish cartographer amused himself by calculating that the circumference of the islet was exactly a league. So Lindstrom in his map of 1654 dubbed it League Island. The London Company, who owned it in the early days, attached little importance to the tract and granted it out to one Thomas Foreman for sheep grazing. At a still earlier day, in 1645, a Dutch frigate was caught in the ice of *Hollander Kill* (Creek) and wintered here. The crew passed the time by trapping birds on the snow-covered island where the gigantic naval cranes now rear their fantastic heads. Except for this interlude, League Island lay for two centuries neglected and forlorn.

There had been a navy yard in Philadelphia for over a century, but it was on the Delaware near the early Swedish settlement called Wicaco. It is chiefly remembered because of the fame of one of its early superintendents, James Humphreys of Haverford, who ranks high on the list of early American shipwrights. Humphreys it was who designed so many of the gallant frigates which brought fame to our young American navy: the *Constitution*, the *Constellation*, and the *President*. Each of these raking men-of-war was at one time or another repaired at the yard on the Delaware. In the end, however, the area of the site began to be inadequate and the Philadelphia city authorities, desirous of retaining a federal navy yard, looked about for a new location. This they found at League Island; but not until 1862, while McClellan was advancing to the Rapahannock, did they acquire the tract for a sum, considered excessive at the time, of $310. After an interlude of inactivity the United States Government moved the yard to the new site in the Centennial year of 1876.

The League Island of today is active and ominous with wartime restrictions, still enforced as the threat of another world conflict hangs in the offing and spurs the navy personnel to unremitting vigilance. It may be that the turnstiles will again swing for the daily admission of a complement of twenty-five thousand artisans, and that the streets of the post will again be blue with uniforms. But at present the mighty warships lie moored rather sleepily in long mournful lines. A visitor strolling along the wharves and noting the names upon the sterns of these leviathans, once the scourge of the seven seas, the *Houston,* the *Brooklyn,* the *Philadelphia,* may think of chained Prometheus and wonder if these engines of destruction will ever be recalled to active duty and whether the Schuylkill's waters will once more echo to the deafening clang of warlike preparation.

Across the river from League Island, the body of land bordering the Schuylkill's mouth on the western side is the site upon which the colonial pesthouse was established in 1742. The advent of the pesthouse made it necessary to push a trail across the river, and Sammy Penrose came to establish a ferry and give it his name. Later Penrose Ferry came into the limelight when the British authorities of Philadelphia, seeking to perfect the defenses of the lower Delaware against the French and Spanish, began to develop the fort on Mud Island (successively known as Fisher's, Province, and State) to the south. The work was entrusted to the engineer officer John Montresor, whose name was later to loom large in the annals of the American Revolution. As Captain Montresor rode the muddy trail through Passyunk and crossed Penrose's Ferry, he could not foresee the time when the King's rebellious subjects would seize this fort which he was building on Mud Island and rechristen it Fort Mifflin. Nor could he prognosticate that he would be given the task of bombarding the very bastions which he was so laboriously constructing.

The marshes of Mud Island, now so neglected, played a prominent part during those autumn days of 1777 when the British were preparing to besiege Fort Mifflin. Brigadier General Foreman of the American army was alerted in the middle of the night of October 29. He wrote at dawn to Washington, who was anxiously awaiting developments in his encampment up the river: "About two o'clock this day (October 29, 1777) one thousand British troops crossed the mouth of Schuylkill and stood paraded on the hills around the Pest House."

The siege and the gallant defense of Fort Mifflin are matters of history. In all the Revolutionary cyclorama there is no prouder picture than that of Colonel Smith, disdaining to surrender, leading the remnants of his garrison in sullen retreat across to the mainland.

After the Revolution, Fort Mifflin was reconstructed by the Frenchman L'Enfant, the architect who laid out the city of Washington. During the Civil War rebel prisoners languished in its dungeons and waxed querulous over the dampness. No memorial park has been laid out at Fort Mifflin to commemorate the siege. Only the "cannon ball house" (formerly Adam Gyers house), with a hole in its walls made by a projectile fired by the Americans during the siege, still stands.

The best view of the confluence of the Schuylkill and

the Delaware is to be obtained from the embankment of
the Federal Ammunition Depot on Mud Island. The
complex installations of League Island are just opposite.
To the south lies Fort Mifflin, from which Colonel Smith
evacuated his garrison by the light of the British frigate
Augusta burning on the sand-spit, while the grapeshot of
Cornwallis whipped on the dejected rear guard of the
patriot forces. Looking eastward, across the broad Delaware one sees Red Bank, where the Hessian Count
Donop, doomed to fall in the assault, rallied his auxiliaries for the attack.

Up from Chester churns a sleek tanker from Bordeaux,
heading into the Schuylkill to take up a cargo of oil at
Girard Point. The tri-color flaps lazily at her stern. One
cannot help wondering whether the captain has ever heard
the story of his Gallic compatriots who fought here, of
Gaston Fleury who layed out the earthworks of Fort
Mifflin, and of Maudit de Plessis who helped direct the
defense of Red Bank.

The mouth of the Schuylkill recalls an era much earlier
than the Revolution. Tinicum, where Governor Johann
Printz had his palace, lies just below. Westward over the
marshes of Skorkillin is Kingsessing, once the seat of
justice, where bewigged counsellors quoted from ponder-
ous tomes in Runic script and promulgated decrees for
the colony of New Sweden. In this storied setting the
Schuylkill merges with the Delaware.

9

CROSSINGS
AND NAVIGATION

CHAPTER 24

The Fords

FORDS were of primary importance along the Schuylkill in the period when there were neither ferries nor bridges. The principal up-country market towns, Orwigsburg, Reading, and Potts Grove, were on the east side of the stream. The west bank farmer must get his ladings of pelts and grain across the river in order to merchandise them. Once on the east side, the farmer was confronted with creeks flowing into the Schuylkill that had to be forded.

The principal tributaries of Schuylkill might be tabulated as follows:

WEST OR SOUTH SIDE	EAST OR NORTH SIDE
Tulpehocken	Little Schuylkill
Alleghany	Maiden Creek
Hay Creek	Monocacy Creek
French Creek	Manatawny Creek
Pickering Creek	Perkiomen
Valley Creek	Wissahickon

Of these tributaries, the broad and swift Perkiomen constituted a major obstacle in colonial travel. There was no bridge across it until 1801, and the stage coaches between Reading and Philadelphia were often held up for days when the creek was in flood. Jacob Hiltzheimer, driving up the Schuylkill with General Tom Mifflin to spend Christmas of 1778 at Angelica, was halted by high water upon reaching the Perkiomen, because the "horses refused to pull. A wagon with four horses coming after us, the driver hitched two of his horses to General Mifflin's and hauled us through the stream and up on the level."

When the first white men came up the Schuylkill, they found well-defined fording places at the points where the Indian trails crossed the river. The Moravian missionaries from Bethlehem and Nazareth, whose travel diaries rival the Relations of the formidable Company of Jesus in clarity and detail, recorded most of the data now available concerning these primitive fords. Heckwelder speaks of the one later called Fincher's near present Schuylkill Haven and of Kern's Ford near Hamburg, a part of an early Minqua trail.

Farther down the river, Reading ford was a link in the chain of the Lenape trail which led from Shamokin to the Delaware. From time immemorial the raiding war parties had traversed this trail until, at the point where it crossed present Penn Square of Reading, even the tough grass roots were obliterated. This ford seems to have been useable in all seasons except after the spring rains. When a bridge was first projected in 1795, some of the towns-people objected to the tax entailed by the improvement and asserted that the ford had been good enough for their ancestors. There was something in this claim, for certainly during the Revolution many important men had ridden through the river and had not complained of a little wetting: De Kalb and Steuben, Gates and Knox.

When the British chased the fugitive Congress out of
Philadelphia, they came up to Reading and waited for the
Schuylkill to subside so that they might continue on towards York, their temporary capital. Charles Carroll of
Carrollton stood at the lower Reading ford (Carroll calls
it Strohecker's Ford), connecting with the Lancaster road,
and each morning sent his Negro slave in to test the force
of the stream. Washington crossed the upper Reading
ford twice, once on horseback in 1793 and once in coach
of state in 1794.

However, in the annals of the Reading fords the most
dramatic episode occurred in 1798. Albert Gallatin, a
Congressman at the time, was very unpopular because of
his supposed sympathy with the French Government,
with which we were in a state of undeclared naval war.
The patriots of Reading had been told that Gallatin came
from Geneva, which they vaguely associated with France.
Accordingly, when Congressman Gallatin took this unpro-
pitious moment to pass through Reading, a mob gathered
before his inn and played the Rogue's March, inter-
spersed with jeers and cat-calls. Gallatin thought it prudent to send his terrified wife out of the front door of
their tavern and make his escape on horseback from the
rear. But he had to cross the Schuylkill ford, and here he
again encountered the jeering crowd. Perhaps to show his
contempt for the proceeding, Gallatin gravely dismounted
and walked waist deep through the river, leading his
horse by the bridle.

Even after the Reading toll bridge was built, the importance of the ford did not diminish, for thrifty travelers
often chose to splash through the stream bed and so save
the crossing fee, while the toll collector watched them

glumly from the parapet above. As late as 1810, Margaret Dwight, a niece of President Timothy Dwight of Yale, bound upon a voyage to Ohio found Reading ford still in use: "We rode through Schuylkill in our wagon. A bridge was begun over it but the man broke & was unable to finish it. It is now grown over with grass & serves as a walk for the ladies."

A faded yellow list survives, giving data on the fords in the Reading district; but the modern tourist derives little profit from the knowledge that Lewis Fall Ford (Poplar Neck) and Green Tree Ford, just above it, are of an average depth of seven inches with sandy bottom.

Downstream at the plantation of the ironmaster Mark Bird there was a ford by which Bird, a vestryman and devout worshiper at St. Gabriel's on the farther bank, used to cross each Sunday. Sometimes when the water was too high, he detoured to the southward crossing at Campbell's ford, whose exact location is no longer known. Most of the fords in the stretch of river just below Birdsboro were used in connection with the iron industry, and there survives a memorandum of the Rutter family, great ironmasters in their day, for the repair of a ford above Potts Grove.

Two fords just below, Royer's and Parker's, gave their names to bustling towns. In this course of the river many fords have entirely disappeared; no living man can locate the Bombay Hook or the Cow and Calf or Frederick's Lower Shoals. But two centuries ago the hardy Reading boatmen marked the approach of these fording places by the contour of the river banks and prepared to guide their craft through the perils entailed by the shallows.

The section of the Schuylkill at Phoenixville and

just below was the scene of the autumn campaign of
1777, during which so many crossings of the river were
made both by Washington and by his opponents, Howe
and Cornwallis, that it might well be called the "Campaign of the Fords." Here, after the defeat at Brandywine, were executed the series of perplexing maneuvers
in which the patriot General, in his own country and yet
handicapped by lack of proper intelligence, remained un-
certain as to whether the real objective of the British
army was the precious munition depot at Reading or the
colonial capital of Philadelphia. So the harried continentals floundered up and down the northern bank of
Schuylkill, marching and countermarching in aimless
fashion, only to learn too late that the wily enemy had
made a moonlit crossing of the stream and was well
on his way to a bloodless occupation of Philadelphia.
General Washington, writing to his brother Augustine
at Mount Vernon, stated that: "This river Schuylkill is
as easily crossed in any place as Potomac Run, Aquia or
any other broad and shallow water."

The patriot army, which had reached the west bank of
the Schuylkill after the repulse at Brandywine and the
rough handling at Paoli, turned in the third week of
September and marched eastward to cross the river at
Parkerford. Pastor Muhlenberg, six miles away in his
parsonage at Trappe, recorded that "In the afternoon
(September 19, 1777) we had news that the British
troops on the other side of the Schuylkill had marched
down toward Providence and with a telescope we could
see their camp. In consequence of this the American
Army, four miles from us forded the Schuylkill breast
high and came upon the Philadelphia road at Augustus

Church. His excellency General Washington was with the troops in person who marched here to the Perkiomen. The procession lasted the whole night and we had numerous visits from officers, wet breast high, who had to march in this condition during the whole night cold and damp as it was and bear hunger and thirst at the same time."

The victorious British, well equipped and confident, were encamped at Valley Forge. They might easily have marched up the west bank, taken Reading with its storehouses, and turned Washington's flank. Instead, they crossed the river and proceeded southward for the capture of Philadelphia. Sergeant Lamb from Dublin, whose memoirs give the best picture of this campaign, shook his head and muttered that the chance to crush this saucy Washington and his rebel crew was lost forever. He was right.

However, if the enemy took the wrong decision, it must be admitted that he masked his intentions well. A pontoon bridge was thrown across at Gordon's Ford (Phoenixville), and frequent forays convinced Washington that this was the point of danger. Then in the moonlight of the twenty-third of September the Hessians forded Schuylkill at Fatland Ford, two miles downstream, and the entire British army followed. The maneuver was reported by Cornwallis' engineer officer, Captain John Montresor:

> 23rd. Just after 12 o'clock this night the whole army moved to the opposite side, on North Side of the River Schuylkill by the way of the Fatland Ford, and by 10 A.M. the whole Baggage and all had happily passed it. After the principal body had got on the North Side of the

Schuylkill about 1 mile the Army halted to dry themselves and rest.

Washington, describing the same maneuver to General Putnam told how "General Howe by various maneuvers marching high up the Schuylkill as if he meant to turn our right flank found means by counter-marching to pass the river several miles below us last night, which is fordable in almost every part, and is now advancing towards Philadelphia."

The fords of the lower river also played their part in the military strategy of that eventful autumn of 1777. Sullivan's crude bridge below Valley Forge and the pontoon bridge at Market Street in Philadelphia enabled the patriots to keep their feet and powder reasonably dry. However, the New England troops who waded the stream at Swede's Ford (Norristown) and recrossed below Spring Mill for Lafayette's ill-advised adventure at Barren Hill must have had lively and not too pleasant recollections of the shaly bed of the Schuylkill.

It was at the Manayunk Fords—Hagy's, named for Jacob Hagy the paper maker of White Marsh, and the crossing which rejoiced in the very Cymric title of Rees ap Edward's—that Washington's army passed over to the west bank shortly after the defeat at Brandywine. One of the staff officers has left his record of this passage:

> Thirty casks of rum having been distributed among the soldiers by special action of Congress as a consolation cup for their ill luck on September 11, the army divested itself of more of its clothes then Adjutant General Pickering thought necessary, and forded the river to the west bank.

And Colonel John Bull had his own personal plaint:
"I caught a rumatic cold when I fell off my horse into
Schuylkill while conducting some general officers over
Rees ap Edward's ford."

These fords of the Manayunk district, including also
Levering's and Young's and Mary Walter's, just below
Flat Rock Tunnel, were of little use when the river ran
high; indeed there were few fords in the deeper water
below Flat Rock. One exception was the ford at about the
site of the later Fairmount Park trolley bridge, which was
called Garret Moreton's Ford in the Scull and Heap
Map of 1750. This is the crossing which later was known
as Robin Hood.

Despite the paucity of fords in the lower Schuylkill,
there is no doubt that many well-marked crossings
through the bed of the stream were used during the dry
season. Such a one existed at the Schuylkill end of High
Street (Market Street) in Philadelphia. By this temporary ford the defeated and dejected remnants of the
regiments of Dunbar and Halket reached Philadelphia,
rather shamefacedly we may suppose, after Braddock's
defeat at Fort DuQuesne. It is also stated, although the
authority is not given, that when the exiled royal brothers,
the Duc d' Orleans (afterwards King Louis Phillipe) and
his brothers the Duc d' Montpensier and the Duc d' Beaujolais, left Philadelphia for their western journey, they
forded the Schuylkill at High Street, perhaps to save the
ferry fee.

The day of the Schuylkill fords is past. We can visualize them in their early beauty: the rushing stream,
the cattle up to their bellies under the shade of the water-

elms, the lumbering Conestoga wagons surging through the river bed as their drivers urged the horses on in Dutch vernacular. They played their part in colonial traffic, these early crossings, but their importance and even their exact locations are long forgotten.

CHAPTER 25

Bridges

THE engineer Trautwine, whose field book has sometimes been called the Surveyor's Bible, once said that the Schuylkill River had inaugurated three important experiments in the pontine craft in America: the permanent bridge at High Street, White and Hazzard's wire-rope footbridge at Falls of Schuylkill, and Ellet's suspension bridge at Fairmount Dam. To this list of claims of distinction might be added that the Girard Avenue bridge for many years was the widest span in the world. Also, Stoudt's Ferry bridge, above Reading, in its time was regarded as the most perfect remaining example of the American wooden bridge and as the longest span, two hundred and sixty-four feet, of any wooden bridge in the world. Nor can any account of the Schuylkill bridges be adequate without reference to the wonderful stone bridges of the Reading Railroad in the upper valley.

Whether many impromptu pioneer bridges were thrown across the Schuylkill in the days of the early settlement, we will probably never know; certainly they could have been neither durable nor elaborate. The first authenticated bridge to span the river was the crude structure, resting upon rafts, which Washington ordered constructed at the High Street Ferry in the critical days of December 1776, when the victorious British had over-run New Jersey and threatened Philadelphia. Washington, foreseeing the possible evacuation of the city and a hasty retreat westward over the Schuylkill, wished to make sure of an avenue of escape.

General Israel Putnam supervised the construction of this floating bridge; and the site seems to have been well chosen, for as early as 1751, when the Pennsylvania Assembly appointed a committee "to sound depths and try bottoms from Peter's Island to Bartram's Gardens," the Middle Ferry was indicated as the most suitable place for a bridge. It was on Putnam's bridge, resting partly on logs and partly on floating scows, that the patriot army marched out for the ill-omened campaign of the Brandywine.

After they had recrossed it, defeated and dispirited, the bridge was broken up and the scows hidden in the reedy marshes of the Schuylkill. With the occupation of Philadelphia by the British, Lord Howe realized the importance of a connection over the Schuylkill and deputed his engineer officer, Captain John Montresor, to construct a pontoon bridge at the same location. Montresor found some of the hidden scows, built others, and made a new bridge. Perhaps it was too hastily put together, for on the night of October 28, 1777, it broke under the impetus of a high tide and was carried downstream. The indefatigable Montresor gathered up the debris and built a second floating bridge, which the Americans inherited and used after the British had evacuated Philadelphia.

Montresor threw another span across the river at
Gray's Ferry, an improvement over the earlier bridge
through the use of logs and chains; but the crossing of
this three-hundred-foot long structure seems to have been
something of an adventure. The English traveler Henry
Wansey left a description of the bridge with its two iron
chains "strained across the river parallel to each other,
about six feet distance; on it are placed flat planks,
fastened to each chain; and on this the horses and carriage pass over. As the horses stepped on the boards they
sank under the pressure and the water rose between
them; no railing on either side, and it really looked very
freightful and dangerous."

The Montreser bridges and their successors, all pontoon structures and all unsatisfactory, spanned the Schuylkill until the erection of the so-called Permanent Bridge
at Market Street in 1800. As early as 1786 Thomas Paine
came forward with a plan for an iron bridge—the first
ever proposed for America. Paine stated that his design
had been suggested by a spider web and made a diminu-
tive model at his home in Bordentown. Dr. Franklin,
just back from France, asked to see the model. It was
accordingly set up in his house off High Street. Nothing
came of the project until 1798, when the legislature incorporated a company for the erection of a permanent
bridge over the Schuylkill at High Street. The design
chosen was not Tom Paine's but that of Timothy Palmer,
self-taught architect from Newburyport.

The crowning day in the story of the Schuylkill bridges
was the radiant autumn afternoon in 1800 when the
Permanent Bridge was dedicated. Governor McKean

made some remarks, and the cornerstone was laid. The curious bystanders noted that this stone was inscribed with a line of cryptic letters:

T F C S O T S P B W L October xviii MDCCC

As time ran on the purport of this cabalistic inscription became lost until finally, during Lafayette's visit in 1824, an old man was found who furnished the key:

The First Corner Stone Of The Schuylkill
Permanent Bridge Was Laid October 18, 1800.

The authorities of the Pennsylvania Railroad, who succeeded the state in the administration of the road, finally woke up to the fact that their line to the west might just as well take a directly westward course instead of disgressing three miles northward to the Belmont plane. The author of *Philadelphia As It Is,* published in 1852, related that "the Market Street Bridge, formerly the Permanent Bridge was made free of toll in 1840. In 1850, it was altered to form a connection for the Pennsylvania Railroad occupying the north side of the bridge while the south side was reserved for carriages."

The story of the High Street bridge runs contemporaneously with that of Lewis Wernwag's celebrated bridge, Colossus of Fairmount, whose graceful curve silhouetted against the waters of the Upper Ferry, three hundred paces to the north. The pride of Philadelphia, this was a Mecca for European visitors. The Englishman Sutcliffe, who trudged out through the snow to visit the bridge on a winter day in 1796, was interested to see crowds of citizens "who were breaking up and taking away large quantities of ice for summer use." This was the origin of the important Schuylkill ice industry which later lined the upper bank with rows of ice houses. Sutcliffe divided his attention between the busy scene below and a chat with an indentured servant whom he described:

> By me on the parapet of the bridge was a black boy in linsey woolsey shirt who had an iron collar chained about his neck. He lived hard by on the banks of Schuylkill and had run away so often that his master took this method of securing him.

Above both portals of the Wernwag bridge were the allegorical wood figures so much admired in their day, the work of the deft carver William Rush. Much dubious poetry, dedicated to this marvel of Fairmount, appeared in the columns of the local press and one enthusiastic peroration claimed that "it was reserved for the genius of America to throw a bridge over a river 340 feet wide without any support other than its abutments. The span is 96 feet longer than any other existing bridge."

This quaint structure, so often illustrated, was burned down in 1838. The bridge tolls, it appears, had not been too lucrative and the City Council, in one of its parsimonious moods, refused to rebuild. Then appeared Charlie Ellett, Jr., who agreed to build a wire bridge in a period of six months if private capital would back him. Ellett's bridge, as notable for the epoch as Wernwag's had been, was finished in the stipulated time, by January of 1842. The artist Birch, for whom all the Schuylkill bridges seem to have had an attraction, sketched it but it has long disappeared in the exigencies of modern traffic.

The townspeople watched the construction of the Philadelphia bridges with interest and walked out on a Sunday afternoon to view them from the verandas of the inns constructed at their abutments. The early artists were quick to adopt them as subjects for their brushes. In Lehman's fine lithograph, now at the Historical Society of Pennsylvania, we may sit on the broad porch at the western end of Ellett's Bridge, sip our julep with the beaux and belles seated about us, and admire the inspiring arch of the bridge, the packet boats (apparently drawn by one tired horse), and the creek flowing in from the east. Bowen's colorful lithographs of 1838 depict both the Upper and the Market Street Bridge. Kennedy, whose aquarelles do so much to restore the old Philadelphia scene, drew the Chestnut Street bridge while the middle span was still incomplete. This was in 1864 during the Civil War. Presumably most of the Philadelphia artisans were at the front and had other occupations than the completion of a Schuylkill bridge.

This same Kennedy did not hesitate to take liberties with his subject in the interest of what he conceived to be the aesthetic result. Seated one blustery March day in 1885 on the east bank of the Schuylkill, with the intention of painting the almshouse then standing along Thirty-Fourth Street on the opposite bank, he perceived that the long wall obstructed the effect of the lawn sloping up from the river to the main structure. Accordingly, he calmly omitted the wall. Birch, in a similar vein, drew the beautiful arch of the High Street bridge while only the framework of the superstructure was to be seen, but carefully sketched in the plan of the completed bridge below his main picture.

An important early Schuylkill bridge was the covered wooden structure at Flat Rock, first projected in 1815. The planners originally were contemplating a bridge in the guise of a dam. Headed by chairman Cadwalader Evans, they journeyed up to Springfield to interview the engineer Ariel Cooley. Cooley, seated on his porch, received the delegation and looked over the specifications somewhat doubtfully.

"Gentlemen," he said, "no engineer can comply with this. 'The proposed dam at Flat Rock shall have a breast at least fifteen feet wide and shall be so constructed as to admit a safe passage for wagons and horsemen over the same.' This would be a bridge not a dam."

The embarrassed committee had to admit that Cooley was right and promised to soften the requirements. So Cooley came to Philadelphia in March of 1816 and went up as far as Reading for a preliminary survey. Flat Rock Dam was finished in 1819 but had no provision for the passage of wagons.

The flimsy wooden bridge first erected at Flat Rock did not last long. In 1818 proposals for a new bridge were circulated, with the proviso that it should be finished in three years. This stipulation frightened off some of the bidders but Captain John Turner, a Manayunk pioneer who was the first lessee of the water power at the dam, agreed to build a bridge. Charlie Hagner, the historian of early Manayunk, tells why Turner never finished it:

> If he'd lived he'd have finished the bridge but he was always an obstinate cuss. We were driving down Barren Hill, very steep in those days. I said "Captain that rear breeching is loose." "I guess it'll reach" said he. Half way down the hill the horse's rear was backing into our dash board and he ran away. I jumped and called to the captain to jump but he stayed in, was thrown against a tree and afterwards died.

The projected bridge was finally built and lasted until the memorable flood of September 1850.

Probably the earliest upstream bridge to be planned was at Reading. A lottery, an approved method for raising funds for public improvements and even for churches, had been projected for a bridge as early as 1790. However, few purchasers appeared to buy the lottery tickets. The bridge promoters, chafing at the delay and with a curious anticipation of modern advertising methods, made a woodcut of the village with a beautiful nonexistent stone bridge in the foreground. There was only one newspaper in Reading at that time, a German weekly, whose stock illustrations portrayed stallions at stud and runaway slaves. As the editor showed no interest in the proposed bridge, the promoters turned to the local almanac for publicity. The title page of this almanac for the years 1798 and 1799 used a cut of the village including the imaginary bridge. By 1800 it would seem that the advocates of the bridge had lost heart, for the almanac shows the village with the Schuylkill as it actually was, unencumbered by any span.

A bridge was finally built in 1818, the wooden structure over which President Van Buren rode in state. This structure was designed by the German engineer Lewis Wernwag. Wernwag, who had come from Reutlingen in Wurtemburg to escape being drafted for the Napoleonic wars, was hailed by the Berks and Schuylkill *Journal* in an enthusiastic peroration as "the Pontifex Maximus of these United States." The bridge was embellished with wood carvings by William Rush of Philadelphia, the same carving which evoked the admiration of the ec-

centric Anne Royal in 1828, when she walked down
Penn Street to inspect the bridge.

The projectors of Reading bridge had temporized so
long that they lost the distinction of constructing the
first bridge in the Reading area. Ulrich Kissinger acted
while his neighbors talked. He was conducting a ferry
two miles above Reading, the same ferry which during
the French Wars had conveyed the ragged militia who
marched up to garrison the Blue Mountain forts. On
the site of the ferry he built a toll bridge, completed in
1810, while the Reading folk were still wading the river.

Shortly after the completion of Kissinger's bridge, the
miller Sam Bell, an associate or lay judge for Berks
County, threw a bridge of sorts across the Schuylkill near
the junction of the Tulpehocken, at the foot of Lynford
Lardner's lane. The lane is forgotten now, along with
the courtly Lardner, one of the founders of the Philadelphia Dancing Assembly. Bell's bridge appears to have
partly floated upon the water and to have been constructed of movable planks chained to crosspieces. It
lasted until the freshet of 1850. Bell's dam is breached
now and the turbulent swarthy foam sweeps through the
gap. However, a hundred yards away on the Tulpehocken
the old mill dam is still intact and the shadow of the
sycamores reflects in the stream just as it did in the
Schuylkill one hundred years ago.

Sammy Bell is a colorful figure as he looks down at us
from the portrait in which Sully depicted him in yellow
waistcoat, fringed with Mechlin lace. He played host to
President Van Buren at Reading in 1839 and on that
occasion is said to have voiced two wishes: first, that

the distinguished visitor, then a widower, would marry
one of the Reading maidens who attended the Presidential Ball given at the Bell mansion; and second that
Mr. Van Buren would come out to see his mill and
bridge.

At the ball that autumn evening in 1839 were two
youths, the sons respectively of the host and of the guest
of honor. Ogling the girls sat the President's son, "Prince
John," whose career had not been too creditable. He had
been plucked at Yale for gambling and had given his
father plenty of trouble. However, in the preceding year
he had made the grand tour in Europe and better things
were expected of him. With Prince John sat a lad in
velveteens, J. Bowman Bell, who was to become a Captain
in the Civil War and die gallantly in the dark days of
1862, leading his company against Beauregard's earthworks at Murfreesboro.

Five miles upstream from Ulrich Kissinger's bridge
Stoudt's Ferry bridge, the graceful span long hailed
as the best example of the wooden bridge in America,
stood until recently.

About the time that American troops were making
their triumphal entry into the city of Mexico, Jacob
Stoudt and his son John operated a ferry over the Schuylkill. Theirs was a sizable ferryboat capable of carrying
an ox team; and the model of it, still preserved in the
museum of the Historical Society of Berks County, gives
us our best idea of the Schuylkill ferryboat of the period.
Business was so good that Jacob conceived the idea of
erecting a toll bridge. It so happened that at the location
of the Stoudt ferryhouse the tow path ended on the east
side of the stream and resumed on the west bank. There-

fore the bridge had to be built with the unique feature of
two side passages, to be used alike by mules and pedestrians. It was built upon the design of Theodore Burr,
who patented the truss and arch bridge in 1817. Stoudt
was a good carpenter himself and meticulous about the
quality of the workmanship which entered into his bridge.
It is true he paid his artisans only sixty-five cents a day,
but living was cheap and everybody had plenty of time
to do thorough work. The completed span was long
hailed as a monument to the efficiency of our forefathers,
and a bill was presented to the Pennsylvania Legislature
to preserve it as a historical monument. Then suddenly,
one autumn afternoon in 1948, the entire structure fell
into the river.

If, just before the middle of the last century, it had
been possible to get a birds-eye view of the winding
Schuylkill from the Delaware to the Tamaqua Hills,
the scene would have disclosed numerous wooden bridges.
Up above the junction of the branches the Pottsville
stage highway crossed the east branch by seven bridges in
a course of three miles. Below these were the spans at
Schuylkill Haven, at Auburn, and at Port Clinton. In
Berks County there had been, in the decades preceding
the Mexican War, a rage for building toll bridges,
usually named for the families which conducted them, so
that north of Reading there came in succession, Bell's,
Kissinger's, Leiss', Stoudt's Ferry, Althouse's, Mohr's,
Windsor Haven—all commercial ventures depending
upon the tolls.

Below Reading there were Birdsboro, Monocacy,
Douglassville (the only wooden bridge still spanning the
Schuylkill), the bridge at Potts Grove, the much admired

covered bridge at Parkerford, and then the bridges of the
middle river, Royer's and Gordon's, Paulings and
Swede's Ford, down to the bridge at Conshohocken which
Peter Wager (sometime cornet of the Philadelphia City
Troop) threw across the stream in 1838.

These bridges, so often painted and sketched, formed
a picturesque feature of the early landscape, but their
doom was at hand. The Schuylkill had always been
subject to impetuous floods. There had been the early
freshet of 1757, the "Pumpkin Freshet" of 1786, so
called because of the great number of pumpkins swept
down from the farms adjoining the river, and the disastrous freshets of 1822 and 1839, in the last of which the
Schuylkill rose twenty-seven feet from its low water
mark in the space of a few hours.

These overflows, however, were trifling compared with
the cataclysm of September 2, 1850, which almost sealed
the doom of the Schuylkill Navigation Company. It
swept away bridges, dams, mills, and workshops. The
anxious watchers at Port Clinton had run a train loaded
with coal out upon their bridge in an effort to give it
solidity. Down the swirling stream came a coal barge
with the ill-omened name of "Here I come." It carried
away not only the Port Clinton bridge but Kern's bridge
farther downstream. This was only the beginning of the
devastation. By nightfall every one of the many graceful
structures which had spanned the stream between Pottsville and Royersford was born away by the raging water.
In the lower river there was equal havoc. Conshohocken
bridge was taken off its piers and swept downstream, a
gigantic battering ram, to demolish Flat Rock bridge.

In the general catastrophe only one upper river bridge

survived, the magnificent stone arch by which the Reading Railway tracks were carried over the Schuylkill above
Tuckerton. The Schuylkill had almost returned to the
bridgeless condition of the days when Lenape squaws
forded out into the river to dry their fish on the rocks.

CHAPTER 26

Pioneer Voyagers

THE earliest craft to ply upon the bosom of the Schuylkill were the canoes which the Lenapes used in the chase and in the wanderings incident to their nomadic life. It may be that war canoes carried painted warriors up the stream for predatory incursions, but there is no certain proof of any such raids. As far as we know, the primitive Schuylkill shallops were used almost entirely for fishing, since the stream was noted for the excellence and abundance of its fish. Governor Samuel W. Pennypacker, who loved the river and composed some of his historical essays while floating down the tranquil course above present Pawlings Bridge, had a collection of spearheads and darts, some of them six inches long, which he had found in the shallow pools near Phoenixville.

These artifacts had been used by the Indians in the spearing of sturgeons; but other fish, notably shad and rock-fish, teemed in those early waters. Great shoals of shad and sturgeon would ascend the stream every spring from the Delaware Bay, a circumstance which inspired the Quaker bard, Thomas Makin:

Large sturgeons numerous crowd the Delaware
Which in warm weather leap into the air

So high that (strange to tell) they often fly
Into the Boats which on the river ply.

Schuylkill shad was highly esteemed for its flavor, and each spring the gourmets of the Quaker City listened eagerly for the cry of the street vendor announcing that this fish was again in the market. Such was the swarm in the upper river that we have a record of nearly four thousand shad being caught in a net near Pottstown in 1784. So abundant was this delicacy, as we now consider it, that when in the spring of 1811 five barrels of shad were salted down for use at the Montgomery County Poorhouse, the inmates protested over the monotony of their diet. Migrating with the shad came shoals of lamprey eels, which were caught in surprisingly large hauls even above the Appalachian Ridge.

In one eighteenth-century engraving of the Schuylkill, a ring of fishermen are shown standing waist deep in the stream, supporting a huge net apparently fifty feet in diameter, which strains under its load of leaping fish. Another method for catching shad was the spearing by horsemen, who seem to have become very dexterous in the practice, for they evoked the admiration of the naturalist William Bartram while on one of his voyages up the river. During Washington's encampment at Valley Forge, his cavalrymen beguiled the time and relieved the monotony of camp diet by forming in line across the shallow stream and driving the fish into a net which seems to have been spread about where the modern highway bridge crosses the Schuylkill at Phoenixville.

Another commodity carried in these primitive Schuylkill canoes, both by the aborigines and by the white settlers who succeeded them, was fur pelts, particularly beaver skins. The importance of this traffic is attested to by the fact that when Anries Hudde, commissary of Fort Nassau by authority of Governor Van Twiller, established a trading post and fort near the end of the present Gray's Ferry Road in Philadelphia, he named it *Beversrede*—the Beaver's Fort. Indeed, the Indian name for the Little Schuylkill was *Tamaquan,* or the Beaver Stream. By the year 1643 over two thousand packages of beaver skins were sent in one shipment to Rotterdam. Naturally, this persistent trapping soon led to the virtual extinction of the beaver, and the navigators on the Schuylkill turned to other ladings, wheat and flour, whiskey, powdered lime, and beeswax.

This canoe navigation greatly facilitated the settlement of the valley. The Dutch and Swedes, both nautical races, were quick to see the advantage of the light draught canoe and quick to put it to practical use. Governor Thomas Pownall, one of the earliest European observers notes that "The Schuylkill is a Fine Branch up which the tide runs five miles above Philadelphia where there is an impassable Falls and three miles further up another not much better. Thence to Reading in a fine gliding current easily set against by canoes." And again, "Tulpehocken, settled by the High Dutchers raises fine wheat which the peasants bring down Schuylkill each Spring and Fall in the high water to Philadelphia."

The Founder himself is supposed, upon the somewhat doubtful authority of "A letter found in the archives of a gentleman in Ireland," to have taken a canoe journey up the Schuylkill as far as Monocacy Hill in Berks County, where a pretentious monument records this semi-apochryphal journey. But whether or not Penn really came far up the river, there can be no doubt that he studied and was impressed with the possibilities of traffic upon its surface. In a letter written in 1683 to his friend Henry Savell at Stoke Pogis, he relates having seen in the Schuylkill Valley a canoe hewed from the trunk of a poplar tree and so large that it carried four tons of bricks. We read, too, of Isaac Smally's canoe which must have been still larger, as it bore forty tons of wheat. This "canoe" must have been a dugout and a sizable one at that.

Among the romantic legends which cluster about the settlement of the village of Douglassville on the upper Schuylkill, the former Swedish village of Morlatton, is one of an early bridal flotilla. The bride and groom, attendant witnesses and guests, their craft festooned with bunting, floated down the river to the strains of minstrelsy.

So important was this means of transportation that Thomas Lewis in 1752, in advertising the sale of his mill property at the mouth of Mingo Creek, stated that "Loaded canoes can come to the mill door." With the development of river traffic, the news soon spread overseas. So illustrious a commentator as Edmund Burke in his "Essay Upon European Settlement," written in 1757, called attention to "the quantities of produce brought down the river Schuylkill in the Province of Pennsylvania."

Incident to the increase in Schuylkill navigation was the inevitable conflict between the fishermen and the boatmen. This was to be expected, since the fishermen had erected dams and racks which extended far out into the stream, forming obstructions which aroused the ire of the boatmen. The latter presented their plant before Squire Boone of Berks County, father of the great frontiersman. The squire listened to their story and issued a warrant. Accordingly, one summer day in 1738, three canoes filled with truculent boatmen and supported by the constables of Amity Township and Oley Township in Berks County came down the stream bent upon the destruction of the weirs. The fishermen, no less determined, assembled in force at the mouth of Pickering Creek below Phoenixville. Then ensued the only naval battle which history records as having been fought on the Schuylkill.

The yellowed affidavits are still to be read wherein it is set out that the leaders of the fishermen army "cursed the Constable of Oley in a gross manner." Whereat the Constable "called from the boat in a loud voice offering five pounds for the offender's head." Several waded into the river, upset the canoes, and struck the boatmen with large clubs. "One John Wainwright was struck with a staff and lay as dead with his body on shore and his feet in the river." Just which faction was acclaimed the winner in this gory skirmish is not clear, but as we read that "the canoes were split to pieces and turned adrift in said river," it is probable that victory perched on the banners of the fishermen.

Following the primeval era of canoe traffic came the advent of the great Schuylkill rafts, the first mention of which is in the period just preceding the Revolution. The sawmills which later studded the banks in the upper valley had not yet appeared; boards and shingles, made from upstream lumber, were manufactured only in the lower valley and were hard to get. The rafts were mostly assembled north of the Appalachian Ridge, some at Finchers Ford and some at Port Clinton, and were usually ten feet in width by twenty in length, that being the size which experience proved was best calculated to negotiate the shoals and rapids. A practical device was the joining of two or even three rafts, forming an imposing spectacle as they drifted down the stream.

Usually three men would be attached to one raft. A crude wigwam was constructed, which sheltered the provisions for the voyage and was used by the men in unfavorable weather. As the draught of these rafts was rarely more than fifteen inches, they were able to dart down the channel and could sometimes make the distance from Pottsville to Reading in seven hours.

The true Odyssey of the rafting days on the Schuylkill is to be found in the recollections of the blacksmith Morgan Thomas, who put his cattle and household goods on a raft at Port Clinton and floated them down to Reading in the year 1806:

> I recollect that I enjoyed the trip greatly. It was in the Spring, late enough for the days to be mild and genial, and we floated along sometimes slowly, when the current was sluggish, at other times rapidly, where there was a greater descent in the stream. The cow was old and gentle and stood up to a post on the raft, apparently enjoying the transport as much as my sister and myself. In the afternoon, we arrived at a long reach of gentle current, and my mother spread the table and arranged dinner for ourselves and the raftsmen, who were old neighbors from the Sharp Mountain district, and the raft was left to its own guidance, while all participated of the fare provided. Whilst thus engaged, there was a sudden

alarm, in consequence of the fore part of the raft striking upon some object. The raftsmen rushed to their oars and succeeded in getting the raft off a stump which had sunk and become embedded in the river, and no damage was done beyond a little fright and a short detention. The twenty miles of river navigation was accomplished before sunset, and we were landed in our new home in Reading.

The imagination of these pioneer Schuylkill navigators never soared high; they evidently thought that the stream would be used for rafting for many decades. One of the first Acts of the Pennsylvania Assembly pertaining to the Schuylkill, that of March 14, 1761, describes the river as "navigable for rafts." And even Benjamin Rittenhouse, who was a man of some vision, reports in his first examination of the Schuylkill, made in 1791 for the Pennsylvania Executive Council, "It appears probable that the principal advantages that can accrue from that part of the River at least for some time, will be in rafting of lumber down to Philadelphia."

Rafting on the Schuylkill was a pleasant enough occupation in the placid reaches of the upper river, but it had its tribulations, even perils, when the swift current swirled amid the reefs of the lower river. A hint of these dangers can be gleaned from an advertisement in the *Gazette* of May, 1768, which told of finding "on the reef in Schuylkill below Mt. Araratt, a large pine raft from which cargo has been washed. This raft may be reclaimed by its proper owner upon payment of charges to George Levering."

However, important as was the part which the Schuylkill rafts played in bringing the wealth of magnificent chestnut, oak, and hemlock to the Philadelphia market—

many houses are still standing which were erected with the timber which they brought down—the ultimate development of the valley demanded a surer form of transportation than the rafts could provide. There ensued accordingly the era of the "Reading Boats," almost as famous as a means of early conveyance as was the Conestoga wagon.

The Reading Boats were long and narrow with shallow draught, suitable for the rock-strewn stream which they descended. The size of the largest of these Schuylkill craft may be judged by the description of the Dutch traveler Theophile Casenove, who came through the central square of Reading in 1794 and described a boat sixty feet long under construction there. The square was half a mile from the river. In the advertisement of the sale of the William Bird mansion on the site of Birdsboro, the *Pennsylvania Packet* of March 6, 1784, states that the Schuylkill, directly before the Bird residence, "is available for navigation for Reading Boats of ten to twelve tons burthen." Considering that no dredging of any importance had been attempted in the Schuylkill at that period, one wonders how boats so heavily laden, as they usually were, could have avoided the many reefs, and also how boatmen were found to undertake the incredibly tedious labor of poling them back upstream at a time when there was no towpath.

The appearance of the Reading Boats is familiar to us, since they were so often depicted in contemporary sketches and were worked into the porcelain platters and plates so popular at the period. Of the countless illustrations perhaps the best is contained in the fine engraving in the *Casket Magazine*, which shows a boat being rowed under old Reading Bridge by a crew of four men, the cargo of barrels neatly arranged in the waist and bow, the stern protected by a canvas awning. The artist Childs, who drew Fairmount Dam in 1810, portrays the Reading boatmen in high hats, knee breeches, and buckled shoes, rather a fanciful costume for the grim work entailed in poling the heavy craft up and sometimes downstream.

In reality these early Schuylkill navigators seem to have been a rough untutored breed, ready for a fight or a quarrel. We have a hint of their real appearance in an early skating lithograph of Fairmount Dam, wherein the uncouth Reading boatmen are shown lounging upon the prow of their ice-nipped craft, leering their rabelasian comments at the abbreviated skirts of the fair Philadelphia skaters. Schuylkill was a hard school, but it produced men of action. Her river-men were among the mariners who propelled the galleys which attacked the British men-of-war in the lower Delaware; they helped to man the scows which took Washington over the icy waters of the Delaware for the midnight attack at Trenton.

It was well that the boatmen were fit and alert, for the descent of the Schuylkill was not without its perils. In the first place, the boats were loaded to the gunwales. At the departure from Reading of one particularly large flotilla, the German newspaper *Readinger Adler* estimated the combined cargoes at twelve hundred barrels of flour, fourteen hundred bushels of wheat, fifteen hundred gallons of whiskey, and five hundred pounds of snuff, the whole amounting to one hundred and sixty tons. When it is recalled that below Spring Mill the Schuylkill descended twenty-four feet in about six miles and that at Flat Rock it was strewn with dangerous reefs, the perils of the voyage in craft so heavily laden can be imagined.

After a spring rain, when the river was in flood, there was usually an expectant throng gathered on the cliff at Manayunk—the Reading Boats were due. Below them the watchers could see the river foaming and swirling between the jagged reefs of Pencoyd. A shout goes up as the first boat rounds the curve. Four rowers are at the bow, with the poleman standing before them. In the waist are rows of barrels, the precious cargo of Berks County flour. The helmsman stands in the stern, surveying the vortex before him; if he falters, all will be lost. He is an excellent athlete, this steersman, Balzer Lesher from Oley, champion wrestler of the upper Schuylkill, the man who defeated the Lancaster champion "Killer" Spangler in three falls at the Reading Fair of 1769. Now the long boat is in the rapids; Balzer Lesher strains at the rudder, shouting directions to the poleman. Over and about the black rocks runs the careening craft. Exultant applause rolls down from the heights; the Reading Boat is through.

The spectacle had the elements of a sacrifice in the Roman Colliseum; each year one or more boats were lost and some of the crews drowned.

During those early years a number of inns—riverside hostelries—punctuated the stretch of stream between Port Clinton Gap and Philadelphia. The last of these crude but not uncomfortable taverns has long since disappeared, but a hint of their conditions comes down to us in the autobiography of the colonial mariner and privateersman, Charles Biddle, who during the Revolution traveled up the Schuylkill to visit his mother, then resident at Reading. He describes how his imperious and distinguished brother Edward Biddle, Speaker of the first Provincial Congress, while descending the river by canoe from Reading disembarked at one of these inns, how he fared and how, when inflamed with rum posset, he quarreled with the Tory landlord.

Schuylkill ferries flourished in those days. As most of the settlers had come from the valleys of the Lahn, Rhone, and Moselle in Germany, they were familiar with the device of propelling the ferry boats by the force of the current. A rope would be stretched across the stream, well secured at either end by two stout trees. Then the ferryboat made its way across by a rope and ring attached to the cross cable. Evilly disposed persons would sometimes cut or steal the rope, an outrage which became so prevalent in the Schuylkill Valley that the Assembly, by act of February 8, 1766, imposed a fine of ten pounds to be paid upon conviction.

These early ferries were not very roomy, a circumstance which induced the dangerous practice whereby travelers remained in the saddle during the crossing. The most notable victim of this risky habit was the Chevalier de Coudray, one of the gallant French volunteer officers who served under Washington. He was drowned at Gray's Ferry.

At a later period larger ferry boats were constructed, some sturdy enough to carry an ox team across the river, as evidenced by the advertisement of Paul Livezey of Whitemarsh in 1796, who offers for sale "A large FERRY BOAT, forty-three feet long, eight and half feet wide, with large iron hinges, and fall at each end, built of white oak, double bottom, each side is of one solid plank, but two years old, and little worse of wear, will carry four horses, wagon and cord of wood across the river Schuylkill."

Under the regime of the Penns, the matter of compensation for the Schuylkill ferrymen was much debated. In particular the greatly used crossing at High Street in Philadelphia, conducted as early as 1722 by Aquilla Rose and later by James Humphreys and then by Sheriff Coultas, was a center of contention. At one period the aggrieved ferrymen, who professed to be much underpaid, refused to operate at all and travelers pulled themselves across the stream as best they might. At length the Provincial Assembly intervened and decreed the legal rates for passage.

Mendenhall's Ferry at Laurel Hill, immortalized in the many lithographs made from Birch's beautiful painting, was another source of litigation; and no less a person than Provost William Smith appeared in court in January, 1758, brandishing a patent from the Penns vesting in him certain rights of ferriage at Falls of Schuylkill.

A problem entailed by the ferries and one which engendered heated arguments, sometimes blows, was the fact that boats being laboriously propelled upstream towards Reading would take advantage of a favoring wind and hoist a mast and sail. As this mast invariably fouled the ferry rope, there was much profane argument as to the respective rights of the master of the flatboat and the ferryman.

How important a part sailboats played in Schuylkill navigation is not certain. Sails as a method of propulsion were hardly practical in the winding gorges of the upper river, but they were certainly used on the lower river and above dams. The German artist Holtzwart sketched Reading Dam in 1835, showing sail boats, and in Strickland's fine drawing of the Wernwag Bridge at Fairmount, sailing boats are shown above Fairmount Dam. Farrand's well-known depiction of the Market Street bridge shows

sizable schooners and brigs, commercial vessels which have come up from the Delaware.

There must have been a period of recession in the lower river about the beginning of the nineteenth century, for an observer writing in 1835 stated that "In the last few years few vessels entered Schuylkill and those few brought pine wood to supply the brickilns on the bank; they were of about one hundred tons burthen now (1835) vessels of 200 to 400 tons come, sometimes two hundred passing up in one day."

This same observer, evidently referring to the floating bridge at Gray's Ferry, noted how much easier it was to pass under sail through the gap in the floating bridge than to pass under a permanent bridge, where "one must cast anchor, furl the sails and adjust the yards."

CHAPTER 27

The Canal

THE Reading Boats were a great improvement over the raft; but as commerce in the valley ramified, their deficiencies (after all, they were useful only in high water) became more apparent and attracted the attention of provincial legislators. The Pennsylvania Assembly on March 14, 1761, appointed commissioners to look into the matter of clearing and improving the all-important Schuylkill channel and into the practicability of a canal. There were doubting Thomases even in that early epoch who opposed the building of a canal. In the columns of the Philadelphia newspapers we find articles by agitated readers, signing themselves "Candidus Justus" and "Schuylkillus Ironicus," protesting against the waste of public funds on a doubtful improvement. And when a meeting of citizens interested in petitioning on behalf of the canal was held at Reifsnyder's Tavern in Orwigsburg, it broke up in a riot.

Far overseas by his comfortable fireside in Craven Street sat the sagacious envoy, Benjamin Franklin. Leafing over his American mail, he read with interest the news of the proposed Schuylkill canal and at once grasped the value of the improvement. In 1771 he had visited Ireland and had been taken to view the construction of the new Leinster and Munster Canal. Now on August 22, 1772, he sat down to write to his good friend, Mayor Rhoades of Philadelphia:

> The Irish have learned at a dear rate in the first attempt of the great Canal. With regard to your question whether it is best to make the Schuylkill a part of the navigation to the back country, or whether the Difficulty of that River, subject to all the Inconveniences of Floods, Ice, &c. I can only say that here they look on the constant Practicability of a canal Navigation, to be a point of the greatest Importance.

Stirred by this suggestion, the Assembly sent a young surveyor up the river to take some soundings. This engineer was Anthony Wayne of Chester County, who was later to write his name in Revolutionary annals in letters of fire as "Mad Anthony Wayne." Following Wayne and also acting under the orders of the Assembly came the scientist David Rittenhouse, accompanied by Provost William Smith of the College of Philadelphia, an odd assignment, surely, for a sedentary pedagogue. These two went up the valley and "leveled the waters of the Schuylkill," as Smith expressed it. Rittenhouse fell sick at a camp somewhere near the present town of Leesport but recovered sufficiently to make an elaborate and favorable report. However, with the Revolution impending and the political horizon perilously over-charged, the Pennsylvania Legislature had other matters to consider.

Although the project of Schuylkill navigation was temporarily shelved when the war began, nevertheless, the military advantage which would accrue from an improved river channel did not escape the alert eyes of the engineers of the patriot army. During the weary weeks that Washington was sojourning at Valley Forge, a quartermaster officer, Charles Pettit, made soundings in the stream and wrote from the camp to Thomas Wharton, Jr., President of the Supreme Executive Council of Pennsylvania: "We have got a number of boats now in use on the Schuylkill which answer the purpose very well when the river is full. Major Eyre has surveyed the river from Reading hither and informs me that the stream may without difficulty be rendered navigable through the summer season."

The hopeful Major Eyre proposed that the patriotic farmers of the neighborhood assemble at the shallow points and do volunteer work in dredging, but there is no evidence of any practical response to his appeal. The sad fact is that too many Schuylkill Valley farmers were more interested in smuggling their produce into the British lines, where they were paid in good gold guineas, than in providing for our own army which paid in doubtful script.

As the Revolution was drawing to its close and after the discomfited Cornwallis had marched out at Yorktown to the strains of "The World Turned Upside-Down," the Pennsylvania Legislature sent another Rittenhouse, Benjamin this time, to further explore the upper Schuylkill and report upon its possibilities for inland navigation. Rittenhouse and his companion John Adlum journeyed up to Hamburg, and then floated down the river making estimates as they went. They calculated the cost of making the stream navigable for boats of ten-ton burthen at the modest sum of £1519, the greater part of this amount to be needed for dredging the dangerous

stretch from Spring Mill to Falls of Schuylkill. Rittenhouse criticised the fishing dams which he observed everywhere in his passage when he noted that "Unless this
mischievous practice, a nuisance of the worst kind, can be
obviated, every attempt to render Schuylkill navigation
efficient will be abortive."

Commissioners had been appointed who were directed,
rather vaguely, to "clear the river and make it passable
for rafts, boats, and other small crafts." That was all.
The commissioners seemed never to have had the courage
to plan a real canal but contented themselves with the
project of blowing up and removing trees, rocks, and
fishing dams which obstructed the stream, and with the
erection of crude dams for raising the river in shallow
places. Even when the canal was finally considered, there
was apologetic reference, and many concessions, to the
rafting and boating industry as it then existed. The dams,
as planned, were to serve as bridges, and it was stipulated
that they must be at least fifteen feet wide and able to
afford safe passage for wagons and carts. Also, the dams
were to be so built as not to obstruct the passage of a raft
floating down the stream, a difficult assignment.

Decades of dormancy ensued until on January 31,
1791, a body of Philadelphia citizens assembled at Independence Hall, with Robert Morris in the chair, and
organized the "Society for the Improvement of Roads
and Inland Navigation." From this meeting in 1791
and subsequent meetings in 1792 came what are claimed
to be the first canal projects in America, under the names
of Schuylkill and Susquehanna Navigation (the ante-
cedent of the Union canal), and Delaware and Schuylkill Canal Navigation (the forerunner of the Schuylkill

canal). Both companies entered into active excavation. By the end of 1794 the first named company had done some excavation on the Loy farm near present Myerstown, the high point between the Schuylkill and the Susquehanna, and could boast of a visit from President Washington to the scene of its operation. The second had built some miles of ditch along the bank of the Schuylkill running south from Norristown.

The uneasy stockholders, disappointed in the slowness of the work, called in the English engineer William Weston. Weston joined himself with Doctor William Smith, who represented the American Philosophical Society, which had sponsored the canal, and who was always ready for a trip up the Schuylkill Valley. The two inspectors reported that two hundred men were working near Norristown and about the same number at the Loy place. They also made the ominous observation that four times the amount of John Adlum's original estimate had been spent and that funds were running low. A lottery, the inevitable resort for the building of all public works, was employed but the project languished and work finally stopped.

After this initial failure the Reading boats came temporarily back to their own and began to operate with renewed vigor. For, whatever their limitations, they could bring produce down the river at about one quarter of the cost of road travel. Meanwhile the disappointed canal projectors licked their financial wounds and awaited developments. Some of them had always contended that the most practical canal would be one following the Schuylkill almost to its source. So when, in 1810, they read in the newspapers of renewed canal activity and of the incorporation of the Union Canal Company (so-called because it was to follow the first route and join the Schuylkill with the Susquehanna), they assembled a group of Philadelphia financiers and formed the Schuylkill Navigation Company in March 1815.

These associates had the ambitious design of completing a Schuylkill canal one hundred and ten miles in length, from Philadelphia to Port Carbon at the very gateway of the present anthracite coal region, although coal, as freight, was subordinated in the minds of the projectors to the produce of the rich agricultural districts of the upper river. Approximately one hundred and eight miles of waterway were proposed in the original plan. Of this distance forty-eight miles were to be negotiated upon the bosom of the river itself, raised to the proper height by dams. These stretches were called "slack water." The remaining sixty-two miles were embraced in connecting canals. Inasmuch as the river fell six hundred and eighteen feet from the mountains to the sea, many locks had to be built to negotiate this fall. One hundred and nine of these were to be constructed at the stupendous cost, for the period, of six hundred thousand dollars. Later the number of locks was reduced to seventy-two. Also there was to be a canal tunnel near Auburn in Schuylkill county, said to have been the first of its kind in America, if not in the entire world. The dam at Poplar Neck below Reading was the junction point between the Union and Schuylkill canals.

The underwriters of the canal seem actually to have expected that their boats would be propelled upstream and downstream by oars or setting poles shod in iron, or be pulled along by men straining on the towpath with rods spanned across their heaving chests. So soon were the lessons of the racking labor entailed in pushing the Reading Boats upstream forgotten. For this reason there was no towpath suitable for mules or horses along the original canal. With the advent of mules the canal boats averaged in "slack" water four miles an hour and about three miles an hour on the canal proper.

When the board of managers of the Navigation Company, headed by Cadwallader Evans, made their historic journey up to Springfield, Massachusetts, in 1815 to enlist the services of the renowned engineer Ariel Cooley, they stipulated that he should enter upon his duties at once. Cooley, a man of his word, came down to Philadelphia within a few weeks and personally went over the whole route of the canal.

Actual canal construction was begun at a point just south of Pottsville in the fall of 1816, with enthusiasm and high hopes. In the crowd who gathered to see the first spadeful of earth thrown out were many who had talked with Washington in his journey up the valley in 1793 and who recalled his interest in the Union Canal then being projected. Curiously enough, in the optimistic comment of those assembled at the inaugural there was very little reference to the coal which was to constitute the main lading of the canal. Indeed, when the first horse-drawn boat, owned by Colonel Huntzinger of Pottsville, made its descent to Philadelphia in the incredibly short time of eleven days, it was loaded with lumber.

The work in the upper valley was supplemented by activity in the lower valley, at Falls of Schuylkill and at Flat Rock. In 1818 the inevitable freshet, the first of many floods which in the succeeding century were to disrupt so sadly the routine of the canal, brought much destruction. Perhaps as the disappointed contractors surveyed the havoc, they may have had the foreboding premonition, all too well founded, that these floods were in the end to prove the undoing of the project. For it was the ceaseless struggle with the unbridled river rather than the competition of the railroad which in the end spelled the financial doom of the Schuylkill canal.

The planning of the early canal was not always well coordinated. Weston, who had criticised the first canal, had gone back to England; and now appeared a new supervising critic in the person of the Lancashire engineer Edward Wilson, who had just completed a survey of the English canal system. Wilson went up the Schuylkill and was astounded to find that the locks were of thirty different lengths and of twenty-one different widths. The English visitor thought that the crowning absurdity lay in the fact that the capacity of the largest lock was 50 percent greater than that of the smallest, although the latter dimension necessarily limited the tonnage of the boat which could use the canal. Indeed the Schuylkill canal was first projected for boats of only twenty-five tons burden, a capacity raised to sixty-five tons only under the spur of the competition of the railroad. It might have been foreseen that the original locks, only eight feet wide and with a draught of three feet, would become impractical for the later and larger demands of commerce. One illustrious stockholder, Joseph Bonaparte, traveled up the valley in 1835 to inspect his property and shook his head over the deficiencies which were apparent even to his unpracticed eye.

The tourist of our own day who admires the beautiful

masonry in the grass-grown Schuylkill locks, some of it ranking as the finest stone work in all America, can only dimly realize the task of drilling this stone by hand without the use of high explosives or advanced machinery, and of then hauling it laboriously from the quarry, often far distant from the dams or locks in which the stone was employed. These locks were systematically vandalized after the abandonment of the canal and their dressed stone is now to be seen in the walls of houses, out-buildings, and even of churches in the upper valley. In this hour of Schuylkill regeneration and obliteration of most of the canal bed, it has been suggested that the beautifully mitred walls of the Peacock locks above Reading be preserved as a monument to the masons who did their work so faithfully and well a century ago.

The problem of masonry was only one of many which confronted the canal engineers in those days long gone. The springs which bubbled up through the lock floors had to be controlled, and this required a gruelling effort. When the spring was of unusual obduracy, twenty-four men operating a hand pump in shifts of three to a minute were required to keep the rebellious waters in check until a temporary lock floor could be constructed. The limestone strata above Reading with its many fissures and leaks made a difficult problem. As President Lewis expressed it in his report of 1836, "The canal at Reading from the moment of its first trial was a continual source of vexation."

No monuments record the achievements of the devoted early engineers of the Schuylkill Navigation Company. Fifty years ago there was a plaque imbedded in the wall of Leesport Lock to commemorate the achievement of the competent George Duncan, who constructed the canal through the troublesome Reading section. The plaque has disappeared and few remember Duncan now, anymore than they recall Michael Tower, who built the section of canal at Vincent, above Phoenixville, or Ariel Cooley, who constructed Fairmount Dam and Flat Rock, or Thomas Oaks, the martyr of the Schuylkill canal who died of malarial river fever at Reading.

The Navigation Company was always straitened for working capital, and the repairs after the numerous freshets caused financial embarrassment. Stephen Girard usually came to the rescue with loans, and the first permanent mortgage of $230,000 was delivered to Girard on February 18, 1825. This first lien upon all the property of the Schuylkill Navigation Company practically controlled the destiny of the canal. At Girard's death it was transferred to the City of Philadelphia, trustee under his will, and ultimately came into the possession of the Philadelphia and Reading Railroad Company.

Despite Girard's cooperation the early period of the Schuylkill canal was an epoch of experimentation and meager funds. Long afterwards Charles Ellet, one of the underwriters, wrote in reflective mood: "That was a period when the very existence of the work was threatened. The $50 shares which a few years later were worth $175, were offered below par with no takers."

However, by 1828 the long course of the winding, dancing river in which the Lenapes had fished and where the Reading Boats had descended in their brief but useful careers was now calmed and ordered. No more shoals, rapids, or mischievous fish weirs. Instead, Schuylkill boats proceeded from the mountain to the Delaware in a sedate and dignified two-mile-an-hour tempo.

In the early days, Samuel Alspach, who knew every eddy of the river, had collated a volume called the *Schuylkill Canal Navigator,* published by the author in 1827 and now very rare. His instructions were very specific:

> Ascending—Tow the whole way to Manayunk. Let the horse go at a slow walk. Keep a look-out for stumps and rocks. Norristown Dam—Run out, keeping about thirty feet from shore, until you come to the island. There is a bar running out from the island which is dangerous to stick upon. Plymouth Dam—Take on the horse at the locks. Go direct to the second wharf and land the horse and continue till you arrive at the next locks. Big Dam below Reading—Throw out the boat by bracing with poles, keeping inside of the stumps above the ferry. Take on the horse and row over. Then tow to the canal.

Alspach's admonitions had only a temporary value, for soon the channel had been made perfectly safe. Horses and mules succeeded the men who drew the first boats and the canal was at the peak of its operative glory.

The ladings of these first Schuylkill boats were diverse and interesting. Going down, they carried live hogs, whiskey, nuts, flour, marble, and lime. Going up they bore store goods, empty kegs, melons, oysters, and sea-food. Oddly enough, the upward-bound boats carried much lumber, this on the same river down which the great lumber rafts had plunged only a few decades before. Another puzzling lading is the pressed hay which the returning barges brought from New York up to the coal regions. One might suppose that the rich agrarian Schuyl-

kill district would have furnished enough hay for the
consumption of the mine mules.

Coal, until 1826, was not the leading commodity. It is
related that when the first coal-laden ark reached Reading Lock from the northward, the lock clerks had a
tariff for many commodities including hazel nuts, but
none for coal. One perplexing item of an upward bound
boat in 1827 was "twenty tons of Virginia coal," a curious
importation for the golconda of anthracite. The most
sinister entry of all is dated 1835: "One steam locomotive, three tons, to be delivered at Reading dock." As the
perspiring stevedores hoisted this locomotive at Fairmount Dam, they little knew that they were accomplishing the ruin of the canal which employed them and that
this fateful contraption was in the end to usurp the hauling of merchandise in the Schuylkill Valley.

With the canal functioning throughout its entire
length, the affairs of the Navigation Company showed
hopeful improvement. The encouraged managers began
to explore the possibilities of passenger traffic and in 1825
instituted packets between Reading and Philadelphia.
Northbound passengers came by stage to Pawling's Bridge
above Norristown and there took the packet for a leisurely
trip to Reading. These trips were made three times a week
and were usually concluded in a long day. The fare was
two and a half dollars.

This was the day of the *Planet*, which later had the
honor of carrying Fanny Kemble, and of the *Comet* of
Norristown, which boasted that Anthony Trollope had
once booked passage upon it. It seems to have been taken
for granted that the voyagers had plenty of time, for the
prospectus of the packets naively warned their proposed

customers that "travelers preferring expeditious travel had better take the stage."

Despite their deficiencies the Schuylkill packets were very popular and always crowded. In the 1830's the wharf at Pawling's was a busy place. Here lay the mule-drawn argosies intended for Reading, the *Comet*, the *Governor Schulze*, and *Pennsylvania's Pride*. There were primitive toilet facilities for women—over the rail for men. Bunks were few and most of the passengers slept cheek by jowl on the hard floors. A Maryland Negro served, from a vile smelling galley over the keel, inter-mittent snacks of bread, scrapple, and Oley ham.

Astern was the popular bar whence a tobacco-chewing attendant dispensed Neversink whiskey, juleps, and claret sangaree. Here all day was the buzz of conversation.

"I tell you, Sah, John C. Calhoun will be our next President. I am to see Governor Hiester at Reading, to-morrow, Sah. He will support Calhoun."

"They are saying at Harrisburg that the new county up Schuylkill is assured. Potts Grove will be its capital. We'll shear the Berks lamb. They'll lose all their South-ern townships."

"Mark my words when the railway gets finished no more coal will be sent down by boat. Why, they'll even burn coal in the locomotives. There'll be no more wood-burning engines."

All this in the bustle of departure. Then the captain blows his conch horn; the mules tauten the tow line and the majestic packet moves northward at two miles an hour.

It soon became apparent that the first boats, constructed mostly in Orwigsburg and hauled by horses to the river at Schuylkill Haven, were too small in their capacity of thirty tons. When Michael Sullivan of Landingville launched the *Irish Hero* of forty tons, his craft was regarded with much the same awe as the liner *Queen Mary* in recent years.

An elderly citizen gave his recollections in 1888 of an old-time launching at the Warner Boat Yards above Schuylkill Haven: "First the false keel, nearly one hundred feet long, was laid on blocks raised several feet above the ground. Then the framework was put up, resembling the skeleton of some monster animal. The inside of the boat was braced and lined, the hatches and cabins constructed. The name was placed across the stern in red or green just above the little cabin windows. Launching day was a gala day and the boys with their ladies were out in full force. The boat was launched sideways instead of stern first and many beakers of Monongahela whiskey were quaffed to its successful career."

Sometimes at the launching the local minister or priest was called in and the canal boat was gravely blessed. This procedure gives the same suggestion of the ludicrous which young Robert Louis Stevenson was conscious of and wrote about when he saw a canal boat suspended from the ceiling of a chapel, with a written aspiration that God should conduct the *Saint Nicholas* of *Creil* to a safe haven:

> You might hang up the model of a sea-going ship, and welcome: one that is to plough a furrow around the world, and visit the tropic or the frosty poles, runs dangers that are well worth a candle and a mass. But the *Saint Nicholas* of *Creil,* which was to be tugged for some ten years by patient draught horses, in a weedy canal,

with the poplars chattering overhead, and the skipper whistling at the tiller; which was to do all its errands in green inland places, and never got out of sight of a village belfry in all its cruising; why, you would have thought if anything could be done without the intervention of Providence, it would be that!

All this is a nostalgic memory for those who can recall the halcyon days when the canal still functioned. There came recollections of the tuneful tinkling of bells as the mules stepped briskly along the towpath, the blast of the conch-horn as the skipper summoned the lock-keeper to open his gates. Then the great barge laden to the gunwales glides by, with the inevitable line of wash suspended at the stern and the skipper's buxom wife peering out of the cabin window.

During the second quarter of the century the Schuylkill Navigation Company experienced an era of prosperity. After the first dividend of 7 per cent had been declared and paid in 1829, the complacent managers voted themselves a silver service apiece, the president, Cadwallader Evans, receiving a silver vase. The tactful directors, remembering how Stephen Girard had saved them in the financial crisis of 1821, voted Stephen Girard a similar vase and requested that they be allowed to paint his portrait. This the great financier modestly declined "both as inconsonant with my feelings and with my general determination."

The days when the projectors must go, hat in hand, to Girard and beg for a loan were over—at least so it was confidently expected. Coal was coming down in larger quantities every year, twice as much in 1831 as in 1830.

One jubilant stockholder, upon the receipt of his fat
dividend check, broke into song:

Dark anthracite! that reddenest on my hearth,
Thou in those inland mines didst slumber long,
But now thou are come forth to move the earth,
And put to shame the men that mean thee wrong;
Thou shalt be coals of fire to those that hate thee
And warm the shins of all that underrate thee.

But the golden age of canal prosperity was not to endure. The Philadelphia and Reading Railroad was pushing its tracks south from Reading and north from Norristown. By 1844 it was through Reading and up to
Mount Carbon. Worse still, not content with passenger
traffic, the railroad was hauling coal in alarming quantities.

The frightened managers of the Navigation Company
turned to meet this new peril. At first they sought to re-
assure their apprehensive stockholders by minimizing the
dangers of railroad competition. Speaking at a meeting of
the canal company in 1845, Charles Ellet told them to
"Remember that the Reading Railroad was not originally
planned for heavy freight. Its structure is of frail contemporary nature, designed to carry only passengers and
to supersede the stages now running between Philadelphia
and Reading."

Whether this disdainful confidence on the part of the
canal authorities was real or assumed, the fact remained
that the railroad was going steadily forward. In 1845 it
carried 573,000 tons of coal as against only 442,000 for
the combined lading of eight hundred canal boats then

in operation. The canal managers might scoff and jeer and point out "that the Reading Railroad had to sell bonds to the amount of $5,000,000 last year, and will give no account to the public of their condition." It was only too evident to the man in the street that railroad competition had come to stay.

The waning canal had a stroke of good fortune in the election of Frederick Fraley as president, who was to serve ably as chief executive for twenty-three years. Fraley made a gallant fight against desperate odds, even though the ruinous flood of September 2, 1850 wrought havoc throughout the valley. Standing on the cliffs by Pencoyd, the discouraged President watched the debris of his up-river dams swirling past him and said, "Never has there been such cataclysm in our valley. The damage done to the canal is incalculable."

Nevertheless, the undaunted Fraley continued his gallant fight. He enlarged the canal, improved the locks on the model of the celebrated Holyoke Lock on the Connecticut River, and achieved a peak of fourteen hundred boats in operation, each barge of one hundred and eighty tons burden. Ever alert for business, this enterprising president leased boats to individual operators and experimented with steam; steam packets ran for awhile but were abandoned because of the damage to the banks caused by their wash. Fraley was the first executive to cope sternly with the criminal bands of river pirates known as the Schuylkill Rangers, who terrorized the boatmen and even made a bold attempt to take Schuylkill Haven. He also made an energetic bid for the New England trade, an idea which Asa Packer had first conceived.

In the early days anthracite coal had been transshipped

at Philadelphia and sent by sailing vessels to New York and Boston. Then Packer had begun operating boats of about fifty tons each, equipped with hatches, which carried coal through the New Jersey canals to the New York market. About 1840 he conceived the idea of sending his boats around by sea to New York and the New England ports.

Many attempts had been made to establish a coal depot at the mouth of the Schuylkill. A canal down the west bank below Philadelphia was projected as early as 1834, and Stephen Girard had agreed to erect a coal depot opposite League Island. Engineers made soundings and advised against the project because of the treacherous "blue mud" in the meadows of the west bank below Gray's Ferry. There were two proposals to build canals across the urban district of Philadelphia, one route being projected across present Gray Street and the other south of Spruce Street. A plan for a circular canal around the west abutment of Market Street bridge was brought before councils in 1834 and met with much debate and vigorous opposition.

Meanwhile, railroad competition was acute and relentless all through the middle decade of the century. The Civil War brought an inevitable diminishment in canal navigation, and in 1863 the president reported to his stockholders: "Owing to the Rebel raid into this State in the month of June last the coal business on the Schuylkill canal suspended for one month."

Two years later, while cannon were still sounding on southern battlefields, the resourceful Fraley secured an agreement with the Reading Company whereby the railroad was to carry 55 per cent of the coal brought down from Schuylkill County and the Canal Company 45 per cent.

One is compelled to admire the gallant effort which the Navigation Company made in the unequal struggle, but the forces of nature were not to be denied. The disastrous flood of October 1869, coming after the destructive inundation of 1850, was a body blow. On January 1, 1870, the Schuylkill Navigation Company gave up the fight and leased itself to the Philadelphia and Reading Railroad for nine hundred and ninty-nine years.

Under the regime of the railroad, canal shipments steadily declined. The boating season of 1886 began apprehensively, for it was whispered that the channel below Schuylkill Haven had been clogged and that no funds were available for dredging. The Pottsville *Journal* gave lugubrious warning that "Boating on the Schuylkill Canal will soon become one of the lost arts."

The end was indeed at hand. To Captain Daniel Cole of Mount Carbon is accorded the doubtful distinction of carrying down the river the last cargo of coal ever shipped by water from Schuylkill Haven, in the spring of 1888. There was some later sporadic navigation on the canal and as late as October, 1919, four boats were with difficulty pulled through the silt from Hamburg to Phoenixville. When the new State Sanatorium at Hamburg was erected, part of the material for its construction was brought down by water. That was the close of navigation on the upper river, although barge traffic between Philadelphia and Manayunk persisted until a still later period. The real finale came April 1, 1947, when the railroad, tiring of the upkeep of a worthless ditch, conveyed the canal bed to the Commonwealth of Pennsylvania. This

acquisition played an important part in the subsequent
river regeneration.

So, unhonored and unsung, passed the once proud
Schuylkill Navigation Company which played so important a part in the development of our Commonwealth.
No monument records its long and honorable career, for
human memory is transient and we are not prone to commemorate our financial failures. The only real memorial
of the Schuylkill Canal is, or was, in the long canal slip
south of Port Clinton. There, twenty years ago, might
have been observed a lugubrious row of rotting hulks
whose names reflected a vanished glory. There lay the
General Banks and the Major Anderson, the Governor
Hiester and the John W. Forney, the Jay Cooke and the
Stephen Girard. Saddest of all was a disintegrating wreck
upon whose stern could still be read the name of the great
leader to whom the Schuylkill Valley and the anthracite
coal regions owed so much, Frederick W. Fraley. *Sic
transit gloria mundi.*

With the termination of navigation on the upper river
there remained only the commerce of the lower or tidal
river. The Schuylkill has a mean tidal range of five and a
half feet in the eight and a half miles from its mouth to
Fairmount Dam. The barks which once clustered about
High Street wharf are long gone to Davy Jones' locker,
but steamships and motor ships have succeeded them in a
channel which laborious dredging has kept open from the
mouth to Gibson's Point and beyond. This river navigation has been maintained against great odds. The tankers
taking oil from Gulf, Atlantic, Standard, and Socony, the
freighters carrying bauxite and sulphur to Du Pont and
gypsum to U. S. Gypsum, have had an increasingly dif-

ficult passage up a choked channel. Yet the peak lading of a million and a half tons in 1941 approximated that passing through the Delaware terminals.

This figure receded sharply in succeeding years because of the inadequate channel, but now a new light breaks over the meadows of Passyunk. The plan of Schuylkill reclamation calls for a thirty-foot draught, a three-hundred-foot wide channel to Twenty-Ninth Street, and a narrower channel to University Avenue bridge. The new Penrose Ferry bridge is to have a clearance of a hundred and thirty feet, so that even the mighty *Missouri* may pass under it. Old Asa Packer, who growled so ferociously a century ago when his barges ran upon the mud flats, would rub his hands over the prospect. So, while the story of Schuylkill navigation has been in the main a tale of commercial defeat, it ends with happy augury, at least for the lower river.

II

RIVER
REGENERATION

——◆—

CHAPTER 28

River Regeneration

G ENERALLY, when writing about a river, the author can undertake the task with the comforting assurance that the physical aspect of his subject will not alter, at least not until a decent interval after publication. The Schuylkill's story, on the contrary, is told during a period of drastic transformation of its channel. A far-reaching project for the cleansing and regeneration of the watershed is now in progress.

This Schuylkill River Project had its formal inception in 1945. In that year the Pennsylvania Assembly passed Act 441, the Desilting Act (sometimes known as the Brunner Act). This bill, together with the Clean Streams Act of 1945, gave the Commonwealth authorities the power and funds to launch a long-considered plan for cleansing the Schuylkill Valley of the deposit of silt and other municipal and industrial wastes which have long defiled it.

The moment was well chosen. By fortunate coincidence the alert Pittsburgh lawyer James H. Duff, serving in 1944 as Attorney General, was an enthusiastic backer of the project; by happy chance he was elected Governor of Pennsylvania in 1947. So, it was State Prosecutor Duff who served stern notice upon the lordly coal operators that a continuation of their time-honored practice of dumping refuse matter into the river would meet with prompt punishment, and it was Governor Duff who later set up the complicated financial engineering fabric for Schuylkill regeneration.

Providence smiled upon the project when by further lucky coincidence the Governor was able to choose as head of his Department of Forest and Waters a brilliant naval veteran, who was equipped with a fund of knowledge gained in his previous station. Admiral Milo F. Draemel had served during World War II as Commandant of the Fourth Naval District, with headquarters in the League Island Naval Base. The Admiral knew the river well and not too favorably. Many times he had been called upon to entertain high ranking allied commanders whose ships were undergoing repairs at the Yard. At a dinner party in his quarters on the waterfront the Admiral's equanimity and the comfort of his distinguished guests were too often disturbed by noxious odors from the river waters. And, a more serious matter for the commandant, one of his problems had been the inevitable corrosion of delicate shipboard installations (almost irreplaceable in the stress of the great conflict) when exposed to the miasmic fumes wafted over from the turbid waters.

Duff found another able administrative ally in Norris W. Vaux, M.D., distinguished Philadelphia physician, to head his Department of Health and its Sanitary Water Board. To him fell the task of preventing the admission of further wastes into Pennsylvania's streams. Draemel, operating through the agency of the Water and Power Resources Board, became the "task force commander" to rid the Schuylkill of its millions of tons of mine wastes.

The undertaking was a joint one by state and nation, with the Commonwealth of Pennsylvania appropriating thirty-five million dollars and the Federal Government pledging the estimated twenty million dollars calculated for the completion of the project. From Norristown to the Delaware, the Schuylkill ranks as a navigable river— a suggestion which has provoked countless jibes from luckless boatmen stranded on the mud bars. Therefore, since navigable rivers are a federal responsibility, this lower section, approximately one-fifth of the river length, was to be the problem of the Army Engineers Corps and to be dredged at the cost of the Federal Government. But this Federal intervention was predicated upon the State's assuming the expense of the removal of the twenty-five million tons of silt which clogged the channel north of Norristown.

The task of the projectors has been materially lightened by the willing cooperation of the coal companies and of the communities and industries along the river banks. The coal operators, led by the Philadelphia and Reading Coal and Iron Company and the Lehigh Navigation Coal Company, loosened their purse strings, placated their stockholders as best they could, and put in expensive de-silting plants. The Sanitary Water Board under the chairmanship of Doctor Vaux ordered the coal operators, the fifty-eight river communities, and approximately five hundred and fifty industries located along the Schuylkill between the mountains and the Delaware, to stop their pollution within four years. The latter prepared more or less cheerfully to comply, even though the expense entailed was enormous. The towns of the upper river have been equally prompt in their cooperation. Philadelphia, which annually discharged sewage containing sixty thousand cubic yards of solids into the river, has taken immediate measures of amelioration.

The miracle is being accomplished while these lines are written. The electrically operated hydraulic dredges, sectionally constructed on nine interlocking pontoons, are assembled and at work; the silt is being sucked up from the river as if by gigantic vacuum cleaners and deposited in the huge basins ashore. The project calls for three desilting dams and twenty-three impounding basins. So, while the bottom is still black, the river runs clear. Bathers have returned and optimistic fishermen are preparing their tackle.

This transmutation has been accomplished with a celerity undreamed of by the most optimistic projector. It was early in the autumn of 1948 that a private dredge under Commonwealth control began to operate. Now the river bed is the scene of feverish effort. A glance at the map of the Schuylkill Valley of today will show it dotted with huge craters, like those which feature an astronomical sketch of the surface of the moon.

They are scarcely ornate, these basins, and the bewildered citizen, looking out from a car window, wonders whether it was really worthwhile to clean up the river when its banks are to be disfigured by these unsightly excavations. "Gigantic Yale football bowls!" as one ironic journalist expressed it. The artist hunting his favorite spot to set up his easel and paint romantic Black Rock Falls might find it hard to ignore the gaping basin just to the northward. And picnickers on the palisades of Valley Forge will find their river view scarcely improved by the desilting basin across the river below.

However, these basins will not remain filled with silt, for this refuse has a distinct value and it is hoped that it can be disposed of by sale. The silt now being pumped is for the most part grained coal known as anthracite fines, technically "anthrafines." Many factories economize by burning anthrafines as fuel, particularly the deposit from upstream. The farther down Schuylkill the silt is carried, the less valuable it becomes because it is mixed with noncombustible solids. This prospect of sale affords a reasonable outlook for the removal of the silt from the basin, the substitution of reclaimed soil, and some financial reimbursement. Afterwards, the Commonwealth can either develop the fifteen hundred acres which it has acquired along the river as recreational park areas, or sell sites to manufacturers.

The aesthetic ravages suggested above represent the most significant liabilities as opposed to the many gains which the project will bring. Certainly, the destruction of historical landmarks is regrettable, and in the case of the Schuylkill the removal of some of the dams. A century ago there were thirty-two dams, but the number of these has steadily lessened. In 1940 when a preliminary survey was made, only eighteen remained. The others had disappeared or had been breached, leaving unsightly gaps.

The dam at Auburn will be preserved, but Blue Mountain Dam, once so broad and stately, mirroring the shadows of its imposing mountain wall, will be replaced by the new Kernsville Dam, almost on the same site, with a proposed forty-two acre artificial lake suitable for summer or winter sports. Felix will still be there but not Herbein's nor Shepp's nor Kissinger's Dams with their reminiscences of the canoeing days of youth. No longer will it be possible to paddle above Reading Dam, look at the summit of Neversink, and speculate on which rock was named Lover's Leap, that attracted the attention of Fanny Kemble when she sat on the upper deck of the river packet on an autumn morning in the year 1837.

Below Pottstown, Vincent Dam will remain, and Black Rock, perhaps the loveliest of all. Pawlings Dam will disappear, and lovely Catfish Dam where in 1805 Audubon made his sketch of roosting egrets, a drawing which is still preserved at the Smithsonian. Norristown Dam will still delight the thousands of commuters who pass over the trolley bridge morning and evening. Flat Rock is to stay and so is Fairmount.

The Schuylkill Isaac Walton, a trifle disappointed perhaps to find that marine life does not immediately return in its former abundance, may console himself with the thought that in this age of rapid commercial development someone will find a way to control the small amount of acid drainage still existing, and that eventually the stream will be restocked with fish. Also any river community is at perfect liberty to restore its dams for recreational purposes.

And thus the fulfillment of this Pennsylvania miracle is well within view. A cleansed and sparkling stream will again flow through rural reaches, including the two new lakes at Auburn and Kernsville. The river water will be potable and palatable, and the rhododendron and wild azalea will again sprout from the blackened banks which they deserted five decades ago.

SELECTED READING LIST

Acts Pennsylvania Legislature. Incorporation of Schuylkill and Susquehanna Navigation Company. Incorporation of Union Canal. Incorporation of Schuylkill Canal.

Acrelius, Israel, *A History of New Sweden,* translated by William M. Reynolds. Philadelphia, 1874.

Alspach, S., *Schuylkill Canal Navigation.* Philadelphia, 1827.

Anburey, Thomas, *Travels Through the Interior Parts of America, 1797–1811,* 2 vols. London, 1789.

Baist, S. W., *Atlas of Schuylkill River from Philadelphia to Norristown.*

Barbe-Marbois, Francois, Marquis de, *Our Revolutionary Forefathers.* New York, 1929.

Berks County Historical Society, publications and magazines of.

Bining, Arthur Cecil, *Forges and Furnaces of Pennsylvania.* Philadelphia, 1914.

——— *Pennsylvania Iron Manufacture in the Eighteenth Century.* Harrisburg, 1938.

Bowen, Eli, *The Pictorial Sketch-Book of Pennsylvania.* Philadelphia, 1852.

Brissot de Warville, J.P., *New Travels in the United States of America, 1759–1760.* London, 1798.

Burnaby, Rev. Thomas, *Travels Through the Middle Settlements of America, 1759–1760.* London, 1798.

Carbon County Historical Society, publications and magazines of.

Chastellux, Marquis de, *Travels in North America, 1780–1782,* 2 vols. Dublin, 1787.

Chester County Historical Society, publications and magazines of.

Day, Sherman, *Historical Collections of Pennsylvania*. Philadelphia, 1843.

Delaware County Historical Society, publications and magazines of.

Dickens, Charles, *American Notes*.

Dewees, Samuel, *Memoirs*. Baltimore, 1844.

Fisher, Sydney George, *The Making of Pennsylvania*. Philadelphia, 1916.

———— *Pennsylvania, Colony and Commonwealth*. Philadelphia, 1897.

———— *The Quaker Colonies*. New Haven, 1919.

———— *The True William Penn*. Philadelphia, 1900.

Gates, Theophilus R., *Battle-Axes and the Weapons of War*. Philadelphia, 1837.

Heckewelder, Rev. John, *History, Manners and Customs of the Indian Nations*. Philadelphia, 1819.

Heiland, Louis, *Schuylkill Navy of Philadelphia*. Philadelphia, 1938.

Hiltzheimer, Jacob, *Extracts from Diary,* edited by Jacob Cox Parsons. Philadelphia, 1893.

Johnson, Amandus, *The Swedish Settlements on the Delaware,* 2 vols. Philadelphia, 1911.

Keith, Charles, *Chronicles of Pennsylvania*. Philadelphia, 1872.

———— *Early Councilors of Philadelphia,* 1872.

Mills, C. K., *Schuylkill Centennial Poem*. 1876.

Montgomery County Historical Society, publications and magazines of.

Penn, *Correspondence of the Penn Family Including William, William, Jr., Thomas, John and Granville*.

Pennsylvania, Historical Society of, *Schuylkill Bridges* (pamphlet collection in archives).

———— *Schuylkill Inclined Plane* (Report of 1848).

Pennsylvania State Archives—all series.

Philadelphia County Historical Society, publications of.

Philadelphia Society of Agriculture, Proceedings of, *Schuylkill Permanent Bridge*. 1806.

Pinkerton, Allan, *The Molly Maguires and the Detectives*. New York, 1877.

Reading Railroad, *The History of the Trunk Line*. Philadelphia, 1890.

Royall, Anne, *Mrs. Royall's Pennsylvania*. Washington, 1828.

Rupp, Isaac, *History of Schuylkill County*. Harrisburg, 1845.

Saxe-Weimar, Memoirs of. Weimar, 1826.

Scharf, J. Thomas, and Westcott, Thompson, *History of Philadelphia*, 3 vols. Philadelphia, 1884.

Schoepf, Johann David, *Travels in the Confederation, 1783–1784,* edited by Alfred J. Morrison, 2 vols. Philadelphia, 1911.

Schuylkill County Historical Society, publications and magazines of.

Shaefer, B. W., *Descriptive Geography of Schuylkill County*.

Wansey, Henry, *Journal of an Excursion to the United States, 1794*. Salisbury, England.

Ward, Christopher, *The Dutch and Swedes on the Delaware*. Philadelphia, 1930.

——— *Jonathan Drew*. New York, 1932.

——— *New Sweden on the Delaware*. Philadelphia, 1938.

Weygandt, Cornelius, *Down Jersey Way*. New York, 1940.

——— *The Dutch Country*. New York, 1939.

——— *Philadelphia Folks*. New York, 1938.

——— *The Red Hills*. Philadelphia, 1929.

——— *The Wissahickon Hills*. Philadelphia, 1930.

Zerbe, Ella, *Blue Book of Schuylkill County*. Pottsville, 1916.

Pennsylvania Newspapers

MANAYUNK: *The Chronicle*
             The Sentinel

NORRISTOWN: *The Daily Gazette*
             The Watchman

PHILADELPHIA :   *Dunlap's Packet*
                  The Inquirer
                  The Ledger
                  The Record
                  The U. S. Gazette

PHOENIXVILLE :   *The Advertiser*
                  The Daily Republican

POTTSVILLE :   *The Anthracite Gazette*
                  The Emporium

READING :   *The Adler*
                  The Berks and Schuylkill Journal
                  The Chronicle of the Times
                  The Daily and Weekly Eagle

INDEX

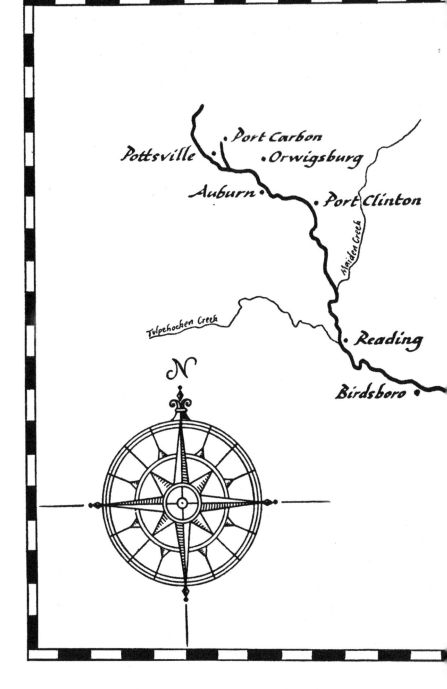